fabulous fat-free cooking

fabulous fat-free cooking

more than 225 dishes—
all delicious, all nutritious,
all with less than 1 gram of fat!

by lynn fischer
TV's Low-Cholesterol Gourmet

Rodale Press, Inc.

Emmaus, Pennsylvania

Printed in Italy by Rotolito Lombarda

Interior and Cover Designer: Debra Sfetsios
Cover Photographer: Angelo Caggiano

Fischer, Lynn.
  Fabulous fat-free cooking : more than 225 dishes—all delicious, all nutritious, all with less then 1 gram of fat! / by Lynn Fischer.
    p. cm.
  Includes index.
ISBN 1-57954-164-X hardcover
1. Cookery. 2. Low-fat diet—Recipes. I. Title.
TX714.F57 1997
641.5'638—dc21   97–872

2 4 6 8 10 9 7 5 3 1   hardcover

— OUR PURPOSE —

"We inspire and enable people to improve their lives and the world around them."

To **Chris**

Contents

Foreword

In 1961, a committee of scientists reviewed the research from around the world on the relationship between heart disease and food. The evidence of a link between diet and heart disease was so strong that in that same year, the American Heart Association issued a warning to the public: Continued consumption of diets high in animal fats is related to the rapidly rising rate of heart attacks among our citizens.

Fortunately, the American public responded to the lifesaving message. In the intervening years, we have reduced our intake of both cholesterol and saturated fat. It is virtually certain that the decline in deaths from heart disease that began in 1965 is directly attributable to changes in our diet.

As a result of the reduction in heart attacks and stroke, Americans are now living longer than ever. More important, we are living healthier than ever.

One of the approaches to reducing the intake of saturated fats has been to warn against the overconsumption of dairy fats, eggs, and fatty meats. A very important supplementary approach, however, is to recommend nutritious, low-fat foods that can displace those dishes that contain the undesirable fats.

In this book, Lynn Fischer provides a very positive message by making fruits, vegetables, and grains more attractive. We can actually enjoy the dietary changes that are recommended by the American Heart Association and by the healthy eating plan outlined in the U.S. Department of Agriculture's Food Guide Pyramid.

Most of us have probably no more than 20 entrées that comprise our regular eating plan. If we identify the dishes that are high in saturated fat and replace them with recipes from this cookbook, we can dramatically improve the health benefits of our diet while increasing our culinary satisfaction.

Eating good food is one of the great pleasures of life. Lynn Fischer has made it possible for us to increase our pleasure while we improve our health.

W. Virgil Brown, M.D.
Professor of Internal Medicine, Emory University School of Medicine
President of the American Heart Association (1991–1992)

Acknowledgments

There are lots of people to give a nod to and thank
publicly when you write a cookbook, because you
can't do it alone. My thanks are both professional
and personal.

Two food companies helped with a few of the
recipes in this book. The White Lily Foods Company
developed several dessert recipes. I asked them to
participate because of their technical expertise in
reducing the fat in cakes and cookies. I learned from
them that soft-wheat flour, which has less gluten,
doesn't need as much fat to tenderize it as all-
purpose flour does. I thank Lloyd Montgomery, Steve
Queisser, and especially Belinda Ellis.

Thanks to the Borden company for developing a
scrumptious rice pudding recipe with their fat-free
sweetened condensed skim milk.

Other talented people who tested or developed recipes were gifted dessert cook Beatrice Ojakangas; Susan McQuillan; Jenna Holst; Andrea Goodman, my former assistant who's such a sweetheart; Rita Calvert, our very talented tester and stylist for nearly all my 200-plus TV shows and food writer for the *Baltimore Sun*; and Leela Berman Greenblat, new mama and prop stylist for my shows.

I especially thank Gail Ross, my literary agent, adviser, lawyer, and friend, who has assisted me with contracts and contacts for nine years. Gail looks out for my best interests, and I greatly admire, respect, and care about her even more today than when I first met her.

My former assistant, Marty Cavendish, was of great help with the beginning of the book, but, darn, I lost her when she was named director of Washington's Women in Film and Video, where I sit on the board of directors.

Chris Loudon is a registered dietitian and the most pleasant, uncomplaining, on-time, always-accurate associate, who is one of the few in the food business who understands low-fat and fat-free cooking. Chris did all the nutritional analyses for this book and analyzes recipes for my television shows, too.

Finally, I thank several at Rodale Press. Tom Ney, food editor for *Prevention* magazine. Gentle managing editor for cookbooks Jean Rogers, for asking me if I would do this book in the first place. Also office manager Roberta Mulliner, who guided me around, literally. JoAnn Brader, manager of the Rodale Test Kitchen, and her helpful staff. Her kind and supportive words came at the right time (cookbooks are tough—good cookbooks are really tough).

I especially thank Sharon Sanders, cooking editor at Rodale Books, with whom I worked most closely and who really knows food and cooking. She has been my toughest, most talented, hardest working, and most demanding editor, but also the one from whom I learned the most. Her skills helped me make every one of these recipes really fabulous.

Thanks to family and friends, because they are so special, and their support and friendship are important. My sweet friend, mentor, and special joy is Virginia Von Fremd (world's best speech coach, too). My dearest friend, Beth Mendelson, jet-setting producer. My tallest friend, Kathy McClain, television station general manager. My lawyer friend, Pat Mahoney. My oldest friends, Jean and Bob Morressy. Susie Hart Wydler, Terry Frantz McKenzie, and my skiing buddies, Jennifer Douglas and Stanford Adelstein. Special friends Bob Furman, Lil Smith, Randy Feldman, Phil Beuth of ABC, Dr. Manuel Trujillo, Karl Viehe, Arna Vodenos, Denise Barta, Linda Ringe and Bob Franken, and Andrea and Marty Kalin all seem to be there when I need words of encouragement, to gossip, to go over a situation or problem—whatever. I adore and lean on them all and try to be there for them, too.

With family, I thank niece Susie Fischer McGarry and her husband, Mark McGarry, who always put me up in St. Petersburg, Florida. My brother Tom Connor and his wife, Mary, in Naples, Florida, and brother Bob Connor in Oakland, California, all of whom put me up when I visit and are always there by phone to offer counsel and support. I thank my sister Ann and her husband, Bill Taylor, who do the same in Oakland and brother Jim Connor and his wife, Trudy, in Troy, Michigan. My pop, Addison Connor, in Naples, who is 91 this year and has hung up his Rollerblades. My daughter, Lisa Jehle, and grandchild Wolf, both in Topanga. My son, Cary Bialac, in Austin. The whole big Gillette family—and especially Christopher Gillette, who's such a doll and is always there for me.

Introduction

I have an appreciation of people and a curiosity
about health, so I wasn't surprised when a sociologist told me that food habits are the most difficult habits to change. Even when we move to a new country and quickly change our style of dress, our language, and even our lifestyle, our food preferences linger.

Because change is difficult, I know why lowering the fat content of familiar foods can be upsetting for some. But we can change. In fact, for some of us, change isn't an option if we want to regain our health. I contend that if the food tastes and looks good, we will incorporate it into our lives and we will learn to love it. It can be done.

I've changed, and I've seen others change, too.

I began reducing the fat in my recipes decades ago. As a newlywed in the early 1970s, I faced a hefty healthy-cooking challenge. My husband, though only in his thirties, was diagnosed with dangerously high cholesterol, caused by too much total fat, saturated fat, and cholesterol in his diet. He eliminated egg yolks, butter, and cheese. He switched from whole milk to low-fat milk. But his cholesterol stayed at a badly elevated 286.

I felt I could improve it more. I attended classes at Eastern Virginia Medical School in Norfolk and buttonholed doctors for information. On Saturdays I scoured the Himmelfarb Health Sciences Library at George Washington University School of Medicine and Health Sciences in Washington, D.C., for every heart and cardiology journal available.

In the kitchen, however, I was on my own. Because I couldn't find anyone who was writing about or teaching low-fat cooking techniques, I improvised. I started to prepare extremely low cholesterol, low fat dishes (surreptitiously at first, because they had to look and taste like the fattier foods that my husband loved).

I served smaller meat portions, but he didn't notice the difference, because the dinner plates looked so abundant. I said I was conserving financially. We were actually eating more food.

A typical meal was cod fillet with a low-fat white lemon sauce speckled with fresh parsley. On the side was a fluffy mound of rice tossed with scallions, a bit of margarine, soy sauce, and ginger. Two or more vegetables, flavored with margarine, rounded out the dinner. In the 1970s, it was considered a pretty healthy meal.

From meat loaf to muffins, hash browns to hollandaise, cream sauces to casseroles, I learned to make lowfat food taste luscious and look lush.

My husband's cholesterol dropped 100 points to 186, and he got back down to his college weight of 186 pounds. Inspired by these improvements, and with a surge in energy, he began to exercise daily. This raised his levels of HDL, the good type of cholesterol that helps transport the bad cholesterol (LDL) from the body.

I also began to reap the rewards of a more healthful lifestyle. Our medical bills dropped. I noticed that I, too, had more energy. Best of all, we had a peace of mind that's gained when you take charge of your health.

An unexpected divorce and the economic climate took me to Washington, D.C. With my newly acquired medical knowledge, I became the television medical anchor for WTTG, part of the Fox Network. In 1989, I co-wrote *The Fischer/Brown Low Cholesterol Gourmet* with W. Virgil Brown, M.D.

With my subsequent books and

television cooking shows on the Discovery Channel and Public Broadcasting System, I've been privileged to bring my message of healthy eating to many more thousands. Allow me to share one more personal story.

Mark White is the talented director of all 230 episodes of my television shows. When I first started working with Mark in the early 1990s, he tipped the scales at 300 pounds. A lifelong struggle with weight, combined with a sedentary job and insufficient exercise, had brought him to his all-time high.

As we taped more and more shows, Mark developed what he called a heightened awareness of low-fat eating. But it was my low-fat apple crumble that really spurred Mark to make a positive change in his life.

Mark is an admitted sweets lover, and his mother was a caterer, so he knows delicious food when he tastes it. One bite of the apple crumble, and he was hooked.

As Mark sampled more of my dishes, he learned that he could feel satisfied without feeling bloated. He made the effort to revamp his eating habits, exercise more, and drink more water. He now weighs 200 pounds and feels better than he has in years.

Mark doesn't diet anymore; he just eats sensibly. But his "sensibly" is nearly fat-free. He eats about 3,000 calories a day, composed primarily of low-fat and fat-free foods.

Because of business travel, Mark must dine frequently in restaurants. So he relies on fat-free meals at home to keep his weight in check.

When I get impatient with slow set changes during program tapings, Mark says, "Be patient, Lynn. It doesn't happen by itself." I can share the same sentiment with all of you struggling with dietary change.

People always ask me if I really do eat this way. Of course I do. How else would I summon the energy to write six cookbooks, create two television cooking shows, launch a radio show, conduct seminars, give speeches and cooking classes, assemble a cookware catalog, create *Lynn Fischer's Healthy Indulgences* CD-ROM, enjoy a fulfilling personal life, and serve on the boards of several associations and charitable organizations?

Eating this way, I am convinced, gives me energy and vitality. I am confident that you will accomplish more in your life when you aim toward good health. I believe that this book can help you achieve your goal. Stay well.

Why **Fat-Free?**

Fat! Can't live with it. But we can't live without it.

Fat is essential for human life. Dietary fat
enables our bodies to absorb vitamins A, D, E and K.
These vitamins help maintain vision, the skeletal
system, and neurological and vascular health.
Without fat to cushion body blows, our organs would
be black and blue. Fat regulates our body temperature, conditions our hair, softens our skin and
soothes our nerves with a protective covering.

But if fat is so good, why is everyone saying that it's so bad?

Ever hear about too much of a good thing?

Overfed and Undernourished

The West's natural abundance provides us with amber waves of grain (good sources of complex carbohydrates and fibre), but it also puts double cream, butter, full-fat cheeses, bacon, well-marbled steaks, greasy burgers, pork spareribs, chips and plump chickens on our tables. The buttercream icing on the cake is a food industry adept at stirring lots of hidden fat into processed foods.

The uninvited guests at this feast are heart disease, some cancers, diabetes and obesity – all life threatening and all directly linked to a diet that's too high in fat. Health experts agree that most of us should reduce our intake of fat, particularly the saturated fat found primarily in animal foods such as red meat, poultry with skin, cheese and butter as well as in tropical plant oils such as coconut and palm.

Most of us eat a diet that gets about 37 percent of calories from fat. About 15 to 17 percent of that is saturated fat. But the Department of Health, the British Heart Association and other health authorities recommend that for the general population, no more than 30 percent of calories should come from fat. Of the total calories consumed, no more than 10 percent should come from saturated fat.

Some health experts recommend the total elimination of saturated fat from the diet – to be replaced by monounsaturated oils, like olive and rapeseed, and polyunsaturated oils, like corn, safflower and soybean. These monounsaturates and polyunsaturates have been found to lower blood cholesterol when substituted for saturated fat in the diet.

Of course, all oils are a concentrated source of calories, containing approximately 120 calories and 14 grammes of fat in each table-spoon. Even healthy individuals at normal weight are advised to eat fats sparingly.

Zeroing In on Fat

No one can, or should, eat a totally fat-free diet. In fact, it would be impossible.

Every food contains some fat as part of its natural composition – some less, some more. 125 grammes of apple has 0.4 gramme of fat, compared with an equal amount of Fuerte avocado, which has 10 grammes. 90 grammes of grilled haddock contain a mere 0.8 gramme, while the same amount of grilled steak contains 30 grammes. 250 ml of skimmed milk has only 0.4 gramme of fat, but 250 ml of double cream has 88 grammes.

Even the fat-free recipes in this book – which all contain *less than 1 gramme of fat per serving* – contain trace amounts of fat.

So it comes down to choices. You have the power to make the right food choices to maximise your health.

My goal in creating these fat-free dishes is not to convince anyone to subscribe to a totally fat-free diet. Rather, I want to provide some truly delicious tools – more than 225 of them – to help you bring your total fat consumption way, way down.

How Much Fat Is Right for You?

That's a hard call. The British Heart Association recommends that the fat intake for the general population go no lower than 15 percent of calories. Other health experts recommend a fat intake as low as 10 percent of total calories for those individuals with coronary heart disease or risk factors for heart disease, such as high cholesterol or obesity.

Dean Ornish, M.D., president and director of the Preventive Medicine Research Institute in Sausalito, California, describes his "reversal diet" in his book *Dr. Dean Ornish's Program for Reversing Heart Disease*. Dr. Ornish recommends an intake of no more than 10 percent of calories from fat to reverse the effects of arterial blockage.

The British Heart Association acknowledges that very low fat diets have been tested with favourable results in studies of persons at high risk, but such diets have not been demonstrated to be of value for the general population.

Consult your doctor to determine your individual dietary needs. Then compute your ideal calorie intake and set up a fat budget based on the percentage of calories from fat that you should consume.

If you're a healthy individual who needs to shed a few pounds, your doctor may recommend 25 percent or less calories from fat, combined with exercise, to trim your weight. If you're recovering from coronary heart disease, 10 percent of calories from fat may be the per-centage recommended by your doctor.

Flexible Fat-Spending Account

Like shoe size, bank account and IQ, each person's fat budget is an individual matter. To determine yours, consult your doctor or a registered dietitian about your ideal weight, calorie needs and the recommended percentage of calories from fat that you should be eating.

Those people recovering from coronary heart disease may be advised to get only 10 percent of their calories from fat.

Persons advised to reduce their body weight may be directed to eat 25 percent of calories from fat (a good reduction from the typical 37 percent that most of us consume).

Consult the chart to find your ideal weight, calorie intake and recommended percentage of fat.

To factor in activity level, for every 100 calories that you burn while exercising, you can add 3 grammes of fat to your daily budget.

Men

Ideal Weight (lb)	Fat Grammes per Day at 25% of Calories	Fat Grammes per Day at 10% of Calories	Total Calories
130	50	20	1,800
140	56	22	2,000
150	58	23	2,100
160	63	25	2,250
170	67	27	2,400
180	72	29	2,600
190	75	30	2,700
200	78	31	2,800
210	82	33	2,950
220	86	34	3,100
230	90	36	3,250
240	94	38	3,400

Women

Ideal Weight (lb)	Fat Grammes per Day at 25% of Calories	Fat Grammes per Day at 10% of Calories	Total Calories
90	31	12	1,100
100	36	14	1,300
110	39	16	1,400
120	42	17	1,500
130	47	19	1,700
140	50	20	1,800
150	53	21	1,900
160	56	22	2,000
170	61	24	2,200
180	64	26	2,300

Using Fat-Free Recipes

After you determine how much fat is right for you, you can step into the kitchen to incorporate my fat-free recipes into your meals.

Those of you who have been advised to dramatically reduce total dietary fat can create entire meals from the recipes in this book. My menu chapter provides a start, but you can create dozens of other meals from these recipes, following your own taste buds. The meals in the menu chapter average about 5 percent of calories from fat. The overwhelming majority of these recipes contain no added fat. I guarantee that you won't miss it a bit.

Those of you who have been advised by your doctor to lose a few pounds will find these fat-free recipes an invaluable aid to reducing the total fat in your eating plan.

When you work within your personal fat budget, it's easy to average your fat intake over several days or even a week. Not every food you eat, or even every meal, needs to meet the recommended percentage of calories from fat. You can decide how and when to spend your fat grammes.

This allows you some flexibility in choosing foods for personal satisfaction, an important mainstay of any eating plan. So go ahead and dip into the guacamole bowl once in a while (with fat-free tortilla chips, of course). Or nibble on some nuts. Both avocados and certain nuts, such as pecans, almonds, peanuts and cashews, contain primarily heart-healthy monounsaturated fat in addition to many other nutrients.

In planning meals, you can supplement your favourite main course with

---

A Few Words about My Nutrient Analyses

All of the recipes in this book were analysed for total fat, saturated fat, calories, cholesterol, sodium, protein, carbohydrates and dietary fibre based on the latest Department of Health figures and more than 1,000 additional scientific sources. Some additional nutrient data came from food manufacturers. Remember that, as with any nutrient analyses, these numbers are guidelines only. They may vary slightly from those in other nutritional programmes, and they may vary from the actual foods you consume.

a fabulous fat-free appetizer or soup, a side dish and a grain dish to bring the total fat for the meal way down.

Adding and Subtracting

Subtracting fat, particularly saturated fat, is important for healthy eating. Adding fruits, vegetables and grains is just as essential to maintain good health.

The diets of most of us need improvement. On a nutritional report card in 1995, only 12 percent had scores of 80 or above on a scale of 100. People were most likely to under-consume foods in the fruit, vegetable and grain groups.

The current dietary guidelines recommend 3 to 5 servings of vegetables, 2 to 4 servings of fruits, and 6 to 11 servings of grains (including bread, cereal, rice and pasta) each day.

If you base your eating plan on these super-nutritious foods, prepared without added fat, your fat consumption will plummet automatically. You won't even need to compute fat grammes because these foods are so low in fat. When you choose fat-free dairy products and only small amounts of red meat and poultry, your saturated fat intake will be reduced as well.

Because my fat-free dishes are all based on nutrient-dense vegetables and whole grains, you can confidently incorporate any of them into even the strictest dietary plan.

Cooking at home gives you control over what goes into your food and into your body. Now that you understand the importance of slashing fat – without sacrificing one iota of flavour – you can turn to "Free of Fat, Full of Flavour" (see page 7) to find out just how easy it is to cook the fabulous fat-free way, right in your own kitchen.

Chances are that you have most of what you need in your kitchen to get started right now. My recipes use common ingredients – the kind found in any supermarket. And my easy fat-free cooking techniques are designed to get the most natural flavour out of each ingredient. I'll show you how you can make your meals sizzle without added fat.

Free of Fat, Full of Flavour

Like three on a date or five wheels on a car, fat

added to food can really ruin a good thing. For food

that tastes naturally wonderful, kick the fat out of

your kitchen. You simply don't need it.

My recipes let the flavours of fresh foods shine.

Taste for yourself the crisp-tender crunch of fresh

vegetables in Sweet-and-Sour Turkey and the succu-

lence of Herb-Breaded Orange Roughy. Savour the

gooey goodness of Pineapple Caramel Cake and the

creamy tartness of Key Lime Cheesecake.

When you allow fresh foods to sing for themselves, you'll never hit an off-note in fat-free cooking.

My shopping list and my larder look quite different today than they did 5 years ago and very different from 25 years ago as I've gained more knowledge.

In this chapter, I share my experience in shopping for fat-free ingredients, stocking a fat-free larder, picking the perfect seasonings and choosing the best cookware for fat-free cooking. I share the cooking techniques that extract maximum flavour from foods without adding fat.

Fat-Free Shopping

With the wide range of ever-improving fat-free and low-fat products in supermarkets today, it's easier than ever to cook absolutely scrumptious meals with a minimum of fat.

Just remember that, even with fat-free products, calories do still count. So enjoy these items in sensible portions, and you'll be well-served.

The first step in buying healthy foods is to read the food labels, so it's important to understand what the terms mean. That way, you can shop confidently, secure in the knowledge that you can select the most nutritious low-fat or fat-free foods on the market. These are the terms that you need to know.

Fat-free. Less than 0.5 gramme of fat per serving.

Low-fat. No more than 3 grammes of fat per serving.

Light (lite). One-third fewer calories (or no more than half the fat) of the higher-calorie, higher-fat version. Can also mean no more than half the sodium of the higher-sodium version.

Cholesterol-free. Less than 2 milligrammes of cholesterol and no more than 2 grammes of saturated fat per serving.

Get into the habit of comparing fat grammes on similar products. You'll be surprised at the savings you can reap on seemingly identical foods. For example, depending on the brand, a 125 ml portion of bottled tomato sauce for pasta can contain anywhere from no fat on up to 6 grammes. It obviously pays to read the Nutrition Facts panel on product food labels before you make your selection.

The Fat-Free Kitchen

Life is hard. Grocery shopping should be easy.

Cooking fat-free recipes is practically effortless when you have the right ingredients at your fingertips.

Below I've listed the essentials that you need for larder, refrigerator and freezer - with some selection and storage tips.

All the old larder standbys that have served you well in regular cooking – such as fresh fruits and vegetables, canned tomatoes, plain flour and even granulated sugar – will continue to perform in your fat-free kitchen.

In the Larder

Applesauce. Use it to replace or reduce fat in baked goods. It works very well in muffins, quick breads and cakes.

Biscuits. Fat-free cinnamon and honey biscuits, low-fat gingersnaps, low-fat digestives and low-fat vanilla wafers make tasty pie shells with a fraction of the fat of traditional pastry shells.

Broth. Canned fat-free low-sodium chicken or vegetable broth on the shelf means practically effortless soups, stews, sauces and grain dishes. If you can't find a fat-free chicken broth, refrigerate the can for several hours, then skim off and discard the chilled fat after opening.

Cocoa powder. Here's deep chocolate flavour with nearly all the cocoa butter removed.

Condiments. Piquant seasonings are the life of the fat-free flavour party. Stock items such as dried chipotle peppers, crystallised ginger and low-sodium soy sauce in addition to herbs, spices and prepared mustard.

Dried fruit. Apricots, cherries, cranberries, dates and raisins add sweetness and fibre – but no fat – to baked goods and savoury dishes alike.

Dry pasta. Most dry pasta contains only 1 gramme of fat per 60-g serving, but lower-fat brands that contain 0.5 gramme of fat per 60-g portion are also available, and I've used them in my recipes. Stock a variety of shapes.

Evaporated skimmed milk. This mimics the consistency of double cream in sauces and soups.

Garlic. Whether you mince it with a knife or squeeze it through a press, this powerful bulb is essential in the fat-free kitchen. Store in a cool, dry place but not in plastic and not in the refrigerator.

Jams and preserves. Just a spoonful can brighten both sweet and savoury dishes. And they're fat-free musts for topping muffins, bagels, crumpets, pancakes and waffles.

Juices. Tomato juice, carrot juice and vegetable juice cocktail are handy to have on hand for soup or stew bases or just for a nutritious snack.

Oils and sprays. I've called for scant amounts

(continued on page 13)

Herbs and spices are indispensable seasonings in the fat-free kitchen, where they enhance everything from appetizers to desserts.

Herbs are the green leaves or seeds of plants grown in temperate regions. They're used both fresh and dried. To preserve flavour and colour, cook fresh herbs only briefly or add them to the dish just before serving. Dried herbs need cooking to rehydrate them and release their flavours. If substituting dried herbs for fresh, add about half the amount.

Spices are the dried bark, flowers, roots, seeds or stems of tropical plants. They are sold whole or ground. You can crush or grind spices in your kitchen using a small electric grinder, a blender, or a pestle and mortar. Lightly toasting spices and herb seeds in a dry frying pan just before using heightens their flavour. Spices benefit from cooking to release their flavours.

Store fresh herbs in loosely closed plastic bags in the vegetable drawer of the refrigerator. Store spices and dried herbs in jars or tightly sealed plastic bags a cool, dark cupboard.

Allspice. The flavour is like a blend of cinnamon, nutmeg and cloves. Use ground allspice with pumpkin, winter squash, baked apple dishes, carrot cake or dried-fruit muffins.

Basil. The flavour is like mint and cloves. Use fresh leaves with raw tomatoes, seafood dishes, pasta or creamy dips. Use dried leaves with Italian tomato sauces, minestrone, fish and poultry.

Bay leaf. The flavour is woodsy with a hint of cloves. Use dried leaves in a bouquet garni (an herb bundle that includes parsley stems and thyme) or to flavour stocks, soups, stews, chowders and bean dishes.

Celery seeds. The flavour is like celery but slightly more pungent. Use whole or crushed seeds in salads, poultry, stuffings, soups, stews, vegetables, dips, yeast breads and relishes.

Chilli peppers. The flavour is a combination of ground hot chilli peppers and warm spices. Use in chilli, chilli sauce, guacamole, barbecue sauce, tomato soup, bean dishes, potato salads, salad dressings, stews, egg dishes and Tex-Mex sauces.

Chives. The flavour is like mild onions. Use sliced fresh chives in salads, egg and vegetable dishes, dips and soups.

Cinnamon. The flavour is warm and sweet. Use ground cinnamon in fruit pies, fruit sauces, quick breads, coffee cakes, pancakes, French toast and biscuits.

Cloves. The flavour is pungent and sharp. Use ground cloves in relishes, fruit sauces, winter squash or pumpkin dishes, gingerbread, biscuits, ham dishes or meat or poultry stews.

Coriander (Fresh). The flavour of these fresh leaves is like citrusy parsley. Use fresh leaves in salsas, seafood dishes, guacamole and soups, as well as Asian, Mexican and North African dishes.

Coriander (Dried). The flavour of the dried seeds is citrusy with a hint of nuts. Use crushed or ground seeds in couscous, curries, bean dishes, beef, poultry, pork, fruit compotes or Middle Eastern dishes.

Cumin. The flavour is caraway-like with a hint of heat. Use crushed or ground seeds in chilli, fajitas and other Tex-Mex dishes, couscous, bean dishes, poultry and pork preparations and creamy dips.

Curry powder. The flavour is a blend of various spices, which could include turmeric, cayenne pepper, coriander, black pepper, cumin, fenugreek, mustard seeds, cinnamon and cloves. Use in sauces for seafood or poultry, in egg dishes, with cauliflower or winter squash, or in rice, couscous or other grain dishes.

Dill. The flavour is refreshing and faintly anise-like. Use fresh or dried leaves with beetroot, cucumbers, seafood, poultry, cream dips, salad dressings, courgettes, potatoes and other mild vegetables. Use whole or crushed seeds to make pickles, borscht or creamy dips and salad dressings.

Fennel seeds. The flavour is sweet and mildly aniselike. Use crushed or ground seeds with seafood, poultry or pork, and in yeast breads and tomato sauces.

Ginger. The flavour is hot and sweet. Use ground ginger in gingerbread, biscuits, curries, marinades, sweet-and-sour dishes, chutneys, stews or braised meat and poultry dishes. Grated fresh ginger can be used in the same types of dishes.

Ground cayenne pepper. The flavour is of ground dried hot red peppers. Use in chilli, stews, marinades, barbecue sauce, tomato sauce or other dishes that need a hint of heat.

Mint. The flavour is sweet and cool. Use fresh leaves with seafood, poultry, mild vegetables such as cucumbers, in creamy salad dressings, fruit salads, desserts, mint tea, sorbet, jelly and in Middle Eastern foods. Use dried

(continued)

leaves in tea or cooked fruit or other dessert sauces (strain and discard the leaves before serving).

Nutmeg. The flavour is warm but sharper and less sweet than cinnamon. Use in cheese sauces, spinach dishes, biscuits, quick breads or egg dishes, and with winter squash.

Oregano. The flavour is pungent, sweet and minty. Use with pizza, pork, seafood, poultry, mushrooms and other vegetables, salads, salad dressing, tomato sauces and Italian or Mexican dishes.

Paprika. The flavour is of dried ground sweet or hot red peppers. Use in meat and poultry stews, chowders, Hungarian foods, tomato-based sauces or as a garnish for seafood or light-coloured vegetables.

Parsley. The flavour is clean, refreshing and grassy. Use fresh leaves just before serving in dips, soups, stews and with seafood, eggs, pasta and vegetables. Use fresh stems tied in a bundle with bay leaf and thyme to make a bouquet garni.

Poppy seeds. The flavour is pleasantly bitter-sweet and nutlike. Use with noodles, eggs, potato salad, coleslaw, creamy salad dressings, or in grain and rice dishes, coffee cakes and yeast breads.

Rosemary. The flavour is piney. Use fresh or dried leaves with roasted pork and poultry, mushrooms, beans, pizza, focaccia, yeast breads, potatoes, stuffing and other starchy dishes.

Saffron. The flavour is rich and warm. Use crushed threads in bouillabaisse, paella, tomato soup, poultry dishes or rice dishes. Saffron needs long cooking to bring out the flavour.

Sage. The flavour is pungent and slightly camphorlike. Use fresh or dried leaves in poultry stuffing and stew or with pork or poultry.

Sesame seeds. The flavour is sweet and nut-like. Use in yeast breads, dips, Middle Eastern or Asian dishes and with pasta or other grains.

Tarragon. The flavour is mildly aniselike. Use with poultry, seafood, cheese, vegetable dishes or salad dressings.

Thyme. The flavour is peppery with overtones of mint and lemon. Use in stocks, soups, stews, seafood dishes, egg or cheese dishes or in combination with bay leaf and parsley stems in a bouquet garni.

of oil in only a handful of recipes. Dark sesame oil (often sold in the ethnic section of supermarkets) is used as a seasoning for its intense flavour. Rapeseed oil is used in my Raisin and Spice Oatmeal Biscuits (the only dessert with added fat) to enhance the texture.

Non-stick spray (either aerosol or pump) is used for lubricating pans. Remember, only a fine mist of the spray is needed.

Fat-free butter-flavoured pump spray makes an acceptable substitute for butter on items such as breads, bagels, muffins or steamed vegetables.

Prune purée. This product traps moisture in baked goods in much the same way that fat does, and it is especially good in recipes containing cocoa powder. You can use convenient baby-food prunes. Or you can make your own purée by processing 125 g stoned prunes with 3 tablespoons hot water in a blender or food processor until smooth.

Sweetened condensed milk. The fat-free version of this classic sweet, thick milk provides a rich consistency in some desserts, such as my Key Lime Cheesecake.

Syrups. Golden syrup can be used in some desserts – such as Citrus-Glazed Carrot Cake – as a fat replacer. You can also stock fat-free caramel topping and chocolate syrup as well as honey, maple syrup and molasses for drizzling on desserts, pancakes or French toast.

Tapioca. Cooked with fat-free creamer or skimmed milk, quick-cooking tapioca makes a wonderfully rich pudding. The dry tapioca granules are also a great thickener for fruit pies.

Vinegar. Vinegar contains absolutely no fat and really brings out the flavour in foods. Try sweet-tart balsamic, cider, red-wine or white-wine vinegar.

In the Refrigerator

Citrus fruits. You'll want to keep lemons, limes and oranges on hand always. Store them in a loosely closed plastic bag in the vegetable drawer of your refrigerator for up to two weeks. Use the grated rind (scrub the fruit well and rinse before grating) and the juice to add zest to everything from appetizers to desserts.

Condiments. For perking up stews, sauces, salads or main dishes, try capers, gherkins (dill and sweet), roasted red peppers or pimientos (jarred), salsa, relishes, ketchup, low-sodium Worcestershire sauce, Dijon mustard, fresh ginger, hoisin sauce, horseradish and hot-pepper sauce.

> It's easy and inexpensive to make your own non-stick spray. Fill a new or well-cleaned plastic pump bottle with rapeseed, olive or other vegetable oil (or a blend). You'll be able to spray a scant ½ teaspoon of oil into the pan – at a cost of only about 2 grammes of fat. Compare that with pouring in 2 tablespoons of oil, which would be a whopping 27 grammes of fat.

Dairy whipped topping. Skimmed milk–based fat-free aerosol whipped topping is a fine substitute for whipped cream on pumpkin pudding, fat-free sundaes and other desserts.

Eggs. Egg whites are both fat-free and cholesterol-free. They're indispensable for lightening and tenderising cakes, soufflés and some biscuits.

Liquid creamers. These fat-free non-dairy and dairy creamers, found in the dairy case, mimic the consistency of double cream in soups and sauces. Choose plain (not flavoured) for cooking. Be sure to check the labels – some contain more sweeteners than others.

Liquid egg substitute. This convenient, pasteurised, fat-free product, which is primarily made from egg whites, is great for omelettes, frittatas, mayonnaise, pancakes, waffles, French toast and baked goods. You can substitute 4 tablespoons egg substitute for each large egg in a recipe.

Mayonnaise. When fat-free mayonnaise is well-seasoned in a sauce or dressing, you won't know it's not the real McCoy.

Milk. Fat-free buttermilk and skimmed milk are good for baking and sauces.

Parmesan topping. Look for fat-free brands that contain some real Parmesan or Romano cheese in the ingredient list.

Polenta in a tube. This ready-to-serve polenta is not only super-convenient but also fat-free. It comes in several flavours, including plain, mushroom and sun-dried tomato.

Poultry and meat. Always select "lean" meats with no visible fat or marbling. Best beef choices are top round and sirloin. Tenderloin is the leanest pork. Lean ham is also a good choice.

30 grammes of cured, smoked pork tenderloin contains only 2.4 grammes of fat, compared with 13.9 grammes in standard bacon.

Boneless, skinless turkey breast, trimmed of all visible fat, is as close to fat-free as poultry can be. And some producers are marketing boneless, skinless chicken breasts with only 0.5 gramme of fat in a 90-g cooked portion. So read labels carefully to always choose the lowest-fat cut possible and always trim off all visible fat.

Fat-free sliced lunchmeat, such as chicken breast, ham or turkey breast, is convenient for sandwiches and salads.

Semifirm cheeses. Look for fat-free Cheddar, mozzarella and Swiss. A few years ago, fat-free cheese was a synonym for rubber, but now there are major brands that melt well. I particularly like individually wrapped slices for melting.

Remember that unless you are on a severely fat-restricted diet, you can enjoy low-fat cheeses blended with fat-free cheeses. Each 30 grammes of low-fat cheese (such as Swiss or mozzarella) adds about 3.5 grammes of fat to the total recipe.

Soft cheeses. Select fat-free cottage cheese, cream cheese, mozzarella and ricotta to add a creamy dairy flavour and consistency to a variety of dishes.

Soured cream. Choose fat-free soured cream, which has the added bonus of not separating when heated, as full-fat soured cream does.

Tortillas. Fat-free flour tortillas keep well in the refrigerator for up to a week (and much longer in the freezer). Use for fajitas or tacos, or serve with scrambled egg substitute or bean dishes.

Yogurt. Fat-free natural yogurt is essential for sauces and for making creamy, tangy Yogurt Cheese (see page 304).

Flavoured and fruit fat-free yogurts are good in sauces and baked goods or eaten as snacks.

In the Freezer

Breads. Keep bagels, bread (40 calories per slice) and pita bread on hand for sandwiches and recipes. Stock muffins and fat-free crumpets for breakfast.

Homemade vegetable or chicken stock. Make a batch (see pages 93 and 94) and freeze it as a handy base for soups, stews, sauces and stir-fries.

Non-dairy fat-free whipped topping. This is convenient for impromptu desserts.

Phyllo, or filo, dough. These paper-thin sheets of fat-free pastry make wonderful pie shells or appetizer wrappers for fat-free fillings. Thaw according to package directions. Lightly coat each sheet of phyllo with non-stick spray so the sheets will stay separate and crisp.

Poultry, seafood and beef. It's convenient to have a variety on hand in recipe-ready portions.

Equipment for Fat-Free Cooking

Non-stick cookware is essential for fat-free cooking. And because it's such a breeze to clean up, you may find yourself cooking much more often.

With just a whisper of non-stick spray in a non-stick frying pan, you can turn onions and other vegetables into flavour gold as the base for great-tasting dishes. You can also brown turkey cutlets, chicken pieces, stewing beef and fish fillets with no added fat.

Fat-free surfaces are tremendously improved from the original coatings that chipped and flaked soon after they were put into use. In general, the heavier the pan, the better the heat is conducted for more even cooking. Aluminium, cast iron and stainless steel (with a bottom pad of aluminium or copper) are all good choices. Check the following list for the pots and pans that you need in your kitchen and then shop for the best that you can afford.

Non-stick bakeware is nice to have but not essential. All the dessert recipes in this book work beautifully with standard bakeware and non-stick spray. Or you can line baking dishes and sheets with greaseproof paper, wax paper or the reusable non-stick sheets that can be cut to fit the dimensions of any pan.

Sharp, good-quality knives are essential for fat-free cooking. They let you trim all fat from meats, as well as skin and fat from fish and poultry. And they make peeling and cutting vegetables and fruits a joy.

High-carbon stainless-steel forged knives are durable, hold an edge well and won't rust as old-fashioned carbon-steel knives did. Good sizes include a 25 cm *chef's knife*, a 25 cm serrated knife, a 10 cm serrated knife and three 7.5 or 10 cm paring knives (I always misplace mine) for peeling fruits and vegetables. A knife sharpener is also a good investment.

I prefer dishwasher-safe knives with molded polyurethane handles, which I always place on the top shelf of the dish-washer away from the drying coils. You may prefer to hand wash and dry your knives to protect them from unwanted bumps that may dull the blades.

Kitchen scissors are great, too, for trimming fat as well as snipping fresh herbs – even for cutting pizza without scratching the pan.

Glass or plastic defatting jugs are a must for removing fat from stocks, soups and meat drippings. I prefer large glass ones because they handle more liquid and remain transparent, unlike some of the plastic cups, which can turn cloudy and crack with heavy use. As a safety precaution, don't pour boiling liquid into a glass jug.

Non-stick Cookware

* Small saucepan (1 litre)
* Medium saucepan (2 litres)
* Large saucepan (3 or 4 litres)
* Flameproof casserole (6 litres)
* Small frying pan (15 or 20 cm)
* Large frying pan (25 or 30 cm)
* Lids (assorted, to fit pans)

Bakeware

* Baking dishes (33 x 23 cm;
  30 x 20 cm; 20 x 20 cm)
* Baking trays
* Bundt tin (3 litres)
* Cake tins (23 cm)
* Loaf tin (20 x 10 cm)
* Pie plates (23 cm regular,
  25 cm deep-dish)
* Soufflé dish (1.5 litres)
* Springform tin (23 cm)
* Tube tin (25 cm)

Kitchen Tools

* Blender, food processor or
  hand blender
* Defatting jug
* Electric mixer
* Kitchen scissors
* Knives
* Whisks

Fat-Free Preparation and Cooking Methods

Trim it and *skim it*. That's all you need to know to rid excess fat from your food before and after cooking.

Before cooking, trim all visible skin and fat from seafood, poultry and meat. Don't trust your supermarket meat cutter with this important job. Your motivation to do a thorough job is the desire for improved health.

After cooking stocks, soups, stews, chilli, a roast with pan drippings or any other dish that contains melted fat, skim as much fat from the surface as you can before serving. Melted fat is clear and rises to the top, where it's easy to capture and discard. You can do this in three ways.

Spoon it. Skim off the melted fat with a large spoon.

Pour it. For clear preparations, such as stock, use a large defatting jug. Pour the liquid into the jug, which has a spout that starts at the bottom. Wait a few seconds until the clear melted fat rises to the top. Slowly pour out the stock (which comes from the bottom of the jug), stopping just before the fat reaches the base of the spout. I usually do two passes with the defatting jug to get rid of every drop of fat.

(continued on page 20)

101 Fabulous Fat-Free Foods

The best foods in life are free – from fat. You can feast on any of these 101 satisfying selections, all with less than 1 gramme of fat. When you base your eating plan on low-fat, nutrient-rich foods, you get more bang for your fat-gramme bucks. When naturally low-fat foods are cooked with excess fat, the cost is high. For example, a measly 10 potato crisps – hardly a satisfying amount of food – will cost you 6.9 grammes of fat. You'd have to eat 34 large baked potatoes to spend the same amount of fat grammes.

Amount	Food	Fat (g.)	Amount	Food	Fat (g.)
Fruits and Fruit Juices			**Vegetables and Vegetable Juices**		
1	apple	0.5	10	asparagus spears, cooked	0.5
250 ml	apple juice	0.3	90 g	beans, canned baked vegetarian	0.6
6	apricot halves, dried	0.1	90 g	beans, green (cooked)	0.4
1	banana	0.6	185 g	beans, red kidney (cooked)	0.9
250 g	blueberries	0.6	185 g	beans, lima (cooked)	0.5
375 g	cantaloupe cubes	0.5	155 g	broccoli (chopped), cooked	0.6
90 g	cherries, sweet	0.9	90 g	cabbage (shredded)	0.2
½	grapefruit, pink or red	0.1	1	carrot	0.1
155 g	grapes, seedless	0.9	125 g	carrots (sliced), cooked	0.3
375 g	honeydew cubes	0.2	125 g	cauliflower (chopped), cooked	0.6
1	kiwifruit	0.3	125 g	courgettes (sliced), cooked	0.1
375 g	mango slices	0.5	90 g	lentils (cooked)	0.8
1	nectarine	0.6	45 g	lettuce, cos(chopped)	0.1
1	orange	0.2	45 g	lettuce, iceberg (chopped)	0.1
250 ml	orange juice	0.7	250 g	mushroom pieces (cooked)	0.7
1	peach	0.1	125 g	peas, frozen (cooked)	0.4
1	pear, Bartlett	0.7	125 g	peppers, green (chopped)	0.1
155 g	pineapple chunks	0.7	1	potato, large with skin (baked)	0.2
1	plum	0.4	185 g	spinach (cooked)	0.5
90 g	raisins	0.3	125 g	spinach (chopped)	0.2
155 g	raspberries, red	0.7	125 g	squash, acorn (cubes), baked	0.3
155 g	cut strawberries	0.5	185	sweetcorn, frozen (cooked)	0.1
1	tangerine	0.2			
250 g	watermelon cubes	0.7			

Amount	Food	Fat (g.)
1	sweet potato, medium (baked)	0.1
1	tomato	0.4
250 g	tomatoes, canned stewed	0.4
250 ml	tomato juice	0.2

Grains, Breads, and Cereals

Amount	Food	Fat (g.)
½	bagel, plain	0.5
3	biscuits, small	0.9
½ slice	bread, cracked wheat	0.7
½ slice	bread, white sliced sandwich	0.6
125 g	bulgur (cooked)	0.4
60 g	cereal, bran flakes	0.7
60 g	cereal, corn flakes	0.1
90 g	cereal, frosted bite-size shredded wheat	0.6
90 g	cereal, bite-size shredded wheat	0.9
60 g	cereal, wheat flakes	0.5
90 g	couscous (cooked)	0.3
2	crackers	0.7
10	crackers, wheat crispbread	0.6
1	digestive biscuit	0.7
125 g	macaroni (cooked)	0.9
½	muffin, plain	0.5
90 g	oatmeal (cooked)	0.8
1	pita bread, white	0.7
90 g	popcorn (air-popped)	0.7
15 g.	pretzels, thin-twist	0.5
250 g	rice, long-grain white (cooked)	0.6
125 g	rice, long-grain brown (cooked)	0.9
2	rice cakes, multigrain brown	0.6
125 g	spaghetti (cooked)	0.9
1	tortilla, corn	0.8

Amount	Food	Fat (g.)

Dairy Foods

Amount	Food	Fat (g.)
250 g	cottage cheese, fat-free	0.0
90 g	cottage cheese, 1% low-fat	0.8
2 Tbsp	milk, instant fat-free dried	0.1
250 ml	milk, canned evaporated skimmed	0.5
60 ml	milk, 1% low-fat	0.7
250 ml	milk, fat-free skimmed	0.4
250 g	yogurt, fat-free with fruit	0.4
250 g	yogurt, lemon fat-free	0.4
250 g	yogurt, natural fat-free	0.4

Seafood and Turkey

Amount	Food	Fat (g.)
90 g	cod, Atlantic (baked or broiled)	0.7
90 g	crab, blue (steamed)	0.7
60 g	flounder (baked or grilled)	0.9
60 g	grouper (baked or grilled)	0.7
90 g	haddock (baked or grilled)	0.8
30 g	halibut (baked or grilled)	0.8
90 g	mahimahi (baked or grilled)	0.8
90 g	orange roughy (baked or grilled)	0.8
60 g	perch (baked or grilled)	0.7
60 g	pollack, walleye (baked or grilled)	0.6
90 g	prawns, large (steamed)	0.9
30 g	scallops (steamed)	0.9
60 g	snapper (baked or grilled)	0.9
60 g	sole (baked or grilled)	0.9
75 g	turkey breast, skinless (roasted)	0.8
90 g	tuna, light, drained, canned in water	0.6

Lift it. Let time do the work for you. This method works especially well for stews and other dishes with lots of chunky ingredients. Refrigerate the finished dish for several hours or overnight, until the fat hardens on the top. Pick off and discard the layer of fat. You'll feel victorious as you toss that fat into the rubbish bin.

Fat-Free Cooking Techniques

You might be surprised to learn that you already know a lot of fat-free cooking techniques. You use them in your kitchen every day. The difference is that now you'll be doing them with non-stick cookware and no added fat. Here's the rundown.

Braising. Braising cooks foods in a small amount of liquid in a tightly covered pan or baking dish on the stove top or in the oven. Seafood, poultry and meat can be browned before braising using the dry-frying technique below. This will boost the flavour of the finished dish. The liquid is often reduced after cooking as the base for an accompanying sauce.

Dry-frying. Dry-frying sears foods to seal in moisture. Lightly coat the food – such as turkey cutlets or fish fillets – with non-stick spray, then sear in a hot frying pan. Cast iron or aluminium non-stick frying pans work best, because they can be heated to higher temperatures.

Grilling and Barbecuing. These direct-heat methods cook vegetables and small cuts of meat, poultry and seafood quickly, sealing in juices and browning the surface without added fat.

Brush the grill rack with a few drops of oil or lightly coat the food with non-stick spray before cooking. To add flavour to low-fat cuts, marinate the food or baste during cooking with seasoned skimmed stock.

To barbecue small pieces of seafood or vegetables, place them on a special cooking rack, perforated with small holes, that sits right on top of the BBQ rack. Or create your own perforated surface by punching holes in a double thickness of foil.

Microwaving. A microwave is especially useful for moist-heat recipes such as braises, soups and stews.

Poaching. This method cooks seafood, poultry and vegetables submerged in simmering seasoned water, juice, wine or other liquids. Always poach at a gentle simmer, never a boil.

Roasting. This method of oven-cooking food in an uncovered tin is ideal for vegetables and tender cuts of poultry, meat and seafood. Enhance flavour with dry seasoning rubs or marinades.

Steaming. This method cooks seafood, poultry or vegetables on a collapsible metal steamer with legs set over boiling liquid in a tightly covered pan.

The steamer unit must sit comfortably inside the pan with some room to spare around the sides, so that the steam rises around the food. Fill the pan with about 2.5 cm of water. Place the steamer rack in the pan and put the food to be steamed on the rack. Cover and bring the water to a boil. Reduce the heat slightly and cook for the amount of time specified in the recipe.

Many foods can also be steamed on a barbecue or in the oven, tightly wrapped in foil packets or in an oven bag, with some seasoned liquid and chopped vegetables added for flavour.

Stewing. Stewing is a method of cooking several foods in a seasoned liquid such as stock or wine. The liquid base, often thickened, is served as part of the dish.

Stir-frying. Cutting seafood, poultry, meat and vegetables into small pieces is the secret to successful stir-frying with just a coating of non-stick spray in a very hot frying pan or wok. For best results, always stir-fry in small batches. If the pan is too crowded, the ingredients will steam instead of brown.

Appetisers, Finger Foods, Dips and Spreads

Appetisers and predinner nibbles don't have to contain fat to be welcoming and delicious. With fat-free recipes, you can show your family and guests real hospitality – food that tastes good, looks good, and is good for them.

I'll show you how to make delicious party fare that proves you care about the well-being of your guests. You won't spend a fortune or countless hours in the kitchen.

The best parties are celebrations of good health.

I love serving fat-free appetisers because I know that I'm not contributing to anyone's health or weight problems. These satisfying morsels won't make you feel guilty. When you can enjoy tasty appetisers that are free of fat, why not indulge?

Serving such festive, delicious appetisers is possible with the wonderful new low fat dairy products. Forget the unhealthy full-fat soured cream, cream cheese and mayonnaise hors d'oeuvres of yesterday.

Something for Every Appetite

Because so many people with lighter appetites can make a meal of appetizers, I have included a section of first courses, several of which could be served together. My seafood appetisers are simple to make and fit this role nicely. Try Grilled Plaice with Fennel, Baked Red Snapper with Clams, Seafood Medley or Parsleyed Bay Scallops.

Some of my vegetable appetisers, such as Roast Parmesan Asparagus and Summer Courgettes are celebrations of seasonal bounty and deserve to be treated as a course of their own. You can also serve them as side dishes at a more casual meal.

Less Work—More Fun

For your casual parties, always put out plenty of fat-free foods to make the offerings look really lavish. Guests will never feel deprived with heaping bowls of fat-free crisps, fat-free corn chips, pretzels, air-popped pop-corn and fat-free crackers. I always include a huge vegetable platter filled with every vegetable possible.

To go with the crisps, crackers and vegetables, make-ahead dips and spreads are always popular and never go out of style. Try my Pinto Bean Dip, Crunchy Onion Dip or Dill Dip.

Don't forget luscious fresh fruit for parties. With their vivid colours, fresh fruits dress up any table. And if you're serving perfectly ripe fruit, you really don't have to do anything to it. Make a large paper cone or use a basket cornucopia spilling out with bananas, bunches of grapes, papayas, plums or whatever fruit is in season. In the summer, cut a melon basket and fill it with bite-size fruit pieces.

For no-cook appetisers, try fat-free ham, chicken and turkey products or fat-free cheese slices. Wrap them around chunks of melon, mangoes, pears, pickled cucumbers or cornichons. Spear with cocktail sticks.

Tomates à la Marseillaise

quick and easy

My terrific former assistant, Marty Cavendish, loved this tomato dish when she lived in France. She has found that its sunny flavours travel beautifully to this country. The tomatoes have to be garden fresh and very ripe. I like them seasoned with a lot of freshly ground black pepper.

1   clove garlic, cut in half
2   ripe medium tomatoes, at room temperature, cut in half
1   teaspoon dried basil
1   teaspoon dried oregano
1   teaspoon dried thyme
    Ground black pepper
    Salt (optional)
4   medium cos lettuce leaves (optional)

1   Coat a large non-stick frying pan with non-stick spray. Warm the pan over medium heat. Rub the cut side of the garlic halves around the pan, then discard the cloves.

2   Place the tomatoes, cut side up, in the pan. Mist with non-stick spray. Sprinkle with the basil, oregano and thyme. Press the herbs down lightly with the palm of your hand. Season to taste with the pepper and salt (if using). Cover and cook for 4 minutes.

3   Turn the tomatoes. Cover and cook for 4 to 5 minutes, or until the tomatoes are hot. Serve, cut side up, on the lettuce (if using).

Makes **4** servings.

nutrition at a glance

per serving
0.3 g. total fat
0 g. saturated fat
17 calories
0 mg. cholesterol
6 mg. sodium
1 g. protein
4 g. carbohydrates
1 g. dietary fibre

Roast Parmesan Asparagus

quick and easy

So simple, yet it tastes like Italy. My special taster and friend Beth Mendelson calls this the best asparagus ever. Thick spears work better than thin for baking.

500	g asparagus
125	ml water
2	tablespoons freshly squeezed lemon juice
	Ground black pepper
	Salt (optional)
45	g fat-free Parmesan topping

1 Preheat the oven to 190°C, Gas 5. Coat a 30 x 20 cm baking dish with non-stick spray.

2 Arrange the asparagus in the dish in rows. Add the water and lemon juice. Season to taste with the pepper and salt (if using). Sprinkle with the Parmesan.

3 Cover loosely with foil. Bake for 20 minutes, or until the asparagus is tender.

Makes **4** servings.

nutrition at a glance

per serving

0.2 g.	total fat
0 g.	saturated fat
60	calories
0 mg.	cholesterol
201 mg.	sodium
8 g.	protein
9 g.	carbohydrates
1 g.	dietary fibre

Summer Courgettes

quick and easy

The flecks of fresh tomatoes, sun-dried tomatoes and yellow peppers add colour and perk up the flavour of this mild summer squash.

125	ml boiling water
2	dry-pack sun-dried tomato halves
500	g courgettes, thinly sliced
1	onion, thinly sliced
1	small yellow pepper, diced
2	cloves garlic, minced
45	g chopped tomatoes
1	tablespoon thinly sliced fresh basil
2	teaspoons balsamic vinegar
	Ground black pepper
	Salt (optional)

1   Place the water and sun-dried tomatoes in a small bowl. Let stand for 10 minutes. Drain and finely chop. Set aside.

2   Coat a large non-stick frying pan with non-stick spray. Add the courgettes, onions, yellow peppers and garlic. Cover and cook over medium-high heat, stirring occasionally, for 4 to 5 minutes, or until the vegetables soften and start to brown. If necessary, add 1 or 2 teaspoons water to prevent sticking.

3   Add the chopped tomatoes and sun-dried tomatoes. Uncover and cook over medium-high heat, stirring occasionally, for 5 minutes, or until the vegetables are tender. Stir in the basil and vinegar. Season to taste with the black pepper and salt (if using).

Makes **6** servings.

nutrition at a glance

per serving

0.2 g.	total fat
0 g.	saturated fat
36	calories
0 mg.	cholesterol
76 mg.	sodium
2 g.	protein
8 g.	carbohydrates
2 g.	dietary fibre

Tabbouleh with Cucumbers

Tabbouleh – a nutrient-rich Middle Eastern bulgur salad – makes a refreshing appetizer for a summer gathering. Thinly sliced tender young courgettes make a nice alternative to the cucumber. I prefer finely ground bulgur rather than the more coarse types of bulgur.

250	ml water
100	g bulgur
	Pinch of salt (optional)
1	small tomato, diced
60	g chopped fresh parsley
60	g finely chopped onions or spring onions
2	tablespoons grated carrots
2	tablespoons freshly squeezed lemon juice
1	tablespoon chopped fresh mint
1	tablespoon dried currants or chopped raisins
½	teaspoon ground cumin
	Pinch of ground allspice
	Coarsely ground black pepper
1	medium cucumber, thinly sliced

1 Bring the water to a boil in a medium non-stick saucepan. Add the bulgur and salt (if using). Reduce the heat to low, cover and cook for 8 to 10 minutes, or until the bulgur is tender and the liquid is absorbed. Remove from the heat. Fluff with a fork, then set aside to cool. Refrigerate for several hours to chill thoroughly.

2 In a medium bowl, combine the tomatoes, parsley, onions, carrots, lemon juice, mint, currants or raisins, cumin and allspice. Toss to mix well. Season to taste with the pepper.

3 Add the bulgur and toss well. Chill if desired.

4 Arrange the cucumbers in a spiral pattern on a platter. Spoon the tabbouleh in the centre.

Makes **6** servings.

nutrition at a glance

per serving

0.4 g.	total fat
0.1 g.	saturated fat
63	calories
0 mg.	cholesterol
11 mg.	sodium
2 g.	protein
14 g.	carbohydrates
3 g.	dietary fibre

Grilled Plaice with Fennel

Many fish can take the place of the mild-tasting plaice. Try sole, halibut, brill, dab, monkfish or turbot. Save the leafy fronds from the fennel to use as a garnish.

1	tablespoon grated lemon rind
2	teaspoons fennel seeds, crushed
1	teaspoon dried thyme
	Pinch of salt (optional)
4	plaice fillets (75 g each)
250	g sliced fennel
	Ground black pepper
2	tablespoons freshly squeezed lemon juice (optional)
2	tablespoons freshly squeezed orange juice (optional)

1 In a small bowl, combine the lemon rind, fennel seeds, thyme and salt (if using); mix well.

2 Rinse the fish and pat dry with paper towels. Coat both sides of the fish with non-stick spray. Place in a single layer on a platter. Sprinkle with the seasoning mix and pat it firmly in place. Cover and refrigerate for 1 to 2 hours.

3 About 15 minutes before cooking the fish, bring 2.5 cm of water to a boil in a large non-stick saucepan. Add the sliced fennel and cook for 6 to 7 minutes, or until tender when pierced with a sharp knife. Drain; return to the pan and mist with non-stick spray. Sprinkle with the pepper. Cover and keep warm.

4 Cover a baking tray with foil. Place the fish on the tray in a single layer. Grill 10 cm from the heat for 4 minutes, or until the fish is opaque in the centre. (Check by inserting the tip of a sharp knife in the centre of 1 fillet.)

5 Serve the fish with the fennel. Sprinkle with the lemon juice (if using) and orange juice (if using).

Makes **4** servings.

nutrition at a glance

per serving

0.9 g.	total fat
0.2 g.	saturated fat
76	calories
33 mg.	cholesterol
70 mg.	sodium
12.5 g.	protein
4 g.	carbohydrates
2 g.	dietary fibre

Baked Red Snapper with Clams

quick and easy

This impressive appetizer was inspired by the Baked Mackerel with Clams in *Jane Brody's Good Seafood Book*. I've substituted lean red snapper, which makes a really pretty presentation, but striped bass or mullet works well, too.

4   red snapper fillets (75 g each), skin on
1   teaspoon dried rosemary, crumbled
1   teaspoon dried oregano
    Pinch of salt (optional)
8   clams, scrubbed
60 ml freshly squeezed lemon juice
60 ml skimmed chicken stock (page 94)
3   cloves garlic, minced
4   tablespoons chopped fresh parsley
    Ground black pepper

1   Preheat the oven to 230°C, Gas 8.

2   Rinse the fish and pat dry with paper towels. Score the skin side with four or five diagonal slashes. Sprinkle on both sides with the rosemary, oregano and salt (if using).

3   Coat a 32 x 23 cm baking dish with non-stick spray. Place the fish in the dish, skin side up, in a single layer.

4   Add the clams to the dish. Sprinkle with the lemon juice, stock and garlic.

5   Bake for 15 to 20 minutes, or until the fish is cooked (check by inserting the tip of a sharp knife in the centre of a fillet) and the clams are opened and hot. Discard any unopened clams. Sprinkle with the parsley and season to taste with pepper.

6   Serve the fish and clams with the pan juices spooned over top.

Makes **4** servings.

Photograph on page 51

nutrition at a glance
per serving

0.9 g.	total fat
0.2 g.	saturated fat
72	calories
24 mg.	cholesterol
35 mg.	sodium
13 g.	protein
3.4 g.	carbohydrates
0.5 g.	dietary fibre

Seafood Medley

This dish of prawns and scallops is a colourful, tasty, and quick appetizer. For a special presentation, serve it in scallop shells (available in cookware shops) or shallow individual baking dishes. Sprinkle with fat-free Parmesan topping and grill for 1 to 2 minutes, or until golden.

155	g peeled prawns
125	g scallops
1	medium tomato, chopped
4	spring onions, sliced diagonally
125	ml clam juice
4	tablespoons thinly sliced fresh basil
60	ml white wine or non-alcoholic white wine
1	clove garlic, minced
¼	teaspoon ground black pepper
	Pinch of salt (optional)
1	tablespoon cornflour
4	teaspoons fat-free Parmesan topping

1 In a large non-stick frying pan, combine the prawns, scallops, tomatoes, spring onions, half of the clam juice, the basil, wine, garlic, pepper and salt (if using). Cover and cook over medium-low heat for 7 minutes, or until the scallops are nearly opaque.

2 Place the cornflour in a cup. Add the remaining clam juice and stir to dissolve the cornflour. Add to the frying pan. Stir for 1 minute, or until the sauce thickens. Sprinkle with the Parmesan.

Makes **4** servings.

Lynn's Kitchen Tip

Prawns are very perishable, so most of the commercial catch is frozen right after it's caught. Unless you are planning to cook prawns immediately after buying, it makes good sense to purchase bagged loose-pack frozen prawns and thaw just the amount you need before cooking. The prawns may indeed taste fresher than thawed prawns that have lingered too long at the fish mongers. To thaw prawns, refrigerate overnight in a plastic bag.

nutrition at a glance

per serving

0.9 g.	total fat
0.2 g.	saturated fat
96	calories
74 mg.	cholesterol
456 mg.	sodium
11 g.	protein
6 g.	carbohydrates
0.6 g.	dietary fibre

Parsleyed Queen Scallops

quick and easy

These succulent queen scallops are bursting with sweet flavour. Serve them with a crisscross of thinly sliced sweet red peppers. For a light main course, try them over linguine, white rice, brown rice or wild rice. (Omit the cornflour and toss the linguine or rice gently with the scallop mixture just before serving.)

3	cloves garlic, minced
1	tablespoon water
250	g queen scallops
2	tablespoons chopped fresh parsley
¼	teaspoon crushed chillies
250	ml white wine or non-alcoholic white wine
2	teaspoons cornflour
	Ground black pepper
	Salt (optional)

1   Coat a large non-stick frying pan with non-stick spray. Warm the pan over medium heat. Add the garlic and water. Cook, stirring, for 2 minutes, or until the garlic is softened.

2   Reduce the heat to low. Add the scallops, parsley, chillies and 180 ml of the wine. Simmer, stirring occasionally, for 5 minutes, or until the scallops are opaque.

3   Place the cornflour in a cup. Add the remaining wine and stir to dissolve the cornflour. Add to the frying pan and stir constantly until the sauce thickens. Season to taste with the black pepper and salt (if using).

Makes **4** servings.

nutrition at a glance

per serving
0.9 g.	total fat
0.2 g.	saturated fat
52	calories
9 mg.	cholesterol
119 mg.	sodium
5 g.	protein
1 g.	carbohydrates
0.1 g.	dietary fibre

Southwestern Polenta

The crisp texture of pant-grilled polenta and the richness of black beans and salsa make this meal opener a tight winner.

1	tube (500 g) prepared fat-free polenta
½	teaspoon ground cumin
½	teaspoon dried oregano
250	ml salsa
185	g cooked black beans
4	spring onions, finely sliced
125	ml fat-free soured cream
1	tablespoon chopped fresh coriander

1 Cut the polenta into 8 slices. Sprinkle evenly on both sides with the cumin and oregano; press gently to adhere.

2 Coat a large non-stick frying pan with non-stick spray. Warm over medium-high heat. Place the polenta in the pan in a single layer. Reduce the heat to medium-low and cook for 5 minutes on each side, or until golden and heated through. Remove the polenta to a platter; cover loosely with foil to keep warm.

3 Add the salsa, beans, and spring onions to the frying pan. Simmer for 2 to 3 minutes, or until hot.

4 Spoon the salsa mixture over the polenta. Top with the soured cream and sprinkle with the coriander.

Makes **4** servings.

Photograph on page 155

Lynn's Fat-Free Flavour

The proliferation of jarred salsas in recent years has ushered great taste and convenience into the low-fat kitchen. They add zest to everything from scrambled fat-free egg substitute to grilled poultry.

---

nutrition at a glance

per serving

0.4 g.	total fat
0.1 g.	saturated fat
· 189	calories
0 mg.	cholesterol
687 mg.	sodium
8 g.	protein
37 g.	carbohydrates
8 g.	dietary fibre

Bruschetta with Tomatoes

quick and easy

My guests have never guessed that these salad-topped garlic toasts – so evocative of the Mediterranean – contain no fat. Bruschetta is so versatile that it can be served hot, warm, at room temperature or chilled. You can prepare the topping and the garlic toasts ahead, but don't spoon on the topping until serving time, or the toasts will get soggy.

16 rounds (about 6 mm thick x 4 cm wide) Italian or
     French bread
3   cloves garlic
1   medium onion, coarsely chopped
2   large plum tomatoes, diced
4   tablespoons thinly sliced fresh basil
2   teaspoons balsamic vinegar
     Ground black pepper
     Salt (optional)

1   Preheat the oven to 165°C, Gas 3. Cover a baking tray with foil.

2   Place the bread on the tray in a single layer. Coat both sides with non-stick spray. Bake for 20 minutes, or until golden.

3   Cut 1 clove of the garlic in half. Rub the cut sides over the tops of the toast; discard the garlic halves.

4   Meanwhile, coat a large non-stick frying pan with non-stick spray. Add the onions. Mist with non-stick spray. Cover and cook over medium-high heat, stirring occasionally, for 3 to 4 minutes, or until the onions start to release liquid. Reduce the heat to medium. Uncover and cook, stirring occasionally, for 3 to 4 minutes, or until golden. If necessary, add 1 to 2 teaspoons water to prevent sticking.

5   Add the tomatoes. Mince the remaining 2 cloves garlic and add to the frying pan. Cook, stirring occasionally, for 2 to 3 minutes, or until the tomatoes soften slightly. Remove from the heat.

Stir in the basil and vinegar. Season to taste with the pepper and salt (if using).

6 Place a spoonful of the topping on each garlic toast.

Makes **16** servings.

Photograph on page 47

Gingery Stuffed Tomatoes

Very Asian and very simple, this refreshing summer appetizer is slightly hot from the fresh ginger.

60 ml rice vinegar or cider vinegar
2 tablespoons sugar
1½ teaspoons minced fresh ginger
1 teaspoon low-sodium soy sauce
½ teaspoon dark sesame oil
1 cucumber, peeled, seeded and grated
20 cherry tomatoes
2 teaspoons toasted sesame seeds (optional)

1 In a medium bowl, combine the vinegar, sugar, ginger, soy sauce, and oil. Add the cucumbers and mix well. The mixture will be watery. Lightly smash with a potato masher or the bottom of a heavy glass. Let stand for 20 to 30 minutes.

2 Slice 2 mm from the stem end of each tomato. Cut a thin slice from the tomato bottoms, if necessary, so the tomatoes can stand without wobbling. With a small metal spoon or small melon baller, remove the flesh from inside the tomatoes; discard.

3 Drain the cucumbers. With your fingers or a small spoon, stuff the cucumber mixture into the tomatoes. Sprinkle with the sesame seeds (if using).

Makes **20** tomatoes.

Japanese Pork Dumplings

These savoury morsels will win raves at your next party. Using bought wonton skins, they really aren't difficult to make. And you can assemble them several hours before serving. Place the sealed dumplings in a single layer on a damp tray, cover loosely with cling film and refrigerate.

Soy Dipping Sauce

5	tablespoons low-sodium soy sauce
2	teaspoons rice vinegar
2	teaspoons minced garlic
1	teaspoon grated fresh ginger
1	teaspoon sugar
	Hot-pepper sauce

Pork Dumplings

250	g thinly sliced baby bok choy or Chinese cabbage
155	g lean minced pork tenderloin, all visible fat removed before grinding
90	g diced or grated carrots
3	cloves garlic, minced
1	tablespoon low-sodium soy sauce
2	teaspoons dry sherry or ½ teaspoon sherry extract (optional)
1	teaspoon brown sugar
½	teaspoon dark sesame oil
32	square or round wonton wrappers

1 *To make the soy dipping sauce:* In a small bowl, combine the soy sauce, vinegar, garlic, ginger and sugar; mix well. Season to taste with the hot-pepper sauce. Set aside.

2 *To make the pork dumplings:* In a large microwaveable bowl, combine the cabbage, pork, carrots and garlic. Cover and microwave on high power for a total of 4 minutes, or until the pork is no longer pink; stop and stir every 60 seconds during this time. Pour off and discard any liquid.

3 Stir in the soy sauce, sherry or sherry extract (if using), brown sugar and sesame oil. Transfer to a blender or food processor. Process until finely chopped. (The mixture can also be chopped in the bowl with a hand blender.)

Lynn's Kitchen Tip

Wontons also make convenient wrappers for home-made ravioli stuffed with fat-free cheeses or mush-rooms. These square or round dough wrappers can be found occasionally nestled in the frozen food case of large super-markets or in Oriental food shops.

4   Place 4 wonton wrappers at a time on a work surface. Have a small bowl of water at hand. Dip your index finger in the water and wet the border of each wonton. Place a marble-size ball of the pork mixture in the centre of each wonton. Fold the wonton in half diagonally to make a triangle or crescent. Fold the seam edges slightly back on themselves. Press to seal tightly.

5   Repeat to use all the remaining wontons and filling.

6   Bring about 2.5 cm of water to a boil in a large pan.

7   Arrange half of the wontons on a steamer rack. Place the rack in the pan, cover and cook for 3 to 4 minutes, or until the stuffing is cooked (test a wonton with the tip of a sharp knife). Transfer the dumplings to a warm platter; keep warm.

8   Repeat with the remaining wontons. Serve with the soy dipping sauce.

Makes **32** dumplings.

nutrition at a glance	
per 2 dumplings	
0.7 g.	total fat
0.2 g.	saturated fat
69	calories
7 mg.	cholesterol
326 mg.	sodium
4 g.	protein
11 g.	carbohydrates
0 g.	dietary fibre

Mediterranean Prawns

You can purchase your prawns already steamed and chilled, which cuts the effort. You can also replace the peppers with mangetout.

16	large prawns, peeled with tails left on
16	thin green pepper slices
80	ml freshly squeezed orange juice
2	tablespoons white-wine vinegar
4	cloves garlic, minced
1	teaspoon crushed fennel seeds
1	bay leaf
½	teaspoon ground cumin
½	teaspoon dried tarragon
4	large lettuce leaves (optional)

Lynn's Fat-Free Flavour

Wine vinegar costs a bit more than distilled vinegar, but it's worth it. The flavour is more mellow, an important consideration when cooking with no added oil or other fats.

1 Fill a large bowl with iced water. Set aside.

2 Bring about 2.5 cm of water to a boil in a large non-stick saucepan. Add the prawns and peppers. Cover and cook, stirring once, for 3 minutes, or until the prawns just begin to turn pink. Drain and transfer to the ice water. Let stand for 2 minutes. Drain and pat dry with paper towels.

3 In a sealable plastic bag, combine the orange juice, vinegar, garlic, fennel seeds, bay leaf, cumin and tarragon. Tightly seal the bag and squeeze the package to mix. Open the bag and add the prawns and peppers. Seal the bag and refrigerate for up to 2 hours.

4 Drain before serving; discard the marinade and bay leaf. Serve on the lettuce (if using).

Makes **8** servings.

Photograph on page 50

nutrition at a glance	
per serving	
0.6 g.	total fat
0 g.	saturated fat
54	calories
80 mg.	cholesterol
94 mg.	sodium
10 g.	protein
4 g.	carbohydrates
0 g.	dietary fibre

Pesto Pita Wedges

quick and easy

These pita wedges are exceptionally tasty and can be served as a snack by themselves or with my Pinto Bean Dip (page 43) or Crunchy Onion Dip (page 44). Be sure to buy the flattest pitas that you can find; they crisp nicely in the oven. I prefer my pepper coarsely ground for this appetizer.

20	g finely chopped fresh basil
1	tablespoon fat-free Parmesan topping
¾	teaspoon ground black pepper
4	fat-free white or whole-wheat pita breads (20 cm diameter)

1 Preheat the oven to 200°C, Gas 6.

2 In a small bowl, combine the basil, Parmesan and pepper. Coat the tops of the pitas with non-stick spray. Spread the basil mixture evenly over the tops of the pitas. Coat with the spray again.

3 Cut each pita into 8 wedges. Transfer to a baking tray and bake for 5 to 8 minutes, or until golden and crisp.

Makes **32** wedges.

Photograph on page 49

nutrition at a glance

per 2 wedges
0 g.	total fat
0 g.	saturated fat
21	calories
0 mg.	cholesterol
32 mg.	sodium
1 g.	protein
4 g.	carbohydrates
0 g.	dietary fibre

Herbed Stuffed Mushrooms

Hot and savoury stuffed mushrooms don't have to be swimming in butter to taste rich. You can make these elegant appetisers ahead, refrigerate them, and then bake just before serving.

Lynn's Lore

The cultivated button mushroom was developed in France by Louis XIV's agronomist, Olivier de Serres. It has since carried the nickname *champignon de Paris*, or Parisian mushroom.

16   medium button mushrooms
60   g lean smoked ham, trimmed of all visible fat and finely chopped
2   chestnut mushrooms, finely chopped
1   small onion, finely chopped
1   tablespoon Madeira wine or Worcestershire sauce
3   tablespoons herbed breadcrumbs
2   teaspoons balsamic vinegar
2   tablespoons chopped fresh parsley
    Ground black pepper
    Salt (optional)
2   tablespoons fat-free Parmesan topping

1   Preheat the oven to 190°C, Gas 5.

2   Remove the stems from the button mushrooms and chop; set aside. Set the caps aside.

3   Coat a large non-stick frying pan with non-stick spray. Add the ham, brown mushrooms, onions and reserved mushroom stems. Mist with non-stick spray. Cook over medium-high heat, stirring often, for 5 minutes.

4   Add the wine or Worcestershire sauce. Cook, stirring, for 1 minute. Add the breadcrumbs, vinegar, and 1 tablespoon of the parsley. Stir to combine. Season to taste with the pepper and salt (if using).

5   Spoon the stuffing into the reserved mushroom caps. Place in a single layer in a large baking dish. Sprinkle with the Parmesan. Cover with foil and bake for 25 minutes, or until the mushrooms are hot. Sprinkle with the remaining 1 tablespoon parsley.

Makes **16** mushrooms.

nutrition at a glance

per 2 mushrooms
0.8 g. total fat
0.2 g. saturated fat
42 calories
4 mg. cholesterol
201 mg. sodium
4 g. protein
6 g. carbohydrates
0.9 g. dietary fibre

Baked Potato Skins

This popular contemporary appetizer is a cinch to make free of fat. To cut down on the baking time, you can microwave the scrubbed potatoes for 7 minutes, turning them 4 times for even cooking. Wet the potatoes and bake at 180°C, Gas 4 for 30 minutes, or until tender. After you've scooped out the potato flesh, save it for another use, such as mashed potatoes or potato pancakes.

4	medium baking potatoes
8	slices fat-free cheese, cut in half
4	tablespoons fat-free soured cream
3	tablespoons finely chopped fat-free ham
½	green pepper, finely chopped
½	sweet red pepper, finely chopped
90	g diced tomatoes
4	spring onions, sliced
	Ground black pepper

1 Preheat the oven to 180°C, Gas 4.

2 Wash and gently scrub the potatoes, but don't dry. Poke each potato several times with a fork. Place at least 10 cm apart on the oven rack and bake for 1 hour, or until tender. Remove from the oven. Cut each potato in half lengthwise. Set aside for 10 minutes, or until cool enough to handle.

3 With a large spoon, scoop out the potato flesh, leaving a sturdy shell; reserve the flesh for another use. Using kitchen scissors, cut each skin in half lengthwise. Place the potato skins on a baking tray.

4 Coat both sides of each skin with non-stick spray. Top each skin with a half slice of cheese. Grill 10 cm from the heat for 4 minutes, or until the cheese partially melts.

5 Remove from the oven. Transfer the skins to a platter. Top with the soured cream and sprinkle with the ham, green peppers, red peppers, tomatoes and spring onions. Season to taste with the black pepper.

Makes **16** skins.

Lynn's Kitchen Tip

Wrapping potatoes in foil before baking actually steams them and softens the skin. So scrap the foil. Instead, scrub the potatoes and then place them (still wet) directly on the oven baking rack. This technique crisps the skin beautifully.

nutrition at a glance

per 4 skins

0.2 g.	total fat
0 g.	saturated fat
210	calories
8 mg.	cholesterol
723 mg.	sodium
13.4 g.	protein
38.5 g.	carbohydrates
3.1 g.	dietary fibre

Baba Ghannouj

Serve this lush Middle Eastern puree as a dip with crackers or pita bread. Or use it as a stuffing for celery or halved hard-boiled egg whites. Top with a sprig of parsley or a slice of pimento.

1	aubergine (875 g - 1 kg)
2	tablespoons freshly squeezed lemon juice
2	tablespoons balsamic vinegar
3	cloves garlic, minced
2	teaspoons grated fresh ginger
90	g finely chopped onions
60	g grated carrots
	Ground black pepper
	Salt (optional)
2	tablespoons capers, rinsed and drained

1   Pierce the aubergine in several spots with a sharp knife. Microwave on high power for a total of 9 minutes, or until soft; turn the aubergine after 4 minutes. Set aside until cool enough to handle.

2   Cut the aubergine in half, scoop out the pulp, and transfer the pulp to a food processor. Discard the aubergine skin. Add the lemon juice, vinegar, garlic and ginger; process until almost smooth but not pureed. Add the onions and carrots; pulse once or twice to combine. Season to taste with the pepper and salt (if using).

3   Chill for several hours. Sprinkle with the capers just before serving.

Makes **6** servings.

Lynn's Kitchen Tip

Here's an alternate way to prepare the aubergine, which is a member of the nightshade family and related to the potato and tomato. Pierce the aubergine in several spots with a sharp knife. Place in a shallow baking dish and bake at 190°C, Gas 5 for 1¼ hours, or until soft, slightly charred, and collapsed.

nutrition at a glance
per serving

0.3 g.	total fat
0 g.	saturated fat
45	calories
0 mg.	cholesterol
113 mg.	sodium
1 g.	protein
11 g.	carbohydrates
3 g.	dietary fibre

Pinto Bean Dip

quick and easy

You can give this bean dip an even more pronounced Tex-Mex flair by adding ½ teaspoon chilli powder. Serve with fat-free tortilla chips, plain toasted pita wedges or small leafy celery stalks as dippers.

1	can (470 g) pinto beans, rinsed and drained
½	sweet red pepper, finely chopped
1	stalk celery, finely chopped
1	small onion, finely chopped
2	cloves garlic, minced
2	tablespoons cider vinegar
2	teaspoons freshly squeezed lemon juice
1	teaspoon dried oregano
½	teaspoon ground cumin
	Ground black pepper
	Salt (optional)

1   Place the beans in a blender or food processor. Process to a chunky puree. Add the red peppers, celery, onions, garlic, vinegar, lemon juice, oregano and cumin. Pulse once or twice to combine. Season to taste with the black pepper and salt (if using).

Makes about **625** ml.

nutrition at a glance

per 60 ml

0.2 g.	total fat
0 g.	saturated fat
46	calories
0 mg.	cholesterol
73 mg.	sodium
3 g.	protein
9 g.	carbohydrates
3 g.	dietary fibre

Crunchy Onion Dip

quick and easy

A confetti of chopped fresh vegetables makes this dip come alive. For a tasty variation, add 125 g tiny steamed shrimp, more lemon juice and hot-pepper sauce to taste.

500	ml fat-free soured cream
90	g finely chopped onions
90	g finely chopped spring onions
125	g finely chopped sweet red peppers
45	g finely chopped carrots
4	tablespoons finely chopped fresh chives
1	tablespoon cider vinegar
1	teaspoon freshly squeezed lemon juice
1	teaspoon chopped fresh parsley
1	clove garlic, minced
½	teaspoon garlic salt
½	teaspoon hot-pepper sauce
¼	teaspoon finely chopped jalapeño peppers (wear rubber gloves when handling)

1 In a medium bowl, combine the soured cream, both onions, red peppers, chives, carrots, vinegar, lemon juice, parsley, garlic, garlic salt, hot-pepper sauce and jalapeño peppers. Stir well.

Makes about **750** g.

Photograph on page 48

nutrition at a glance

per 60 g

0 g.	total fat
0 g.	saturated fat
58	calories
0 mg.	cholesterol
128 mg.	sodium
3 g.	protein
10 g.	carbohydrates
0 g.	dietary fibre

Dill Dip

quick and easy

Dill is one of those refreshing, delightful herbs that's pleasing to almost everyone. This appetizer gets a double dill kick with the addition of dill pickled cucumbers.

250	g fat-free cottage cheese
1	tablespoon skim milk (optional)
250	ml fat-free natural yogurt cheese (page 304)
4	tablespoons chopped onions
4	tablespoons chopped fresh dill
4	teaspoons chopped low-sodium dill pickled cucumbers
½	teaspoon sugar
½	teaspoon ground black pepper

1 In a blender or food processor, process the cottage cheese for at least 2 minutes. Add the milk, if necessary, to facilitate blending. Add the yogurt cheese; process to combine.

2 Add the onions, dill, pickled cucumbers, sugar and pepper. Pulse just to combine.

Makes about **500** g.

Lynn's Kitchen Tip

Dill isn't used just to flavour pickled cucumbers, which is how some of us know it best. The ferny herb can be snipped over salads, vegetables, fish, stews, soups, sauces and meats. It gives foods a clean, crisp flavour.

nutrition at a glance

per 60 g

0.1 g.	total fat
0 g.	saturated fat
55	calories
3 mg.	cholesterol
127 mg.	sodium
7 g.	protein
6 g.	carbohydrates
0 g.	dietary fibre

Cream Cheese and Chutney

quick and easy

**The old standby of sweet and spicy, this updated simple 1950s
appetiser is a tasty spread on melba toast rounds or any fat-free
cracker. Our testers loved it in celery stalks and mangetout.**

500	ml mild or hot chutney
2	nectarines, peeled and cut into quarters
4	tablespoons fat-free liquid creamer
8	spring onions, chopped
1	package (250 g) fat-free cream cheese, at room temperature

1 In a blender or food
processor, combine the chutney, nectarines and
creamer. Process to break up any large chunks of fruit
and make a coarse puree. Add all but 2 tablespoons of
the spring onions; pulse once or twice to combine.

2 Place the cream cheese on a
serving dish. Pour the chutney sauce over the cream
cheese, letting it drip down the sides. Sprinkle with the
remaining 2 tablespoons spring onions.

Makes **8** servings.

nutrition at a glance
per serving

0.7 g.	total fat
0.2 g.	saturated fat
154	calories
2 mg.	cholesterol
295 mg.	sodium
6 g.	protein
34 g.	carbohydrates
3 g.	dietary fibre

Bruschetta with Tomatoes (page 34)

Crunchy Onion Dip (page 44)

Pesto Pita Wedges (page 39)

Mediterranean Prawns (page 37)

Baked Red Snapper with Clams (page 30)

Springtime Asparagus Soup (page 65)

Sweetcorn Chowder (page 89)

Fresh Tomato Soup (page 67)

New Orleans Spicy Bean Soup (page 80)

Gazpacho with Prawns and Avocado (page 66)

Tossed Antipasto Salad (page 97)

Caesar Salad with Turkey (page 99)

Tomato, Basil and Mozzarella Salad (page 106)

Spinach-Orange Salad (page 109)

Turkey Salad with Orange Dressing (page 100)

Moulded Cran-Blackberry Salad (page 110)

Soups and Chowders

Soups are so easy to love because soups are so

easy to make. Even a novice can create fine soups.

Most require only one pan and little attention as

they simmer. In my kitchen, soups are among the

most gratifying dishes to prepare free of unwanted

fat. It's easy to start your soup with fat-free

homemade stock or canned broth, if you follow my

easy recipes on pages 93 and 94.

Big-batch soups are a powerful arsenal in the

war against fat. With my larger recipes, you can serve a delicious meal and have extra portions to refrigerate or freeze for packed lunches or fast weeknight meals. Most soups keep beautifully, actually improving in flavour. (Cook no-yolk noodles, potatoes or other starches just before serving.)

Bowling for Health

For ladling out good nutrition, you can't make a better choice than a big bowlful of low-fat home-cooked soup. Made primarily from vegetables, legumes and grains, a serving or two of soup each day can deliciously help you meet the healthful eating guidelines of the Food Pyramid.

The vegetables in soup are complex carbohydrates that provide a density of nutrients – vitamins A, C, and sometimes B, plus various minerals. They also fortify your body with fibre and powerful substances called antioxidants, which may destroy the free radicals that can lead to cancer and heart disease.

The grains, rice and pasta in soup provide complex carbohydrates, an important source of energy. They also contain fibre, vitamins and minerals. The Food Pyramid suggests 6 to 11 servings of these foods each day.

The dry beans, lentils and peas in soup are excellent sources of fibre, vitamins, minerals and lean protein. Cook them from scratch (page 259) or use rinsed and drained canned beans.

Ready to Serve

How much soup is a serving? 250 ml or less is an appropriate appetiser size. Chicken stock with tiny pasta or a refreshing gazpacho is the type of lighter soup that makes a perfect meal opener. Eating a nutritious soup can actually curb your appetite to prevent overeating later in the meal.

For a soup-and-sandwich lunch, I recommend 375 ml of soup per serving. Cream of Broccoli Soup and my other cream soups are great companions for savoury sandwiches made with fat-free cheeses, roasted vegetables or bean spreads.

Sometimes you'll want to make a meal of soup, accompanied by whole-grain bread. Try my robust Gumbo z'Herbes, U.S. Senate Bean Soup or Winter Potato and Fish Chowder. For those occasions, 375 to 500 ml is a reasonable serving.

I've given recipe yields in volume. The nutrient analyses are calculated per 250-ml serving. You can adjust your nutritional totals depending upon the amount that you actually eat.

Springtime Asparagus Soup

quick and easy

This thick soup is an edible celebration of springtime's finest vegetable. Garnish it with a squeeze of lemon or a dollop of fat-free natural yogurt. For a cream soup variation, substitute 500 ml fat-free liquid creamer or buttermilk for the final 500 ml water. Stir in 2 teaspoons fat-free Parmesan topping just before serving.

500	g asparagus
1	chicken bouillon cube
1	medium leek, white and some green stem, chopped
1	small onion, coarsely chopped
1	small potato, coarsely chopped
1	large stalk celery, cut into 1 cm pieces
750	ml water
	Ground black pepper
	Salt (optional)
2	tablespoons plain flour
	Pinch of ground nutmeg

1   Remove the tough ends from the asparagus. Chop the tips finely and set aside. Cut the stalks into 1 cm pieces.

2   Place the stalks in a medium non-stick saucepan. Add the bouillon cube, leeks, onions, potatoes, celery and 250 ml of the water. Cover and simmer over medium-low heat for 15 minutes, or until the asparagus is very tender.

3   Season to taste with the pepper and salt (if using). Whisk in the flour.

4   Pour the soup into a blender or food processor. Process for 3 to 4 minutes, or until very smooth. Return the soup to the saucepan. (The soup can also be puréed in the saucepan with a hand blender.)

5   Whisk in the remaining 500 ml water. Add the nutmeg and reserved asparagus tips. Cover and simmer, stirring occasionally, for 4 minutes, or until the tips are tender and bright green.

Makes about **1** litre.

Photograph on page 52

Photograph on page 52

Lynn's Kitchen Tip

Keep asparagus chilled and cook it as soon as possible. If refrigerated longer than a few days, asparagus spears wilt, dry out, and toughen. If you can't use asparagus soon after purchase, freeze it. Boil or steam the spears for 2 to 3 minutes, then plunge them into a large bowl of iced water. Drain and pat dry. Place in a heavy-duty resealable plastic bag and freeze.

nutrition at a glance

per 250 ml

0.4 g.	total fat
0.1 g.	saturated fat
68	calories
0 mg.	cholesterol
314 mg.	sodium
3 g.	protein
14 g.	carbohydrates
2.4 g.	dietary fibre

Gazpacho with Prawns and Avocado

quick and easy

If your ingredients are cold from the refrigerator, you won't have to chill the gazpacho before serving. Pass additional hot-pepper sauce and some lemon wedges at the table so that people can make the soup as spicy or tart as they like. For extra crunch and fibre, I like to reserve the pepper seeds and stir them into the chunky soup.

½	large cucumber, cut in half crosswise
1	large very ripe tomato, cut into quarters
½	green pepper, cut into quarters
½	sweet red pepper, cut into quarters
½	large yellow or Spanish onion, cut into quarters
3	tablespoons chopped fresh coriander
2	sprigs fresh parsley
1	small clove garlic, minced
2	tablespoons cider vinegar
5	tablespoons freshly squeezed lemon juice or lime juice
	Hot-pepper sauce
500	ml tomato juice
250	ml cold water
	Salt (optional)
4	tablespoons finely diced avocado
3	cooked large prawns, chilled and cut in half lengthwise
6	sprigs fresh coriander

1 In a food processor, combine half of the cucumber, half of the tomatoes, half of the green peppers, half of the red peppers and half of the onions. Add the chopped coriander, parsley, garlic, vinegar and 4 tablespoons of the lemon juice or lime juice. Process until nearly puréed. Season to taste with the hot-pepper sauce.

2 Add the remaining cucumber, tomatoes, green peppers, red peppers and onions. Pulse 2 or 3 times, so that the mixture remains chunky. Stir in the tomato juice and water. Season to taste with the salt (if using).

Lynn's Nutrition Note

Avocados are high in fat, but most of it is heart-healthy monounsaturated fat. They also contain folate, potassium and vitamin C. The Fuerte avocado, a smooth-skinned variety usually grown in Israel or Florida, has one-third less fat than the alligator-skinned Haas, usually grown in California. With very little saturated fat, avocados (especially the Fuertes) can and should be enjoyed in moderation in a low-fat diet.

3 In a small bowl, toss the avocado with the remaining 1 tablespoon lemon juice or lime juice. Serve the soup garnished with the avocado, prawns and coriander sprigs.

Makes about **1.5** litres.

Photograph on page 56

Fresh Tomato Soup

quick and easy

You'll want to pick the ripest red tomatoes from your garden or farmers market for this summery soup. This version is chunky, but you can purée it if you like. Garnishing ideas: fat-free soured cream, fat-free natural yogurt, lemon or lime wedges, chopped jalapeño peppers or fat-free croutons. For extra spice, add a dash of hot-pepper sauce.

4	tablespoons plain flour
500	ml vegetable stock (page 93) or water
5	large ripe tomatoes, coarsely chopped
1	medium onion, coarsely chopped
1	stalk celery with leafy top, coarsely chopped
2	cloves garlic, minced
2	teaspoons dried oregano
1	teaspoon brown sugar
	Juice of ½ lemon
	Salt (optional)
8	large fresh basil leaves, thinly sliced

Lynn's Nutrition Note

We eat about 9 kg of tomatoes each year, in quantities second only to the potato. That's smart eating. A single tomato can provide nearly half the vitamin C that you need each day. Tomatoes also contain lycopene, an awesome antioxidant that may aid in cancer prevention.

1 Place the flour in a large non-stick pan. Gradually whisk in the stock or water until smooth. Add the tomatoes, onions, celery, garlic, oregano and brown sugar.

2 Cook over medium-high heat, stirring constantly, until the soup almost comes to a boil. Reduce the heat to medium-low, cover and simmer, stirring occasionally, for 15 minutes, or until the vegetables are soft. Stir in the lemon juice and season to taste with the salt (if using). Sprinkle with the basil just before serving.

Makes about **1.5** litres..

Photograph on page 54

Cavendish Green-Pepper Soup

My former assistant, Marty Cavendish, shared her mother's unique recipe for green-pepper soup for those of us who never get enough green peppers. I love all that vitamin C! I scatter the sweet, crunchy pepper seeds over the soup before serving.

1	medium onion, chopped
2	cloves garlic, minced
4	medium green peppers, coarsely chopped
½	teaspoon dried thyme
1	teaspoon dried marjoram
2	cans (440 g each) low-sodium chicken broth, skimmed
5 - 8	tablespoons instant potato flakes
1	tablespoon Worcestershire sauce
2	tablespoons chopped fresh parsley
¼	teaspoon hot-pepper sauce
500	ml fat-free liquid creamer or evaporated skimmed milk
	Freshly ground black pepper
	Salt (optional)

1   Coat a large non-stick pan with non-stick spray. Add the onions and garlic. Sauté over medium heat for 4 minutes, or until translucent. (Add 1 to 2 tablespoons water to the pan if the onions start to stick.) Add the green peppers, thyme, marjoram and 250 ml of the broth. Simmer for 12 to 15 minutes, or until the peppers are tender.

2   In a blender or food processor, purée 500 ml of the soup mixture. Return to the pan. Pour the remaining broth into the pan. Cover and simmer over medium heat for 10 minutes.

3   Add 5 tablespoons of the potato flakes and cook, whisking, for 4 minutes, or until thickened. (Add 2 to 3 tablespoons more flakes, if needed, to thicken.) Stir in the Worcestershire sauce, parsley and hot-pepper sauce. Add the creamer or milk. Season to taste with the black pepper and salt (if using). Cook for 3 minutes, or until the soup is hot.

Makes about **2.5** litres.

nutrition at a glance

per 250 ml

0.2 g.	total fat
0.1 g.	saturated fat
68	calories
2 mg.	cholesterol
133 mg.	sodium
6.7 g.	protein
9.9 g.	carbohydrates
1 g.	dietary fibre

Cabbage and Potato Soup with Ham

To make this soup even quicker, start with shredded cabbage, which can be purchased at most large markets in convenient cellophane bags.

185	g chopped onions
2	litres water
500	g shredded green cabbage
2	large potatoes, diced
6	tablespoons diced lean ham
2	vegetable bouillon cubes
1	teaspoon crushed dill seed
2	tablespoons cider vinegar
	Ground black pepper
	Salt (optional)
2	tablespoons chopped fresh parsley

1 Coat a large non-stick pan with non-stick spray. Add the onions. Cover and cook over medium heat, stirring occasionally, for 5 to 6 minutes, or until the onions start to colour. Uncover and cook for 3 to 4 minutes, or until golden. If necessary, add 1 or 2 teaspoons water to prevent sticking.

2 Add the water, cabbage, potatoes, ham, bouillon cubes and dill seed. Cover and bring almost to a boil.

3 Reduce the heat to low and simmer for 15 to 20 minutes, or until the potatoes are very tender. If a slightly thicker soup is desired, mash some of the potatoes against the side of the pan with the back of a large spoon. Stir in the vinegar. Season to taste with the pepper and salt (if using). Sprinkle with the parsley.

Makes about **2.5** litres.

Lynn's Lore

For the ancient Romans, cabbage was an expensive delicacy. It was so beloved that the emperor Claudius once convened the Roman Senate to vote on whether any dish was superior to corned beef and cabbage.

nutrition at a glance
per 250 ml

0.5 g.	total fat
0.1 g.	saturated fat
65	calories
2 mg.	cholesterol
139 mg.	sodium
3 g.	protein
13 g.	carbohydrates
2 g.	dietary fibre

Carrot and Almond Soup

I like this vitamin-rich purée served with a dollop of fat-free yogurt cheese on top. I take a sip of soup and then a bite of cheese. You can also serve it with a spoonful of fat-free natural yogurt, which blends more easily with the soup when you stir it in at the table.

6	medium carrots, cut into 5 cm pieces
1	medium potato, cut into eighths
½	stalk celery, sliced
1	small onion, cut in half
2	shallots, cut in half
6	unblanched almonds
½	teaspoon sugar
½	teaspoon salt (optional)
¼	teaspoon ground nutmeg
	Pinch of ground allspice
	Pinch of ground ginger
500 - 750	ml vegetable stock (page 93) or water
4	whole cloves
2	cloves garlic, unpeeled
	Ground black pepper
250	ml fat-free natural yogurt cheese (page 304) or fat-free natural yogurt
1	tablespoon snipped chives or spring onion stems

1 In a large non-stick saucepan, combine the carrots, potatoes, celery, onions, shallots, almonds, sugar, salt (if using), nutmeg, allspice, ginger and 500 ml of the stock or water. Place the cloves and garlic in a mesh tea ball or wrap in a small piece of muslin and tie with kitchen string. Place in the saucepan.

2 Cover and bring almost to a boil over medium-high heat. Reduce the heat to low and simmer for 35 minutes, or until the carrots and potatoes are tender. Remove the tea ball or muslin bundle; discard the cloves. Squeeze the garlic from its skin and add the soft paste to the soup.

3 Working in batches if necessary, pour the soup into a blender or food processor. Process for several minutes, or until puréed. (The soup can also be puréed in the saucepan with a hand blender.) Return the soup to the pan. If the soup is too thick, thin with the remaining 250 ml stock or water. Season to taste with the pepper. Serve topped with the yogurt cheese or yogurt and chives or spring onions.

Makes about **1.5** litres.

nutrition at a glance

per 250 ml

0.8 g.	total fat
0.2 g.	saturated fat
108	calories
1 mg.	cholesterol
95 mg.	sodium
6.2 g.	protein
19.7 g.	carbohydrates
2.5 g.	dietary fibre

Salt Substitutes

Nearly everyone wants a little salt in soup, and frankly, most soups taste better with it. Salt intensifies flavours. Of course, you should follow your doctor's advice about sodium consumption. If you have to watch your salt intake, here are some seasonings that will heighten flavours without contributing sodium.

Try a tablespoon or two of vinegar or a few squeezes of lemon juice or lime juice. Worcestershire sauce and soy sauce, which contain some salt, also do the trick. Just remember that standard Worcestershire sauce (a low-sodium brand is also available) contains a third less sodium than even low-sodium soy sauce. Crushed chillies, fresh or pickled chilli peppers and commercial salt-potassium seasoning blends are also good flavour boosters.

On occasions when you want real salt, remember that, by weight, sea salt has more sodium chloride than table salt, which contains anticlumping agents and starches. (Valid comparisons are difficult to make by volume measurement, because the density of these salts differs.)

Better-Than-French Onion Soup

quick and **easy**

This simple soup with a secret ingredient (coffee!) has all the flavour of the finest onion soup you ever tasted. It requires some attention while cooking, but the results are well worth it. A small piece of toast and 2 tablespoons finely grated fat-free mozzarella will add close to 1 gramme of fat per serving. Ladle the soup into 6 ovenproof bowls, then top with the toast piece and cheese. Bake in a preheated 230°C, Gas 8 oven for 10 minutes, or until the cheese melts.

2   large onions, sliced
3   tablespoons brewed coffee
1   beef bouillon cube
1   litre water
4   tablespoons port wine (optional)

1   Coat a large non-stick saucepan with non-stick spray. Warm the saucepan over medium-high heat. Add the onions and coffee. Cook, stirring constantly, to coat the onions well with the coffee. Cook for 3 minutes, or until the coffee is nearly evaporated.

2   Add the bouillon cube and 125 ml of the water. As the cube melts, mash it with the back of a large spoon and stir into the water. Cook, stirring, until the water is nearly evaporated.

3   Add 60 ml of the remaining water and cook, stirring occasionally, for 7 minutes, or until the water evaporates. Add 60 ml of the remaining water and cook for another 7 minutes, or until the onions are soft.

4   Add the port (if using) and the remaining 750 ml water. Cook over medium-high heat until the soup comes to a light boil.

Makes about **1.5** litres.

nutrition at a glance
per 250 ml
0.1 g.   total fat
0 g.   saturated fat
18   calories
0 mg.   cholesterol
149 mg.   sodium
0.6 g.   protein
3.9 g.   carbohydrates
0.5 g.   dietary fibre

Lemongrass Egg-Drop Soup

This aromatic Oriental broth studded with vegetables is sure to be a welcome addition to your soup repertoire. You can add 45 g prawns, 60 g turkey breast or 60 g no-yolk noodles to the recipe and still keep it fat-free. If you don't have a fresh hot red pepper, use ¼ teaspoon crushed chillies.

2 tablespoons dried flaked lemongrass or 1 stalk fresh
1 litre skimmed chicken stock (page 94)
1 medium tomato, chopped
1 small hot red pepper, chopped (wear rubber gloves when handling)
2 tablespoons chopped spring onions
1 tablespoon freshly squeezed lemon juice
2 teaspoons sugar
1 teaspoon grated fresh ginger
2 tablespoons chopped fresh coriander
   Salt (optional)
1 egg white
½ teaspoon dark sesame oil

1   If using dried lemongrass, place it in a mesh tea ball. Place the ball in a medium non-stick saucepan. Add 250 ml of the stock. Warm over medium-low heat; turn off the heat and let soak for 1 hour. Add the remaining 750 ml stock.

2   (If using fresh lemongrass, peel the root end of the stalk to expose the pinkish-white centre. Thinly slice and place in a medium non-stick saucepan. Add all the stock; do not soak.)

3   Add the tomatoes, peppers, spring onions, lemon juice, sugar, ginger and 1 tablespoon coriander. Bring to a boil over medium-high heat; reduce the heat to medium. Cover and simmer for 5 minutes. Season to taste with the salt (if using).

4   In a small bowl, lightly beat the egg white with a fork. While stirring the soup, add the egg white in a thin stream and cook for 1 minute. Remove from the heat. Stir in the sesame oil and the remaining 1 tablespoon coriander. If using dried lemongrass, remove the tea ball and discard the lemongrass.

Makes about **1** litre.

nutrition at a glance
per 250 ml
   0.9 g. total fat
   0.1 g. saturated fat
      52 calories
   5 mg. cholesterol
   41 mg. sodium
      5 g. protein
      7 g. carbohydrates
   0.8 g. dietary fibre

Cream of Broccoli Soup

The little bit of mature Cheddar really enlivens the taste of this simple soup. You can make this soup into a meal by serving it over no-yolk noodles, rice or mashed potatoes. The starch will raise the fat content by about 1 gramme.

1	kg broccoli
500	ml vegetable stock (page 93) or skimmed chicken stock (page 94)
1	medium onion, finely chopped
4	tablespoons grated carrots
1	small clove garlic, minced
250	ml skimmed milk
250	ml fat-free liquid creamer
3	tablespoons plain flour
	Juice of 1 lemon
	Ground black pepper
	Salt (optional)
6	tablespoons grated fat-free mature Cheddar cheese
1	tablespoon grated mature Cheddar cheese

1   Take one bunch of the broccoli and cut the florets away from the stalks; cut the florets into slivers lengthwise and set them aside.

2   Finely chop the stalks and the remaining broccoli; place in a medium non-stick saucepan.

3   Add the stock, onions, carrots and garlic. Cover and cook over medium heat, stirring often, for 6 to 7 minutes.

4   Add the reserved broccoli florets. Cook, stirring, for 2 to 3 minutes, or until the florets are bright green.

5   Whisk in the milk and creamer. Bring almost to a boil over medium heat.

6 Hold a large, fine sieve over the saucepan; add the flour to the sieve and shake into the soup, whisking to incorporate. Cook over low heat, stirring, for 3 to 4 minutes, or until the soup is thick. Stir in the lemon juice. Season to taste with the pepper and salt (if using).

7 Serve sprinkled with both the fat-free Cheddar cheeses.

Makes about **2** litres.

Barley Soup with Beef

Beef and barley soup is a thick, aromatic soup traditional among Middle European Jewish families. The soup should be hearty. You can make it thick or thin it with water or broth. I love it both ways.

1	beef knuckle or marrow bone with meat attached
3	litres vegetable stock (page 93) or water
2	bay leaves
2	beef bouillon cubes (optional)
155	g extra-large dry lima beans
2	medium onions, chopped
2	stalks celery, chopped
2	carrots, chopped
60	g chopped fresh parsley
100	g barley
4	cloves garlic, minced
	Ground black pepper
	Salt (optional)
2	tablespoons chopped fresh parsley

1 In a large non-stick pan, combine the beef knuckle or marrow bone, stock or water, bay leaves and bouillon cubes (if using). Simmer for 1¼ hours over low heat.

2 Strain the liquid into a large bowl and skim it (see page 17).

3 Wash the pan with soapy water and rinse.

(continued)

Lynn's Lore

Barley has nourished humans for thousands of years. It was grown 10,000 years ago in Jericho, 5,000 years ago in Japan, and 3,000 years ago in Babylonia for both food and beer. In the Dark Ages, bread was made primarily of barley.

4   Discard the bay leaves. Cut the lean meat from the bone; discard the fat. Dice the meat and set aside 6 tablespoons; reserve any remainder for another use.

5   Return the liquid and the meat to the pan. Add the beans, onions, celery, carrots, parsley, barley and garlic. Cover and cook over low heat for 2½ hours, or until the beans are tender. (If the soup becomes too thick, add some water. If the soup is too watery, remove the lid for the last 30 minutes of cooking.)

6   Season to taste with the pepper and salt (if using). Sprinkle with the parsley.

Makes about **3** litres.

nutrition at a glance
per 250 ml

0.5 g.	total fat
0.1 g.	saturated fat
115	calories
4 mg.	cholesterol
37 mg.	sodium
6.4 g.	protein
22.2 g.	carbohydrates
5.6 g.	dietary fibre

Mushroom and Wild Rice Soup

Garnish this chunky soup with lemon slices and paprika. To make a creamy variation, stir 375 ml fat-free liquid creamer into the soup just before serving. Heat through but do not boil.

90	g wild rice
2	litres skimmed chicken stock (page 94) or vegetable stock (page 93)
750	g large closed cap mushrooms, thickly sliced
1	large onion, chopped
1	carrot, chopped
1	stalk celery, chopped
3	shallots, chopped
3	cloves garlic, minced
1	teaspoon dried basil
¼	teaspoon ground nutmeg
4	tablespoons dry sherry or 2 teaspoons sherry extract (optional)
3	tablespoons plain flour
60	g chopped fresh parsley

1   Cook the rice according to the package directions. Set aside and keep warm.

2   Meanwhile, in a large non-stick pan, combine the stock, mushrooms, onions, carrots, celery, shallots and garlic. Bring to a boil over medium-high heat. Add the basil, nutmeg and 2 tablespoons of the sherry or 1 teaspoon of the sherry extract (if using). Reduce the heat to medium, cover and simmer for 30 minutes.

3   Hold a large, fine sieve over the saucepan; add the flour and shake over the soup, whisking to incorporate. Cook over medium-high heat, stirring, for 3 to 4 minutes, or until thick. Add the parsley and the remaining 2 tablespoons sherry or 1 teaspoon sherry extract (if using). Mix well. Cook for 1 minute but do not boil. Serve the soup over the wild rice.

Makes about **3** litres.

Lynn's Fun Food Fact

The North American plant wild rice isn't rice at all. It's an aquatic wild grass that looks like a branched candlestick. It was historically a staple food of North Central Native Americans, and much of the commercial crop is still collected in canoes by their descendants. The grains grow in colours ranging from beige to black, as short as a few millimetres or as long as 2.5 cm. Wild rice takes longer to cook than white or brown rice, but it isn't complicated or difficult.

nutrition at a glance
per 250 ml
0.4 g.	total fat
0.1 g.	saturated fat
68	calories
0 mg.	cholesterol
23 mg.	sodium
3 g.	protein
14.3 g.	carbohydrates
2 g.	dietary fibre

Wheat Berry Soup

If you've never tasted wheat berries – hulled whole grains of wheat – you'll be delighted by their nutty flavour and chewy texture. If wheat berries are unavailable, you can use bulgur, which will cook in only 40 minutes. Serve the soup garnished with a little grated fat-free mozzarella and some pimiento-stuffed olive slices. If you don't have Cajun spice blend, substitute ¼ teaspoon cayenne pepper and ¼ teaspoon sugar.

200	g wheat berries
1	litre water or skimmed chicken stock (page 94)
500	g closed cap mushrooms, sliced
3	ripe plum tomatoes, diced
1	medium onion, finely diced
6	cloves garlic, minced
1	teaspoon dried thyme
1	teaspoon dried rosemary, crumbled
½	teaspoon Cajun spice blend
	Salt (optional)

1   Place the wheat berries in a large bowl. Cover with at least 1.5 litres cold water. Set aside to soak for at least 4 hours. Drain and place in a large non-stick saucepan.

2   Add the water or stock. Cover and bring to a boil over medium-high heat. Reduce the heat to medium and simmer for 1 hour. Add the mushrooms, tomatoes, onions, garlic, thyme, rosemary and Cajun spice blend.

3   Cover and simmer, stirring occasionally, for 30 to 45 minutes, or until the wheat berries are tender. Season to taste with the salt (if using).

Makes about **2.25** litres.

Wheat berries are whole, unprocessed kernels of ripe wheat that are high in fibre and other nutrients. Look for them in health food shops or large supermarkets. Soak wheat berries for several hours in cold water before cooking and cook them in a generous amount of water for 1½ hours, or until tender. You can cook a large amount of wheat berries, drain them, and freeze them in recipe-ready portions. They're a nutritious addition to soups, casseroles and mixed-grain pilafs.

nutrition at a glance

per 250 ml
0.5 g.	total fat
0.1 g.	saturated fat
50	calories
0 mg.	cholesterol
21 mg.	sodium
2.6 g.	protein
11.1 g.	carbohydrates
2.2 g.	dietary fibre

If a soup is properly thickened to a luscious consistency, you'll never notice that it has no fat.

For clear or translucent soups, such as Oriental broths or chicken soup, use cornflour, arrowroot, rice flour or tapioca flour.

For opaque soups that don't already contain starchy ingredients, use plain flour, breadcrumbs, mashed potatoes, puréed cooked rice, red lentils (which disintegrate quickly) or mashed potatoes.

Of course, the simplest and purest way to thicken a soup made with vegetables or legumes is to pour a small portion of the soup into a blender or food processor, purée it and stir it into the soup.

Cooked rice. For each litre of liquid, process 125 to 250 g cooked rice with 60 ml water until puréed. Whisk into the soup over medium heat for 4 minutes, or until thickened.

Cornflour. For each litre of liquid, whisk 2 tablespoons cornflour into 125 ml cold water. Whisk into the hot soup over medium heat for 30 seconds, or until thickened. Any refrigerated leftover soup may need to be rethickened after reheating.

Mashed potatoes. For each litre of liquid, whisk 155 g mashed potatoes into the soup over medium heat for 4 minutes or until thickened.

Plain flour. For each litre of liquid, whisk 2 tablespoons flour into 125 ml cool water. Whisk into the hot soup over medium heat for at least 3 minutes, or until the soup thickens and the flour loses its raw taste. Flour-thickened soups can usually be reheated without losing their consistency.

Potato flour or mashed potato powder. For each litre of liquid, whisk 2 tablespoons potato flour or mashed potato powder into 125 ml cool water. Whisk into the soup over medium heat for 4 minutes, or until thickened.

Rice flour. For each litre of liquid, whisk 2 tablespoons rice flour into 60 ml cool water. Whisk into the soup over medium heat for 2 minutes, or until thickened.

Tapioca flour. For each litre of liquid, whisk 2 tablespoons tapioca flour into 60 ml cool water. Whisk into the soup over medium heat for 30 seconds, or until thickened.

New Orleans Spicy Bean Soup

I like many of the Creole seasonings which can be bought in most large supermarkets, for this Crescent City speciality. Creole seasoning is spicy hot, so you may want to start with the minimum amount and add more later if the soup needs it.

3	litres water
1	smoked ham knuckle with meat attached
1	bay leaf
500	g dry navy or kidney beans
2	large onions, chopped
2	stalks celery with leafy tops, chopped
1	carrot, grated or chopped
½	sweet red pepper, chopped
125	g chopped fresh parsley
1	tablespoon chopped fresh coriander
2	teaspoons ground cumin
1	teaspoon dried oregano
1–2	teaspoons Creole seasoning
4	cloves garlic, minced
	Hot-pepper sauce

1 In a large non-stick pan, combine the water, ham knuckle and bay leaf. Bring to a boil over medium-high heat. Reduce the heat to medium-low, cover and simmer for 1 hour. Uncover and simmer for 30 minutes.

2 Strain into a large bowl. Discard the bay leaf. Remove the meat from the bone. Trim off all visible fat and cut the meat into small dice. Set aside about 90 g of the meat; reserve any remainder for another use. Skim the stock (see page 17).

3 Wash the pan with soapy water and rinse. Return the stock to the pan.

Lynn's Kitchen Tip

When using several cloves of garlic in a long-cooked dish, don't bother to peel and dice them. Place the cloves in a mesh tea ball, clip it shut and put it right in the pan to cook with the soup. After cooking, remove the ball, rinse the cloves to cool them and squeeze out the sweet, cooked garlic. Whisk the garlic paste into the soup for a mellow flavour accent.

4 Add the beans, onions, celery, carrots, red peppers, parsley, coriander, cumin, oregano, Creole seasoning and garlic. Set over medium-high heat and bring almost to a boil. Reduce the heat to low, cover and simmer for 2½ to 3 hours, or until the beans are tender.

5 Transfer 1 litre of the soup to a blender or food processor. Purée, then stir back into the soup. If the soup is not thick enough, continue puréeing in 250-ml batches until the soup is the desired consistency. (The soup can also be partially puréed in the pan using a hand blender.) Stir in the reserved ham. Season to taste with the hot-pepper sauce.

Makes about **3.5** litres.

Photograph on page 55

Photograph on page 55

U.S. Senate Bean Soup

This thick soup has a rich history and great depth of flavour. Scatter some chopped parsley, chives, spring onion greens, or shreds of sweet red peppers over the top for colour. A few dashes of hot-pepper sauce will add some spunk.

3   litres water
1   smoked ham knuckle with meat attached
500   g dry navy or cannellini beans
3   medium onions, chopped
3   stalks celery, chopped
1   large baking potato, chopped
4   tablespoons chopped fresh parsley
3   cloves garlic, minced
    Ground black pepper

1 In a large non-stick pan, combine the water and ham knuckle. Bring to a boil over medium-high heat. Reduce the heat to medium-low, cover and simmer for 1 hour. Uncover and simmer for 30 minutes.

2 Strain into a large bowl. Remove the meat from the bone. Trim off all visible fat and cut the meat into small dice. Set aside about

(continued)

Lynn's Lore

The original recipe for this bean soup has been made for decades in the dining room of the United States Senate. Some of the more senior stewards tell me that the recipe came from the family of the late Henry Cabot Lodge and features foods from many parts of the country, such as celery and garlic from Florida or Washington State, potatoes from Maine, onions from California, ham from Virginia and beans from Michigan. Like a seasoned politician, this all-American potage adapts beautifully to the (low-fat) times.

90 g of the meat; reserve any remainder for another use. Skim the stock (see page 17).

3 Wash the pan with soapy water and rinse. Return the stock to the pan.

4 Add the beans, onions, celery, potatoes, parsley and garlic. Set over medium-high heat and bring almost to a boil. Reduce the heat to low, cover and simmer for 2½ to 3 hours, or until the beans are tender.

5 Working in batches, transfer half of the soup to a blender or food processor. Purée, then stir back into the soup. (The soup can also be partially puréed in the pan with a hand blender.)

6 Stir in the reserved ham. Season to taste with the pepper.

Makes about **4.5** litres.

nutrition at a glance	
per 250 ml	
0.8 g.	total fat
0.3 g.	saturated fat
114	calories
2 mg.	cholesterol
32 mg.	sodium
7.7 g.	protein
19.4 g.	carbohydrates
5.7 g.	dietary fibre

Chilli Soup

quick and **easy**

Garnish with chopped spring onions or fresh coriander.

185	g lean minced beef, all visible fat removed before grinding
1	large onion, coarsely chopped
1	green pepper, cut into 2.5 cm pieces
1	sweet red pepper, cut into 2.5 cm pieces
3	cloves garlic, minced
1	litre water
1	can (880 g) crushed tomatoes (with juice)
1	can (470 g) dark red kidney beans, rinsed and drained
1	can (250 g) tomato sauce
2	teaspoons chilli powder
1	teaspoon ground cumin
1	teaspoon dried oregano
1	teaspoon hot-pepper sauce
½	teaspoon cocoa powder
	Salt (optional)

1 Coat a non-stick flameproof casserole with non-stick spray. Warm over medium heat. Add the meat and cook, stirring occasionally, for 4 to 5 minutes, or until no longer pink. Place the meat in a colander to drain and then rinse under hot tap water to remove any residual fat. Set aside.

2 Wipe the casserole with paper towels. Add the onions, green peppers, red peppers and garlic. Mist with non-stick spray. Cover and cook over medium-high heat, stirring occasionally, for 4 minutes, or until the onions start to release liquid. Remove the cover and reduce the heat to medium. Cook, stirring, for 2 to 3 minutes, or until golden.

3 Add the water, tomatoes (with juice), beans, tomato sauce, chilli powder, cumin, oregano, hot-pepper sauce, cocoa powder and the reserved meat. Bring to a boil. Reduce the heat to medium, cover and simmer for 8 minutes. Remove the cover and simmer, stirring occasionally, for 10 minutes. Season to taste with the salt (if using).

Makes about **3** litres.

nutrition at a glance

per 250 ml

0.9 g.	total fat
0.2 g.	saturated fat
74	calories
9 mg.	cholesterol
188 mg.	sodium
6.6 g.	protein
10.9 g.	carbohydrates
3.3 g.	dietary fibre

Double Lentil Soup

Oh, you lucky lentil lovers! This soup has lots of invaluable nutrients and fibre. You can add 15 g crumbled feta cheese (or 30 g low-fat feta) per serving and still come in under 1 gramme of fat. Or try a few tablespoons of diced tomatoes mixed with 1 tablespoon sliced spring onions as a fresh topper.

2	tablespoons water
125	g diced or grated carrots
185	g diced celery stalks with leafy tops
1	large yellow onion, chopped
3	cloves garlic, minced
1.25	litres vegetable stock (page 93) or skimmed chicken stock (page 94)
185	g brown or green lentils
90	g red lentils, rinsed
2	teaspoons Worcestershire sauce
½	teaspoon dried thyme
⅛	teaspoon ground allspice
1	bay leaf
	Ground black pepper
	Salt (optional)

1   Coat a large non-stick pan with non-stick spray. Add the water. Warm over medium-high heat. Add the carrots, celery, onions and garlic. Cook, stirring frequently, for 6 minutes, or until the carrots are tender. If necessary, add 1 or 2 teaspoons more water to prevent sticking.

2   Add the stock, brown or green lentils, red lentils, Worcestershire sauce, thyme, allspice and bay leaf. Bring to a boil. Reduce the heat and simmer for 35 to 40 minutes, or until the red lentils disintegrate.

3   Remove and discard the bay leaf. Season to taste with the pepper and salt (if using).

Makes about **2** litres.

nutrition at a glance
per 250 ml

0.5 g.	total fat
0.1 g.	saturated fat
152	calories
0 mg.	cholesterol
47 mg.	sodium
11 g.	protein
27.4 g.	carbohydrates
6.3 g.	dietary fibre

Split Pea Soup

Split pea soup is always welcome at my house. It's a cinch to make fat-free, even with all the savoury ham flavour. Serve with low-fat crackers.

2.5	litres water
1	smoked ham knuckle with meat attached
1	bay leaf
2	carrots, chopped
2	stalks celery with leafy tops, chopped
1	large onion, chopped
1	large potato, coarsely chopped
250	g dry green split peas
125	ml beer or non-alcoholic beer (optional)
½	teaspoon dried thyme
	Ground black pepper

1   In a large non-stick pan, combine the water, ham knuckle and bay leaf. Bring to a boil over medium-high heat. Reduce the heat to medium-low, cover and simmer for 1 hour. Uncover and simmer for 30 minutes.

2   Strain into a large bowl. Discard the bay leaf. Remove the meat from the bone. Trim off all visible fat and cut the meat into small dice. Set aside about 6 tablespoons of the meat; reserve any remainder for another use. Skim the stock (see page 17).

3   Wash the pan with soapy water and rinse. Add the stock to the pan.

4   Add the carrots, celery, onions, potatoes, split peas, beer (if using) and thyme. Cover and simmer for 45 minutes, or until the split peas are soft.

5   Working in batches, transfer the soup to a blender or food processor. Purée and return to the pan. (The soup can also be puréed in the pan with a hand blender.) Season to taste with the pepper. Serve sprinkled with the reserved ham.

Makes about **3** litres.

nutrition at a glance

per 250 ml

0.9 g.	total fat
0.3 g.	saturated fat
107	calories
3 mg.	cholesterol
50 mg.	sodium
8.4 g.	protein
16.7 g.	carbohydrates
2.3 g.	dietary fibre

Gumbo z'Herbes

This New Orleans gumbo is traditionally made with seven different greens, but the results are just as delicious using only two or three. Choose from spinach, greens, kale, beetroot greens, dandelion, mustard greens, lettuce, young radish tops, coriander or celery leaves.

2.25 litres water
1 smoked ham knuckle with meat attached
185 g quick-cooking brown rice (ready in 30 minutes)
1 onion, chopped
60 g chopped spinach leaves
90 g chopped fresh greens or kale
60 g chopped fresh parsley
90 g chopped cabbage
60 g chopped watercress
1 bay leaf
Pinch of dried thyme
Pinch of dried tarragon
75 g plain flour
500 g okra, sliced into rounds
Pinch of salt
Pinch of ground black pepper
Hot-pepper sauce
Wine vinegar or lemon wedges

1 In a large non-stick pan, combine the water and ham knuckle. Bring to a boil over medium-high heat. Reduce the heat to medium-low, cover and simmer for 1 hour. Uncover and simmer for 30 minutes.

2 Strain into a large bowl. Remove the meat from the bone. Trim off all visible fat and cut the meat into small dice. Set aside about 90 g of the meat; reserve any remainder for another use. Skim the stock (see page 17).

3 Wash the pan with soapy water and rinse. Return the stock to the pan.

4 Add the rice. Cover and cook over very low heat for 25 minutes, or until the rice is nearly tender.

5   Add the onions, spinach, greens or kale, parsley, cabbage, watercress, bay leaf, thyme and tarragon. Simmer for 20 minutes, or until the rice is tender.

6   Meanwhile, place the flour in a large non-stick frying pan. Cook over medium-high heat, stirring frequently, for 3 to 4 minutes, or until golden. Set aside to cool slightly.

7   Transfer the flour to a large plastic bag. Add the okra, salt and pepper. Holding the bag closed with one hand, shake to coat the okra with flour.

8   Coat the same frying pan with non-stick spray. Remove the okra from the bag, shaking lightly to remove excess flour. Discard the re-maining flour. Place the okra in the frying pan. Coat lightly with non-stick spray. Cook over medium heat, tossing occasionally, for 10 minutes, or until cooked.

9   When the rice is cooked, re-move and discard the bay leaf. Stir the okra and reserved ham into the gumbo. If the gumbo is too thick, stir in a little extra water to thin it slightly. Serve with the hot-pepper sauce and vinegar or lemon wedges for seasoning.

Makes about **4** litres.

nutrition at a glance

per 250 ml

0.8 g.	total fat
0.2 g.	saturated fat
56	calories
2 mg.	cholesterol
34 mg.	sodium
3.7 g.	protein
8.8 g.	carbohydrates
1.1 g.	dietary fibre

Cream of Celery Soup

quick *and easy*

This simply wonderful creamed soup – which is also delicious chilled – can serve as a blueprint for many tasty variations. Just substitute broccoli, cauliflower, asparagus or fennel for the celery. A dash of ground nutmeg is always welcome in any cream soup.

250	g chopped celery stalks with leafy tops
125	ml water
4	tablespoons chopped onions
2	tablespoons plain flour
250	ml skimmed milk
125	ml fat-free liquid creamer
	Ground black pepper
	Salt (optional)
4	small leafy celery sprigs

1 In a medium non-stick saucepan, combine the chopped celery, water and onions. Bring almost to a boil over medium-high heat. Reduce the heat to medium-low. Cover and cook for 12 to 15 minutes, or until the celery is tender.

2 Meanwhile, place the flour in a small bowl. Gradually whisk in the milk until blended. Whisk the milk mixture into the saucepan. Whisk in the creamer.

3 Pour the soup into a blender or food processor. Process for several minutes, or until puréed. (The soup can also be puréed in the saucepan with a hand blender.) Return the soup to the saucepan.

4 Cook over medium heat, stirring constantly, for 4 minutes, or until the soup thickens. Season to taste with the pepper and salt (if using). Serve garnished with the celery sprigs.

Makes about **1** litre.

nutrition at a glance
per 250 ml
0.2 g.	total fat
0.1 g.	saturated fat
69	calories
1 mg.	cholesterol
84 mg.	sodium
3.1 g.	protein
13 g.	carbohydrates
1.2 g.	dietary fibre

Sweetcorn Chowder

quick and easy

This soup reminds me of the many summer trips I took with my mother to her childhood Iowa, where sweet, heavenly sweetcorn filled the fields along the narrow roads. If you like more vegetables, add 90 g chopped carrots. Plenty of chopped parsley makes a pretty and nutritious garnish.

250	ml water
375	g fresh sweetcorn
2	medium onions, chopped
1	medium potato, diced
1	medium leek, white and some green stem, chopped
185	g finely diced sweet red peppers
60	g finely diced green peppers
½	teaspoon sugar
½	teaspoon ground cumin
¼	teaspoon dried thyme
½	teaspoon curry powder
	Salt (optional)

1   In a blender or food processor, combine the water, half of the sweetcorn, half of the onions and half of the potatoes. Process to a coarse purée.

2   Pour into a large non-stick saucepan. Bring almost to a boil over medium-high heat. Reduce the heat to low and simmer, stirring occasionally, for 10 minutes.

3   Add the leeks, red peppers, green peppers, sugar, cumin, thyme and curry powder. Add the remaining sweetcorn, onions and potatoes. Cover the pan and cook for 10 to 12 minutes, or until the potatoes are tender. Add more water if a thinner consistency is desired. Season to taste with the salt (if using).

Makes about **2** litres.

Photograph on page 53

Photograph on page 53

Lynn's Kitchen Tip

To cut sweetcorn kernels from the cob, use a sharp, heavy 20 or 25 cm chef's knife. First, trim the wider end of the ear so that it will stand steadily on a cutting board when held upright. Holding the ear upright with one hand, carefully but firmly slice the kernels in rows, from top to bottom, as close to the cob as possible. Rotate the ear to repeat slicing the kernels in rows. Then, with the blunt side of the knife, scrape the cob to remove all the sweet, milky juice.

nutrition at a glance

per 250 ml
- 0.7 g. total fat
- 0.1 g. saturated fat
- 82 calories
- 0 mg. cholesterol
- 14 mg. sodium
- 2.4 g. protein
- 18.9 g. carbohydrates
- 2.6 g. dietary fibre

Winter Potato and Fish Chowder

If you like fish chowder and you like creamy potato soup, this savoury merger will suit you just fine. I like to use red snapper or tilapia, both of which hold their shape well. (You could also substitute pike, pollack, kingfish or monkfish.) You adventurous eaters may want to substitute smoked chub or the milder smoked sablefish for half the amount of fish in the recipe.

1	medium onion, coarsely chopped
2	stalks celery, sliced
½	teaspoon fennel seeds, crushed
2	tablespoons water
750	ml skimmed milk
1	large yellow or white potato, cut into 1 cm cubes
500	ml fat-free liquid creamer
185	g red snapper or tilapia fillets, cut into 2.5 cm cubes
185	g fresh or frozen sweetcorn
	Ground black pepper
	Salt (optional)

1 Coat a medium non-stick saucepan with non-stick spray. Add the onions, celery and fennel seeds. Mist lightly with non-stick spray. Add the water. Cook over medium heat, stirring, for 10 minutes, or until the onions are translucent.

2 Add the milk and potatoes. Simmer over medium-low heat, stirring occasionally, for 15 minutes, or until the potatoes are soft.

3 Pour the soup into a blender or food processor. Pulse about 5 times, or until the soup is partially puréed but still chunky. (The soup can also be partially puréed in the saucepan with a hand blender.)

4 Return the soup to the saucepan. Add the creamer, fish and sweetcorn. Cook over medium-low heat for 5 minutes, or just until the fish is cooked. Season to taste with the pepper and salt (if using).

Makes about **1.5** litres.

nutrition at a glance
per 250 ml
0.9 g.	total fat
0.3 g.	saturated fat
169	calories
9 mg.	cholesterol
89 mg.	sodium
9.7 g.	protein
28.9 g.	carbohydrates
1.6 g.	dietary fibre

Manhattan Clam Chowder

Try to find streaky slab bacon that has a wide streak of lean meat running through it.

155	g lean streaky bacon
500	ml water
3	medium potatoes, diced
1	medium onion, finely chopped
2½	stalks celery, finely chopped
1	can (440 g) diced tomatoes (with juice)
1	medium tomato, diced
60	g diced green peppers
125	ml white wine or non-alcoholic white wine
½	teaspoon dried thyme
1	can (315 g) baby clams (with juice)
500	ml tomato juice
60	g chopped fresh parsley
	Ground black pepper

1 In a large non-stick saucepan over medium-high heat, fry the bacon, turning often, for 4 minutes, or until some of the fat is rendered. Add the water and bring to a boil.

2 Reduce the heat to medium, cover and simmer for 20 minutes. Strain into a bowl and skim off the fat (see page 17). Remove the bacon to a work surface. Cut the lean meat from the fat; discard the fat. Dice the meat and set aside 3 tablespoons; reserve any remainder for another use.

3 Wash the saucepan with soapy water and rinse. Return the broth and meat to the saucepan. Add the potatoes, onions, celery, canned tomatoes (with juice), diced tomatoes, green peppers, wine and thyme. Drain the juice from the clams into the saucepan; set the clams aside.

4 Cover and cook over low heat for 15 minutes, or until the potatoes are soft. Stir in the tomato juice, parsley and the reserved clams. Cover and bring to a boil over medium-high heat. Reduce the heat to medium-low and cook for 4 minutes. Season to taste with the black pepper.

Makes about **2** litres.

Lynn's Fat-Free Flavour

Some clam soups and chowders are made with a large, rubbery clam called, appropriately enough, the chowder clam. It's usually cut up for soups and fritters. Any clam can be used, however. Hard-shell clams – like littleneck, cherrystone and venus – are fine. So are soft-shelled clams such as the razor and the geoduck. Clams can be bought canned or frozen. If purchased live, refrigerate them and make the chowder within two days. These very low fat shellfish are high in protein, vitamin B_{12} and iron.

nutrition at a glance
per 250 ml

0.9 g.	total fat
0.2 g.	saturated fat
111	calories
14 mg.	cholesterol
426 mg.	sodium
7.8 g.	protein
17 g.	carbohydrates
2 g.	dietary fibre

I like to create visual excitement with a contrasting garnish colour, such as finely chopped spring onion greens sprinkled over an ivory potato soup or a dollop of fat-free soured cream on black bean soup.

Here are some garnishes that complement various types of soups.

Clear Soups

* Fresh herb sprigs – coriander, parsley, basil, watercress, dill or mint
* Thinly sliced spring onions
* Cooked pasta stars, alphabets or other tiny shapes

Cream Soups or Vegetable Purées

* Grated fresh ginger
* Chiffonade-cut lettuce or spinach leaves
* Ground nutmeg or paprika
* Chopped apples
* Fat-free plain or herb croutons
* Poppy seeds or toasted sesame seeds
* Air-popped popcorn

Bean and Legume Soups

* Raw vegetables such as diced tomatoes, cucumber slices, celery-leaf sprigs, sliced spring onions or sweet red or yellow pepper strips
* Banana slices
* Fat-free plain or herb croutons
* Diced hard-boiled egg whites
* Hot-pepper sauce or chopped fresh jalapeño peppers or serrano peppers
* Fat-free soured cream or natural yogurt

Chunky Vegetable Soups

* Bean sprouts or alfalfa sprouts
* Toasted squash seeds or toasted pumpkin seeds
* Fat-free Parmesan topping

Seafood Chowders

* Cooked mussels, clams, or oysters in or out of the shell
* Cooked small crab claws or crayfish in the shell
* Cooked scallops or prawns
* Lemon, lime or orange slices

Vegetable Stock

Vegetable stock is easy to make as a tasty, nutrient-rich base for many soups. It's so satisfying to know exactly what ingredients are in your soup base. If you like, double the recipe and freeze in recipe-ready amounts.

4	litres water
250	g butternut squash, peeled, seeded and cut into 5 cm chunks
3	stalks celery, coarsely chopped
2	large tomatoes, diced
2	large onions, coarsely chopped
2	carrots, coarsely chopped
60	g chopped fresh parsley
3	shallots, coarsely chopped
4	cloves garlic, minced
1	teaspoon dried basil
1	large bay leaf
¼	teaspoon dried thyme
¼	teaspoon dried rosemary

Lynn's Kitchen Tip

You can make a puréed vegetable soup from this recipe if you like. After the vegetables are cooked, remove the mesh tea ball or muslin bag and discard the herbs. Purée the soup in a blender or food processor (or in the pan with a hand blender). Season with salt to taste.

1 In a large non-stick pan, combine the water, squash, celery, tomatoes, onions, carrots, parsley, shallots and garlic.

2 Place the basil, bay leaf, thyme and rosemary in a mesh tea ball or wrap in a small piece of muslin and tie with kitchen string. Add to the pan. Bring to a boil over medium-high heat. Reduce the heat to medium-low, cover and simmer for 1 hour.

3 Strain the stock through a colander into a large bowl. Discard the vegetables and herbs. Refrigerate or freeze for use in recipes.

Makes about **3** litres.

nutrition at a glance
per 250 ml

0.1 g.	total fat
0 g.	saturated fat
11	calories
0 mg.	cholesterol
14 mg.	sodium
0.5 g.	protein
2.1 g.	carbohydrates
0 g.	dietary fibre

Chicken Stock

Here's a flavourful fat-free stock that can be the basis of many recipes. To turn it into chicken and vegetable soup, add 1 tablespoon chopped cooked chicken and 90 g cooked vegetables to each 250 ml of stock. For another variation, add 60 g cooked no-yolk noodles, low-fat pasta, white rice, wheat berries or bulgur plus 1 tablespoon chopped chicken to each 250 ml of stock.

4	litres water
1	boiling chicken
2	carrots, cut into large chunks
1	medium onion, cut into quarters
1	large stalk celery with leafy tops, cut into large chunks
1	large leek, white and some green stem, cut into large chunks
4	tablespoons chopped fresh parsley
3	cloves garlic
	Pinch of dried thyme
	Pinch of dried rosemary
	Pinch of dried tarragon

1 In a large non-stick pan, combine the water, chicken, carrots, onions, celery, leeks, parsley, garlic, thyme, rosemary and tarragon.

2 Bring almost to a boil over medium-high heat. Reduce the heat to low, cover and cook for 1¼ to 1½ hours.

3 With a large slotted spoon, remove the chicken and vegetables. Discard the vegetables. Remove the skin, bones and fat from the chicken and discard. Reserve the cooked chicken for another use.

4 Skim off the fat from the stock (see page 17). Refrigerate or freeze for use in recipes.

Makes about **3.5** litres.

nutrition at a glance
per 250 ml

0.1 g.	total fat
0 g.	saturated fat
14	calories
0 mg.	cholesterol
20 mg.	sodium
0.4 g.	protein
3.3 g.	carbohydrates
0 g.	dietary fibre

Salads and Dressings

Salads are natural fat fighters. Composed primarily of fresh vegetables and fruits, salads can easily help us fulfil the Department of Health's Food Guide Pyramid recommendations of three to five servings of vegetables and two to four servings of fruit a day.

Vegetable and fruit salads are bundles of colour, texture and flavour that are loaded with fibre, vitamins and minerals. Try my Spinach-Orange Salad,

Oriental Coleslaw and Fruit Salad with Cantaloupe Dressing to taste just how delicious good nutrition can be.

Add a small amount of protein-rich cooked beans, lean poultry, fat-free cheese or seafood to a simple vegetable salad, and it turns into a fat-free feast. My Turkey Salad with Orange Dressing and Mexicali Pasta Salad make great light meals.

Dressed for Success

Salads are indeed fat-free wonders, but salad dressing is the serpent lurking in this Garden of Eden.

Just 1 tablespoon of vegetable oil – less than many people unthinkingly pour on a serving of salad – contains 13.5 grammes of fat. You can see that by liberally pouring on the oil-based dressing, you can quickly send the fat content of a salad into the double digits.

Fortunately, great-tasting fat-free dressings are a cinch to make, as my Creamy Italian Dressing, Thai Peanut Dressing and others attest. There are many alternatives that perform the same role as oil: namely, to buffer the sharpness of the vinegar.

Choose from fat-free soured cream, fat-free buttermilk, fat-free natural yogurt, fat-free mayonnaise, skimmed chicken stock, vegetable stock, fruit juices or vegetable juices as a base for your homemade dressings.

If you still think that you simply must have some oil, mist it lightly on your salad from a plastic spray bottle. And be sure to choose an oil that offers plenty of flavour – such as extra-virgin olive oil or dark sesame oil – in exchange for the fat calories that you'll be spending.

Sharpen Flavours

I often dress my salads with only vinegar, but I suspect that most people don't care for salads quite that sharp. Vinegar or citrus juices should heighten natural flavours without over-powering them. Unlike most other vinegars, balsamic vinegar has a nat-ural sweetness that makes it mellow enough to drizzle alone on a salad.

Other options include red- or white-wine vinegar, malt vinegar, cider vinegar, Oriental rice vinegar, lemon juice, lime juice and orange juice.

After combining the fat-free base and vinegar or citrus juice, season the dressing with ketchup, mustard, Worcestershire sauce, hot-pepper sauce, fresh or dried herbs, ground spices, crushed herb seeds, ground black pepper, minced garlic, grated fresh ginger, chopped fresh hot peppers, chopped pickles or capers.

Tossed Antipasto Salad

quick and easy

This satisfying main-dish salad is a colourful blend of chickpeas, roasted peppers and fresh vegetables. The parsley takes the place of traditional greens. Serve with a crusty country bread and soup for a delightful meal.

Lynn's Health Watch

Add cooked chickpeas to any tossed salad to boost fibre intake.

1	sweet red pepper
1	yellow pepper
45	g coarsely chopped fresh parsley
125	g diced celery
60	g canned chickpeas, rinsed and drained
1	medium onion, chopped
6	cherry tomatoes, cut in half
3	tablespoons water
2	tablespoons balsamic vinegar
2	teaspoons dried basil
½	teaspoon dried oregano
1	large clove garlic, minced
	Ground black pepper

1 Cut the red and yellow peppers in half lengthwise. Discard the stems, membranes and seeds. Line a baking tray with foil and place the peppers, cut side down, on the sheet. Grill 10 cm from the heat for 10 minutes, or until the skins are blackened. Wrap the foil around the peppers, sealing the edges securely, and set aside for 10 minutes, or until the peppers are cool enough to handle.

2 In a medium bowl, combine the parsley, celery, chickpeas, onions, tomatoes, water, vinegar, basil, oregano and garlic. Toss to blend.

3 Remove the peppers from the foil. With a sharp paring knife, remove and discard the blackened skin. Cut the peppers into thin strips. Add to the bowl. Season to taste with the black pepper. Toss to combine.

Makes **4** servings.

Photograph on page 57

nutrition at a glance
per serving

0.8 g.	total fat
0.1 g.	saturated fat
71	calories
0 mg.	cholesterol
57 mg.	sodium
2.9 g.	protein
14.9 g.	carbohydrates
3.7 g.	dietary fibre

Mexicali Pasta Salad

If you want more heat, add ½ teaspoon finely diced jalapeño peppers. Garnish with a few tablespoons grated fat-free cheese. Make the salad a few hours ahead of time for the flavours to blend. If desired, replace the macaroni with other small pasta shapes.

125	g low-fat macaroni (0.5 g. fat per 60-g serving)
1	ear sweetcorn
125	ml skimmed chicken stock (page 94)
4	tablespoons chopped fresh coriander
2	cloves garlic, minced
1	tablespoon Dijon mustard
1	teaspoon chilli powder
90	g canned pinto beans, rinsed and drained
250	g finely diced celery
185	g finely diced onions
1	yellow pepper, diced
1	can (125 g) diced mild green chilli peppers
1	large head cos lettuce, chopped or shredded

1 Bring a large pan of water to a boil over high heat. Add the macaroni and cook for 5 minutes. Add the sweetcorn and cook for 4 minutes, or until the pasta is just tender.

2 Remove the sweetcorn with tongs and place in a large bowl of iced water for several seconds to cool.

3 Drain the pasta and let stand in the colander.

4 Remove the sweetcorn from the iced water. With a sharp knife, cut the sweetcorn kernels from the cob. Set aside.

5 In a large bowl, combine the stock, coriander, garlic, mustard and chilli powder. Whisk to combine. Add the pasta, sweetcorn, beans, celery, onions, yellow peppers and chilli peppers; toss gently to mix. Cover and refrigerate for at least 1 hour. Just before serving, add the lettuce. Toss to mix.

Makes **8** servings.

Photograph on page 145

Lynn's Kitchen Tip

Pinto beans are often used to make the Mexican speciality refried beans. For an easy fat-free version, rinse and drain 1 can pinto beans. Mash well and season to taste with chilli powder and garlic powder. Add 1 to 2 tablespoons water or chicken stock if the beans are dry. Shape into patties. Coat with non-stick spray and cook in a non-stick frying pan for 2 to 3 minutes per side, or until the patties are hot in the centre.

nutrition at a glance

per serving

0.8 g.	total fat
0.1 g.	saturated fat
123	calories
0 mg.	cholesterol
155 mg.	sodium
5.2 g.	protein
24.6 g.	carbohydrates
4.5 g.	dietary fibre

Caesar Salad with Turkey

quick and easy

This classic salad has become positively trendy in fashionable restaurants. It's so easy to make at home as a luncheon main dish. Fat-free egg substitute replaces the raw egg used in traditional recipes.

½ large head cos lettuce
185 g cubed cooked boneless, skinless turkey breast
125 ml freshly squeezed lemon juice
4 tablespoons fat-free egg substitute
2 large cloves garlic, minced
1 teaspoon Worcestershire sauce
¼ teaspoon anchovy paste (optional)
Ground black pepper
4 tablespoons fat-free Parmesan topping
Garlic croutons (optional)

1 Tear the lettuce into large pieces and place in a large bowl. Add the turkey.

2 In a small bowl, combine the lemon juice, egg substitute, garlic, Worcestershire sauce and anchovy paste (if using). Whisk to combine. Season to taste with the pepper. Pour over the lettuce and turkey. Toss to combine.

3 Sprinkle with the Parmesan and croutons (if using). Toss to combine.

Makes **4** servings.

Photograph on page 58

nutrition at a glance

per serving
0.9 g. total fat
0.2 g. saturated fat
129 calories
45 mg. cholesterol
247 mg. sodium
22 g. protein
8.8 g. carbohydrates
1.2 g. dietary fibre

Turkey Salad with Orange Dressing

This turkey salad is so special that I served it at a friend's wedding. I can guarantee that none of the wedding guests missed the fat. As a cool main-dish summer salad, it's beautiful served with a rainbow of fresh fruit: grapes, strawberries, cantaloupe, honeydew, watermelon or fresh pineapple.

Orange Dressing

125	ml orange juice
125	ml fat-free natural yogurt
2	cloves garlic, minced
2	teaspoons freshly squeezed lime juice
2	teaspoons low-sodium soy sauce
1	teaspoon Dijon mustard
1	teaspoon dried tarragon

Turkey Salad

250	g boneless, skinless turkey breast, trimmed of all visible fat and cut into 1 cm cubes
1	teaspoon lemon-pepper seasoning
90	g coarsely chopped celery
155	g seedless red or green grapes, cut in half
155	g coarsely chopped fresh pineapple
125	g canned sliced water chestnuts, cut into matchsticks
4	spring onions, thinly sliced
6	hard-boiled egg whites, sliced into wedges
1	head butterhead lettuce
4	tablespoons chopped pimientos
250	g garlic sourdough croutons (optional)

1 *To make the orange dressing:* In a small bowl, combine the orange juice, yogurt, garlic, lime juice, soy sauce, mustard and tarragon. Cover and refrigerate.

2 *To make the turkey salad:* Season the turkey with the lemon-pepper seasoning. Place in an ovenproof plastic cooking bag. Microwave on high power for 4 minutes, or until the turkey is no longer pink in the centre when tested with the point of a sharp knife. Transfer to a large bowl and refrigerate for 30 minutes, or until chilled.

3 Add the celery, grapes, pineapple, water chestnuts, spring onions and egg whites.

Lynn's Kitchen Tip

To make croutons, preheat the oven to 180°C, Gas 4. Dice sourdough, French, Italian or other crusty bread. Place on a baking tray and coat the bread cubes lightly with non-stick spray. Sprinkle lightly with garlic salt, parsley and fat-free Parmesan topping. Bake for 10 to 15 minutes, tossing occasionally, or until golden.

nutrition at a glance

per serving

0.9 g.	total fat
0.2 g.	saturated fat
139	calories
26 mg.	cholesterol
314 mg.	sodium
15.3 g.	protein
18.7 g.	carbohydrates
2.8 g.	dietary fibre

4 Remove 6 lettuce leaves and place on a platter. Chop the remaining lettuce and add to the turkey mixture. Pour the dressing over the salad. Toss gently to coat. Spoon over the lettuce. Sprinkle with the pimientos and croutons (if using).

Makes **6** servings.

Photograph on page 61

Prawn Salad

quick and easy

You can also make this special seafood salad with lobster, crab, scallops, imitation crab or a combination of seafood. It makes a wonderful appetizer or sandwich filling. Serve with chilled fresh melon slices and grapes for a refreshing summer luncheon salad.

4	tablespoons fat-free mayonnaise
4	tablespoons fat-free soured cream
2	tablespoons freshly squeezed lemon juice
2	tablespoons water
¼	teaspoon hot-pepper sauce
155	g diced cucumbers
2	large stalks celery, diced
1	medium onion, diced
2	tablespoons diced gherkins
1	tablespoon capers, rinsed and drained
1	teaspoon chopped fresh dill
250	g cooked and chilled peeled prawns, cut into bite-size pieces
	Ground black pepper
	Paprika

1 In a small bowl, combine the mayonnaise, soured cream, lemon juice, water and hot-pepper sauce. Whisk until smooth.

2 In a medium bowl, combine the cucumbers, celery, onions, gherkins, capers and dill. Toss lightly to mix. Add the dressing and prawns; toss gently to combine. Season to taste with the pepper and paprika.

Makes **4** servings.

nutrition at a glance
per serving

0.8 g.	total fat
0.2 g.	saturated fat
102	calories
111 mg.	cholesterol
473 mg.	sodium
14 g.	protein
10 g.	carbohydrates
1 g.	dietary fibre

Barley-Lentil Salad

quick and easy

Make this hearty main-dish grain salad when you have leftover cooked barley and lentils on hand.

8	chestnut mushrooms, sliced
2	cloves garlic, minced
125	ml skimmed chicken stock (page 94)
3	tablespoons balsamic vinegar
2	teaspoons Dijon mustard
1	teaspoon freshly squeezed lemon juice
250	g cooked barley
185	g cooked lentils
155	g cooked peas or thawed frozen peas
3	spring onions, sliced
8	baby carrots, sliced
1	medium tomato, diced
	Ground black pepper
	Salt (optional)
6	curly lettuce leaves (optional)
1	tablespoon chopped fresh parsley

1 Coat a large non-stick frying pan with non-stick spray. Add the mushrooms and garlic and mist with non-stick spray. Cover and cook over medium heat for 3 to 4 minutes, or until the mushrooms start to lose their moisture. Uncover and cook, stirring, for 1 to 2 minutes, or until the mushrooms are tender.

2 In a large bowl, combine the stock, vinegar, mustard and lemon juice; whisk until smooth. Add the barley, lentils, peas, spring onions, carrots, tomatoes and mushroom mixture. Toss gently to coat the salad with dressing. Season to taste with the pepper and salt (if using).

3 Line a platter with the lettuce leaves (if using). Top with the salad. Sprinkle with the parsley.

Makes **6** servings.

nutrition at a glance

per serving

0.7 g.	total fat
0.1 g.	saturated fat
123	calories
0 mg.	cholesterol
57 mg.	sodium
6.2 g.	protein
24.5 g.	carbohydrates
5.6 g.	dietary fibre

Artichoke Salad

quick and easy

If frozen artichoke hearts aren't available, you may use canned ones, but they'll be higher in sodium. Garnish with capers and paprika, if you like, for extra piquancy and colour.

2	packages (280 g each) frozen artichoke hearts, thawed
250	g grated carrots
1	sweet red pepper, cut into matchsticks
1	small onion, thinly sliced
90	g fat-free mozzarella cheese, diced
1	teaspoon dried thyme
3	tablespoons balsamic vinegar
3	tablespoons freshly squeezed lemon juice
2	tablespoons water
	Ground black pepper
1	head iceberg lettuce
3	tablespoons chopped fresh parsley

1   Place the artichokes on several layers of paper towels. Let them drain for 5 minutes, then pat dry. Cut the artichokes in half lengthwise. Place in a large bowl.

2   Add the carrots, red peppers, onions, mozzarella, thyme, vinegar, lemon juice and water. Toss to combine. Season to taste with the black pepper.

3   Remove the outer leaves of lettuce and arrange on a platter.

4   Coarsely chop the remaining lettuce. Add to the bowl; toss to combine. Spoon the salad over the lettuce on the platter. Sprinkle with the parsley.

Makes **4** servings.

nutrition at a glance
per serving

0.9 g.	total fat
0.2 g.	saturated fat
136	calories
3 mg.	cholesterol
230 mg.	sodium
12 g.	protein
23.4 g.	carbohydrates
7.9 g.	dietary fibre

Greek Salad

quick and easy

**Garnish each salad with ½ teaspoon diced kalamata olives, and
you'll increase the fat to only 1 gramme per serving.**

4	tablespoons skimmed chicken stock (page 94)
2	tablespoons red-wine vinegar
2	teaspoons freshly squeezed lemon juice
1	teaspoon sugar
1	teaspoon thinly sliced fresh basil or ½ teaspoon dried
½	teaspoon dried oregano
1	head cos lettuce, torn into pieces
12	thin slices cucumber
125	g chilled cooked French beans cut into 2.5 cm pieces
4	tablespoons finely chopped red onions
2	tablespoons finely chopped fresh parsley
1	tablespoon crumbled low-fat feta cheese
1	large tomato, cut into 8 wedges
4	peperoncini
	Ground black pepper

1 In a large bowl, combine the
stock, vinegar, lemon juice, sugar, basil and oregano.
Whisk until smooth. Add the lettuce, cucumbers,
beans, onions and parsley. Toss to combine the salad
with the dressing.

2 Serve topped with the feta,
tomatoes and peperoncini. Season to taste with the
pepper.

Makes **4** servings.

Photograph on page 143

nutrition at a glance

per serving

0.9 g.	total fat
0.4 g.	saturated fat
46	calories
1 mg.	cholesterol
222 mg.	sodium
2.4 g.	protein
8.5 g.	carbohydrates
2.2 g.	dietary fibre

Cuke and Zuke Raita

quick and easy

This raita – an Indian salad with yogurt dressing – is a refreshing blend of cucumbers, courgettes and mint. It beautifully balances any spicy main dish.

185	ml fat-free natural yogurt
4	tablespoons fat-free soured cream
4	tablespoons chopped fresh chives
3	tablespoons chopped fresh mint
2	cloves garlic, minced
1	cucumber, diced
90	g diced courgette

1 Line a fine sieve with muslin or a coffee filter. Add the yogurt. Set over a bowl to drain for 5 minutes. Discard the whey that drains into the bowl.

2 Transfer the yogurt to a medium bowl. Add the soured cream, chives, mint and garlic. Stir to mix well. Add the cucumbers and courgette. Toss to coat with the dressing. Let stand for 10 to 15 minutes to blend the flavours. Pour off any excess water that accumulates.

Makes **4** servings.

nutrition at a glance

per serving

0.3 g.	total fat
0.1 g.	saturated fat
69	calories
1 mg.	cholesterol
60 mg.	sodium
5 g.	protein
11 g.	carbohydrates
2 g.	dietary fibre

Tomato, Basil and Mozzarella Salad

quick and easy

Make this superb Italian salad in the summer, when garden tomatoes, courgettes and yellow squash are abundant. If yellow tomatoes aren't available, simply use all red ones. You'll need only a few drops of balsamic vinegar to enhance the sweetness of the tomatoes.

30	large fresh basil leaves
60	g small spinach leaves
4	small yellow tomatoes, thinly sliced
1	courgette, thinly sliced
125	g fat-free mozzarella cheese, thinly sliced
4	small red tomatoes, thinly sliced
1	yellow squash, thinly sliced
	Balsamic vinegar
4	stoned black or green olives, sliced (optional)
	Ground black pepper

1 Stack 6 of the basil leaves on top of each other. Roll lengthwise into a tight bundle and then cut into thin slices. Unfurl the slices into shreds and set aside.

2 Line the outer edge of a round platter with the spinach leaves. Alternate the remaining basil leaves, yellow tomatoes, courgette, mozzarella, red tomatoes and yellow squash, slightly overlapping, in circles going around the plate.

3 Sprinkle lightly with the vinegar. Sprinkle with the reserved basil and olives (if using). Season to taste with the pepper.

Makes **4** servings.

Photograph on page 59

Photograph on page 59

Lynn's Kitchen Tip

Chiffonade is a French term meaning "made of rags", according to *The New Food Lover's Companion* by Sharon Tyler Herbst. Strips of green herbs, such as basil, make a pretty garnish in a soup or salad. To cut any herb leaves, lettuce or other greens into chiffonade, stack the leaves, then roll them into a tight bundle. Cut crosswise into thin slices.

---

nutrition at a glance

per serving

0.9 g.	total fat
0.1 g.	saturated fat
117	calories
4 mg.	cholesterol
218 mg.	sodium
12 g.	protein
18 g.	carbohydrates
4 g.	dietary fibre

Oriental Coleslaw

quick and easy

Roasting brings out the flavour of seeds and nuts. Use a bit of dark sesame oil or dark roasted peanut oil, and you'll experience the distinctive flavour note that just a few drops of roasted nut oils add to foods.

3	tablespoons white-wine vinegar or cider vinegar
1	teaspoon sugar
1	teaspoon low-sodium soy sauce
½	teaspoon minced fresh ginger
¼	teaspoon five-spice seasoning
1	clove garlic, minced
1	teaspoon sesame seeds (optional)
¼	teaspoon crushed chillies (optional)
1	medium cucumber, diced
125	g shredded bok choy or cabbage
90	g grated carrots
½	sweet red pepper, finely diced
1	can (185 g) sliced water chestnuts, drained and cut in half
1	tablespoon chopped fresh coriander
	Dark sesame oil in a spray bottle

1 In a large bowl, combine the vinegar, sugar, soy sauce, ginger, five-spice seasoning and garlic. Add the sesame seeds (if using) and chillies (if using). Whisk to combine.

2 Add the cucumbers, bok choy or cabbage, carrots, red peppers, water chestnuts and coriander. Spray lightly with the oil; toss to combine.

Makes **4** servings.

Photograph on page 144

Photograph on page 144

Lynn's Kitchen Tip

Storing flavourful oils, such as extra-virgin olive oil or dark sesame oil, in a plastic spray bottle is a convenient way to flavour salads with a scant amount. To make sure that you're spritzing the amount that you want, do a test. Spray oil into a ½ teaspoon measuring spoon, counting the number of spritzes. Make a note of the number and you'll always know exactly how much oil you're spraying. Remember that each ½ teaspoon oil contains 2.3 grammes of fat.

---

nutrition at a glance

per serving

0.8 g.	total fat
0.1 g.	saturated fat
54	calories
0 mg.	cholesterol
71 mg.	sodium
2 g.	protein
11 g.	carbohydrates
2 g.	dietary fibre

Potato Salad with Caramelised Onions

quick and easy

On the day of testing, several guests arrived just at the moment this potato salad was finished. Some testers barely got a taste of the salad because it disappeared so fast. Garnish with extra finely chopped parsley, if you like, to perk up the colour.

750	g small red potatoes
1	large onion, chopped
2	tablespoons white-wine vinegar
2	tablespoons finely chopped fresh parsley
1	clove garlic, minced
4	tablespoons fat-free mayonnaise
4	tablespoons fat-free soured cream
2	tablespoons freshly squeezed lemon juice
½	teaspoon sugar
1	sweet red pepper, diced
	Ground black pepper
	Salt (optional)

1 Place the potatoes in a medium non-stick saucepan. Add enough water to cover. Bring to a boil over medium-high heat. Reduce the heat to medium. Cook for 15 minutes, or until the potatoes are tender when pierced with a fork.

2 Meanwhile, coat a large non-stick frying pan with non-stick spray. Add the onions and coat with non-stick spray. Cover and cook over medium-high heat, stirring occasionally, for 5 minutes, or until the onions start to give off moisture. Uncover and cook over medium heat, stirring occasionally, for 6 to 8 minutes, or until golden. If necessary, add 1 to 2 teaspoons water to prevent sticking.

3 Drain the potatoes, then cut into large bite-size pieces. Place in a large bowl. Sprinkle with 1 tablespoon of the vinegar; toss. Sprinkle on the parsley and garlic; toss and set aside.

4 To serve the salad cold, cover the potatoes and refrigerate for several hours before adding the dressing.

5 In a small bowl, combine the mayonnaise, soured cream, lemon juice, sugar and the remaining 1 tablespoon vinegar. Whisk to combine.

6 Pour over the potatoes. Add the red pepper. Season to taste with the black pepper and salt (if using). Toss gently to combine.

Makes **4** servings.

Spinach-Orange Salad

quick and easy

This salad is a bright addition to the winter table when fresh tomatoes are out of season.

125	ml fat-free buttermilk
2	teaspoons Dijon mustard
1	clove garlic, finely chopped
250	g torn spinach leaves
2	navel oranges, peeled and separated into segments
1	small red onion, sliced
4	tablespoons finely chopped spring onions
	Ground black pepper

Lynn's Fat-Free Flavour

Mustard – such as Dijon, stone-ground, honey or horseradish – offers a mighty amount of flavour with barely any fat. Use a teaspoon or two to spark flavour in salad dressings and sauces.

1 In a large bowl, combine the buttermilk, mustard and garlic; whisk to mix well. Add the spinach, oranges, onions and spring onions. Toss to coat with the dressing. Serve sprinkled with the pepper.

Makes **4** servings.

Photograph on page 60

Cran-Blackberry Gelatine Salad

The contrast of tart berries and rich, sweet soured cream is irresistible in this moulded gelatine salad. It's ideal for a party. In fact, you can make it several days ahead and store, tightly covered, in the refrigerator.

Soured Cream Layer

4	tablespoons orange juice
1	teaspoon powdered gelatine
1	tablespoon sugar
250	ml fat-free soured cream

Cran-Blackberry Gelatine

375	g fresh or frozen cranberries
105	g sugar
2	tablespoons freshly squeezed lemon juice or lime juice
¼	teaspoon ground cinnamon
680	ml orange juice
250	g blackberries
5	teaspoons powdered gelatine
	Butterhead lettuce leaves or fresh mint leaves (optional)

Lynn's Lore

To speed up the setting of any gelatine mixture, place the bowl with the gelatine in a larger bowl filled partially with iced water. Set aside for 15 minutes, stirring occasionally, or until the mixture gets thick enough to coat a spoon.

1 *To make the soured cream layer:* Place the orange juice in a medium microwaveable bowl. Sprinkle with the gelatine. Let stand for 2 minutes, or until the gelatine softens. Microwave on high power for 45 seconds, or until hot. Stir in the sugar.

2 Whisk in the soured cream until well-combined. Pour into a 1.5-litre ring mould. Refrigerate while preparing the cran-blackberry gelatine.

3 *To make the cran-blackberry gelatine:* Meanwhile, in a medium non-stick saucepan, combine the cranberries, sugar, lemon juice or lime juice, cinnamon and 500 ml of the orange juice. Bring to a boil over medium heat. Reduce the heat to low, cover and simmer for 5 minutes, or until the sugar dissolves.

4 Add the blackberries. Cover and simmer, stirring occasionally, for 10 minutes.

5 Place the remaining orange juice in a small microwaveable bowl. Sprinkle with the gelatine. Let stand for 2 minutes, or until the gelatine softens. Microwave on high power for 1 to 2 minutes, or until hot; stir to dissolve the gelatine.

6 Add to the berry mixture and stir well. Transfer to a large bowl. Refrigerate for 45 minutes, stirring occasionally, until the mixture is thickened enough to mound when dropped from a spoon.

7 Pour the berry mixture into the mould. Refrigerate for at least 4 hours, or until set.

8 To unmould, run a knife around the outer and inner edges of the mould. Dip the bottom of the mould into hot water for a few seconds. Cover with a serving plate and flip the mould over. Allow to stand for a few seconds before gently lifting off the mould.

9 Tuck lettuce leaves or mint leaves (if using) under the edges of the salad.

Makes **8** servings.

Photograph on page 62

nutrition at a glance

per serving
0.3 g.	total fat
0.1 g.	saturated fat
161	calories
0 mg.	cholesterol
27 mg.	sodium
4.2 g.	protein
36 g.	carbohydrates
2.2 g.	dietary fibre

Fruit Salad with Cantaloupe Dressing

quick and easy

The creamy cantaloupe dressing is also refreshing for any fruit, poultry or prawn salad. The following recipe yields about 250 ml dressing. The cantaloupe can be puréed in a blender for a smoother dressing, if you like.

Cantaloupe Dressing

4	tablespoons fat-free lemon yogurt
2	teaspoons freshly squeezed lime juice or lemon juice
1	teaspoon Dijon mustard
½	teaspoon honey
315	g finely chopped cantaloupe

Fruit Salad

2	bananas
1	tablespoon freshly squeezed lemon juice
2	ruby red grapefruit, peeled and cut into wedges
2	pears, cut into chunks
250	g blueberries
185	g thinly sliced celery
2	kiwifruit, cut into wedges
2	plums, cut into wedges
1	tablespoon finely chopped fresh mint

1 *To make the cantaloupe dressing:* In a medium bowl, combine the yogurt, lime juice or lemon juice, mustard and honey. Whisk to combine. Add the cantaloupe and stir to combine. Set aside.

2 *To make the fruit salad:* Cut the bananas into slices and place in a medium bowl; toss with the lemon juice. Arrange on a large platter. Arrange the grapefruit, pears, blueberries, celery, kiwifruit, plums and mint in a pretty design.

3 Drizzle with the dressing just before serving.

Makes **6** servings.

nutrition at a glance
per serving

0.9 g.	total fat
0.1 g.	saturated fat
163	calories
0 mg.	cholesterol
30 mg.	sodium
2.8 g.	protein
40 g.	carbohydrates
6 g.	dietary fibre

Thousand Island Dressing

quick and easy

For those of you who have given up on your old favourite chunky salad dressing because of the outrageous fat content, I've created this fat-free version that tastes zestier than the original.

250	ml fat-free mayonnaise
4	tablespoons chunky chilli sauce
4	tablespoons finely chopped green peppers
3	tablespoons finely chopped onions
3	tablespoons sweet pickle relish
2	tablespoons chopped fresh parsley
½	teaspoon paprika
4	tablespoons skimmed milk or fat-free soured cream (optional)
3	hard-boiled egg whites, finely chopped

1   In a medium bowl, combine the mayonnaise, chilli sauce, peppers, onions, relish, parsley and paprika. Stir to mix well. Add the milk or soured cream (if using) for a thinner dressing. Fold in the egg whites.

Makes about **500** ml.

nutrition at a glance

per 2 tablespoons

0 g.	total fat
0 g.	saturated fat
22	calories
0 mg.	cholesterol
194 mg.	sodium
0.8 g.	protein
4.2 g.	carbohydrates
0.2 g.	dietary fibre

Green Goddess Dressing

quick and easy

This old-favourite salad dressing can double as a condiment for grilled or barbecued beef, fish or shellfish.

185	ml fat-free mayonnaise
125	ml fat-free soured cream
2	tablespoons white-wine vinegar
2	teaspoons freshly squeezed lemon juice
1	teaspoon anchovy paste or Worcestershire sauce
½	teaspoon Dijon mustard
3	tablespoons chopped fresh parsley
2	tablespoons chopped fresh chives
1	spring onion, finely chopped
1	clove garlic, minced
¼	teaspoon dried tarragon

1 In a medium bowl, combine the mayonnaise, soured cream, vinegar, lemon juice, anchovy paste or Worcestershire sauce and mustard. Mix with a whisk until blended. Stir in the parsley, chives, spring onion, garlic and tarragon.

Makes about **300** ml.

nutrition at a glance

per 2 tablespoons

0 g.	total fat
0 g.	saturated fat
22	calories
0 mg.	cholesterol
194 mg.	sodium
0.8 g.	protein
4.2 g.	carbohydrates
0.2 g.	dietary fibre

Creamy Italian Dressing

quick and easy

If you don't have fresh basil for this dressing, you can substitute 1½ teaspoons dried basil.

80	ml fat-free soured cream
4	tablespoons fat-free buttermilk
2	tablespoons red-wine vinegar
2	tablespoons thinly sliced fresh basil
2	cloves garlic, minced
¾	teaspoon dried oregano
	Ground black pepper
	Salt (optional)

1 In a small bowl, combine the soured cream, buttermilk, vinegar, basil, garlic and oregano. Whisk to combine. Season to taste with the pepper and salt (if using).

Makes about **160** ml.

nutrition at a glance

per 2 tablespoons

0 g.	total fat
0 g.	saturated fat
23	calories
0 mg.	cholesterol
24 mg.	sodium
1.5 g.	protein
4 g.	carbohydrates
0 g.	dietary fibre

Thai Peanut Dressing

quick and easy

This distinctive dressing is wonderful over greens, sprouts, mangetout, carrots, sugar snap peas and many other vegetables. It's also delicious spooned over grilled fish or poultry. Some minced chives or spring onions are a nice addition.

1½	teaspoons low-fat peanut butter
6	tablespoons freshly squeezed lime juice or lemon juice
2	tablespoons low-sodium soy sauce
2	tablespoons water
1	teaspoon sugar
¼	teaspoon hot-pepper sauce
3	tablespoons chopped fresh coriander
2	tablespoons thinly sliced fresh basil
2	teaspoons chopped fresh mint
3	cloves garlic, minced

1 Place the peanut butter in a medium bowl. Gradually add the lime juice or lemon juice, whisking constantly until smooth. Add the soy sauce, water, sugar and hot-pepper sauce. Whisk to blend. Add the coriander, basil, mint and garlic. Stir to combine.

Makes about **180** ml.

Photograph on page 319

nutrition at a glance

per 2 tablespoons

0.6 g.	total fat
0.1 g.	saturated fat
22	calories
0 mg.	cholesterol
211 mg.	sodium
1 g.	protein
3.9 g.	carbohydrates
0.3 g.	dietary fibre

Poppy Seed Dressing

quick and easy

This tangy dressing is great for coleslaw. Toasting the poppy seeds in a small frying pan for a few minutes over medium heat will bring out their flavour.

125	ml cider vinegar
1	tablespoon honey
1	tablespoon freshly squeezed lemon juice
1	teaspoon poppy seeds

1   In a small bowl, combine the vinegar, honey, lemon juice and poppy seeds. Mix well with a fork.

Makes about **160** ml.

Lynn's Fun Food Fact

The colour and flavour of honey are affected by the flower that the bee visits. Buckwheat is dark and intensely flavoured. Thyme flowers make a clear and golden honey. Sage is a lightly pungent taste. Wildflower honey is vigorous. Orange blossom is light and delicate.

nutrition at a glance

per 2 tablespoons

0.1 g.	total fat
0 g.	saturated fat
13	calories
0 mg.	cholesterol
0 mg.	sodium
0 g.	protein
3.3 g.	carbohydrates
0 g.	dietary fibre

Slim Salad Sidekicks

Transform a tossed salad from simple to sensational with any of these fat-free additions.

* Matchsticks of fat-free ham, turkey or chicken
* Diced fat-free, Cheddar or Mozzarella cheese
* Fat-free Parmesan topping
* Diced or sliced hard-boiled egg whites
* Chopped dried dates, figs, apricots or raisins
* Chopped or sliced fresh apples, nectarines, peaches or grapes
* Sliced pickled peppers, such as peperoncini or jalapeños
* Sliced pickled vegetables, such as okra, capers, beetroot, green beans, asparagus or baby onions
* Frozen peas or sweetcorn (sprinkle on the salad and they'll thaw in minutes)
* Rinsed and drained canned kidney beans, pinto beans, navy beans or chickpeas

Ranch Dressing

quick and easy

If you don't have dried celery flakes, use chopped celery leaves or finely chopped celery.

250	ml fat-free soured cream
125	ml fat-free buttermilk
2	teaspoons cider vinegar
¼	teaspoon sugar
90	g grated carrots
1	tablespoon finely chopped fresh parsley
1	large clove garlic, minced
½	teaspoon celery seeds
½	teaspoon dried celery flakes
½	teaspoon onion powder

1 In a medium bowl, combine the soured cream, buttermilk, vinegar and sugar. Mix to blend. Add the carrots, parsley, garlic, celery seeds, celery flakes and onion powder. Mix to combine.

Makes about **500** ml.

Lynn's Fat-Free Flavour
Use some ranch dressing as a zippy sandwich spread instead of high-fat mayonnaise.

nutrition at a glance
per 2 tablespoons

0 g.	total fat
0 g.	saturated fat
21	calories
0 mg.	cholesterol
22 mg.	sodium
0.1 g.	protein
3.7 g.	carbohydrates
0.1 g.	dietary fibre

Fish

Shellfish

Fish and Shellfish

Seafood, an excellent source of lean protein, is like manna from heaven to the fat-free cook. Plenty of fish and shellfish contain less than 1 gramme of fat for each 105-g portion (see "The Skinny on Seafood" on page 125), which is about the size of a deck of cards. And that fat is overwhelmingly the better-for-you unsaturated variety.

Seafood is generally lower in total fat – and certainly lower in saturated fat – than pork, beef, lamb and poultry. Although the cholesterol content from clam to lamb and turkey to jerky is comparable, cholesterol doesn't impact weight control and is a far less important contributing factor to heart disease than saturated fat.

Don't be scared off by fish that has more than 1 gramme of fat per serving. The types that have the most fat, like mackerel and herring, are also high in health-enhancing omega-3 fatty acids, which may help reduce the risk of stroke and heart attacks. Other seafood, such as sea bass, turbot and oysters, has only a few grammes of fat per 105 g and fits nicely into a healthful diet.

Preparing the Catch

Start by shopping at a reliable fishmonger – one with a brisk trade to help guarantee a fresh product.

Before cooking, rinse the fish gently in cold water. Scrub the shells of mollusks and crustaceans. (Discard any mollusks that don't close after a light tapping.) Pat the seafood dry.

You can marinate seafood for up to one hour before cooking to add flavour. Zesty fat-free marinades can include vinegar, citrus juice, white or red wine, vegetable juice, low-sodium soy sauce, teriyaki sauce, Worcestershire sauce, skimmed stock or broth, bouillon, clam juice and fat-free salad dressing. Herbs, spices and other aromatics can also add intrigue.

Seafood is spectacularly easy to prepare with no added fat. Be sure to cook it just until done so it remains moist. For finfish, check by inserting a sharp knife into the centre of a fillet. It should be opaque and no longer translucent. A good rule of thumb is to allow 10 minutes of cooking time for each 2.5 cm thickness of the fish.

For lobster, prawns, crab and scallops, cook until the flesh turns opaque and is set but not overly firm to the touch. Cook mussels and clams until the shells open and the flesh is hot.

Perfect Portions

Remember that my seafood main dishes are designed to be just part of a meal. To boost your nutrients and satisfy your appetite, you'll want to include plenty of fresh vegetables, a low-fat salad, and a whole-grain side dish.

Every serving of my seafood dishes contains less than 1 gramme of fat. Of course, the number of servings you'll eat will vary depending upon your gender, body type and personal calorie needs. Even if you double the servings, however, your total fat intake will still be extremely low.

Red Snapper with Creamed Dill Sauce

quick and easy

This creamy sauce, pungent with fresh dill, tastes decadent. You can replace the snapper with other low-fat seafood, such as orange roughy, halibut, cod, flounder or scallops.

4	red snapper fillets (90 g each), skin on
½	teaspoon crushed black peppercorns
375	ml fat-free liquid creamer
2½	tablespoons plain flour
2	tablespoons chopped fresh dill or 2 teaspoons dried dill
1	tablespoon white wine or white-wine Worcestershire sauce (optional)
	Salt (optional)

1 Rinse the fish and pat dry with paper towels. Score the skin side with several diagonal slashes. Rub ¼ teaspoon of the pepper into the flesh.

2 Coat a large non-stick frying pan with non-stick spray. Warm the pan over medium-high heat. Add the fish and cook for 1 minute on each side, or until golden. Reduce the heat to low.

3 Partially cover the pan and cook for 10 minutes, or until the fish is cooked. (Check by inserting the tip of a sharp knife in the centre of 1 fillet.)

4 Meanwhile, in a small non-stick saucepan, combine the creamer, flour, dill, wine or Worcestershire sauce and the remaining ¼ teaspoon pepper. Whisk over low heat for 5 minutes, or until thickened. Season to taste with the salt (if using).

5 Put the fish on dinner plates. Pour the sauce across of each fillet.

Makes **4** servings.

nutrition at a glance

per serving

0.8 g.	total fat
0.2 g.	saturated fat
136	calories
21 mg.	cholesterol
26 mg.	sodium
12.3 g.	protein
16 g.	carbohydrates
0.2 g.	dietary fibre

Mahimahi with Prawns and Tropical Salsa

quick and easy

> This dish looks like a tropical sunset and tastes like paradise. For a summer dinner party, it doesn't get any better than this vibrant mélange of seafood and fruity salsa. If you like, you can cook the seafood in a non-stick frying pan on the stove top.

Mahimahi and Prawns

4	mahimahi fillets (75 g each)
2	teaspoons freshly squeezed lime juice or lemon juice
125	g peeled prawns, tails left on

Tropical Salsa

125	g fresh pineapple chunks
90	g diced mangoes or peaches
1	slice (1 cm thick) honeydew or cantaloupe, cut into 1 cm pieces
¼	green pepper, cut into 1 cm pieces
¼	sweet red pepper, cut into 1 cm pieces
80	ml freshly squeezed lime juice or lemon juice
4	tablespoons chopped fresh coriander
4	spring onions, sliced
½	teaspoon finely diced jalapeño peppers (wear rubber gloves when handling)

1 *To make the mahimahi and prawns:* Rinse the fish and pat dry with paper towels. Place in a large shallow baking dish. Drizzle with the lime juice or lemon juice; turn to coat both sides. Coat both sides with non-stick spray.

2 Prepare a barbecue grill. Coat the grill rack with non-stick spray.

3 Place the fish on the rack. Barbecue for 3 to 5 minutes, or until opaque on the bottom. Turn the fish. Carefully place the prawns on the barbecue. Cook for 3 to 5 minutes, or until the mahimahi and prawns are opaque in the centre. (Check by inserting the tip of a sharp knife in the centre of 1 fillet and 1 prawn).

To dice a fresh mango, cut it in half lengthwise, slightly off centre, just grazing the flat, oval stone. Score the flesh into 1 cm cubes with a small, sharp knife, cutting down to, but not through, the skin. Holding the piece with both hands, push the skin side upward to display the fruit cubes. Cut the fruit cubes away from the skin. On the remaining half, use the tip of the knife to cut the stone away from the flesh. Cut the flesh as above.

4 *To make the tropical salsa:*
While the fish is cooking, in a medium bowl, mix the pineapple, mangoes or peaches, melon, green peppers, red peppers, lime juice or lemon juice, coriander, spring onions and jalapeño peppers. Serve with the fish and prawns.

Makes **4** servings.

Photograph on front cover

Sole Française

quick and easy

This succulent fat-free version of a timeless French classic is always perfect for a special occasion. Serve with parsleyed potatoes, tender young green beans, crisp lettuce salad and sorbet with fruit. If sole is not available, use flounder. I like to serve the fish with lemon wedges.

4   Dover sole or lemon sole fillets (90 g each)
60   ml white wine or non-alcoholic white wine
4   tablespoons chopped fresh parsley
1   tablespoon freshly squeezed lemon juice

1   Rinse the fish and pat dry with paper towels. Coat both sides with non-stick spray.

2   Warm a large non-stick frying pan over medium-high heat. Add the fish and cook for 2 minutes, or until lightly browned on the bottom.

3   Add the wine, parsley and lemon juice. Reduce the heat to low, cover and cook for 4 minutes, or until the fish is opaque. (Check by inserting the tip of a sharp knife in the centre of 1 fillet.)

4   Remove the fish to warm plates. Boil the sauce over medium-high heat for 1 minute to reduce slightly. Pour over the fish.

Makes **4** servings.

Lynn's Health Watch

Colour is a clue to the fat content of fish. Light-coloured flesh usually indicates leaner fish. White-fleshed halibut and sole, for example, are low in fat. Darker mackerel, salmon, and tuna contain more fat.

Cod with Ginger-Orange Sauce

quick and easy

This recipe makes plenty of sprightly ginger-orange sauce. Spoon it over angel hair pasta, cellophane noodles or spaghettini as a low-fat accompaniment to the cod. A green vegetable, sweet grapes and a salad will complete the menu. You may replace the orange with a 185-g can of mandarin oranges, drained and cut into chunks.

4	cod fillets (100 g each)
1	tablespoon minced fresh ginger
1½	tablespoons freshly squeezed lemon juice
1	teaspoon Dijon mustard
1	teaspoon low-sodium soy sauce
375	ml freshly squeezed orange juice
2	tablespoons cornflour
185	g orange pieces
4	spring onions, chopped

1 Rinse the fish and pat dry with paper towels. Set aside.

2 Coat a large non-stick frying pan with non-stick spray. Add the ginger and cook over medium-high heat, stirring often, for 2 minutes, or until lightly browned. Add the lemon juice, mustard, soy sauce and 250 ml of the orange juice; stir to combine.

3 Add the fish in a single layer. Cover and cook over low heat for 6 to 8 minutes, or until the fish is opaque. (Check by inserting the tip of a sharp knife in the centre of 1 fillet.) Remove the fish to a plate; cover to keep warm.

4 Place the cornflour in a cup. Add the remaining orange juice and stir to dissolve the cornflour. Add to the frying pan. Cook, stirring constantly, for 1 minute, or until the sauce thickens. Stir in the oranges; cover and cook for 1 minute, or until the oranges are hot. Serve the sauce over the fish. Sprinkle with the spring onions.

Makes **4** servings.

Photograph on page 149

nutrition at a glance	
per serving	
0.8 g.	total fat
0.1 g.	saturated fat
141	calories
26 mg.	cholesterol
97 mg.	sodium
12.1 g.	protein
21.5 g.	carbohydrates
0.5 g.	dietary fibre

The Skinny on Seafood

Get your hooks into these low-fat seafoods for delicious, nutritious meals. The fat content listed is for 100 g fish (raw weight).

Seafood	Fat (g.)
Alaska king crab leg	0.6
Pacific cod	0.6
Atlantic cod	0.7
Haddock	0.7
Mahimahi	0.7
Orange roughy	0.7
Abalone	0.8
Queen scallops	0.8
Walleye pollack	0.8
Northern lobster	0.9
Ocean pout	0.9
Perch	0.9
Atlantic pollack	1.0
Clams (large)	1.0
Dungeness crab	1.0
Grouper	1.0
Octopus	1.0
Blue crab	1.1
Flounder	1.2
Queen crab	1.2
Sole	1.2
Snapper	1.3
Squid	1.4
Spiny lobster	1.5
Atlantic ocean perch	1.6
Large prawns	1.7
Sea bass	2.0
Atlantic/Pacific halibut	2.2
Blue mussels	2.2
Pacific oysters	2.3
Striped bass	2.3
Tilefish	2.3
Tilapia	2.4
Eastern oysters	2.5
European turbot	2.9

Pollack with Cajun Sauce

quick and easy

Serve this spunky fish dish over rice, with okra on the side, for an authentic taste of Louisiana. Orange roughy makes a good substitute for the pollack. If you don't have Cajun spice blend, use ground red pepper.

4	pollack fillets (125 g each)
500	ml tomato juice
1	small onion, cut into quarters
½	stalk celery, cut in half crosswise
¼	sweet red pepper, sliced (optional)
3	cloves garlic, minced
¼	teaspoon dried basil leaves
¼	teaspoon dried oregano
¼–½	teaspoon Cajun spice blend
	Salt (optional)
4	tablespoons chopped fresh parsley

1   Rinse the fish and pat dry with paper towels. Set aside.

2   In a blender or food processor, combine the tomato juice, onions, celery, red peppers (if using), garlic, basil and oregano. Process until pureed. Pour into a large non-stick frying pan. Stir in the Cajun spice blend.

3   Bring to a boil over medium-high heat. Reduce the heat to medium-low and cook, stirring occasionally, for 15 minutes, or until the mixture thickens into a sauce.

4   Add the fish. Cover and cook for 7 minutes, or until the fish is opaque. (Check by inserting the tip of a sharp knife in the centre of 1 fillet.) Season to taste with the salt (if using).

5   Spoon the sauce onto dinner plates. Top with the fish. Sprinkle with the parsley.

Makes **4** servings.

nutrition at a glance

per serving

0.9 g.	total fat
0.2 g.	saturated fat
116	calories
70 mg.	cholesterol
561 mg.	sodium
18.5 g.	protein
8 g.	carbohydrates
1 g.	dietary fibre

Cod Baked in Foil Packets

quick and **easy**

Preparing fish in foil packets is quick, easy, and fat-free – a cook's dream. Serve with a green vegetable or two plus new potatoes, baked potatoes or rice.

4	cod fillets (125 g each)
2	medium carrots, julienned
1	large stalk celery, julienned or chopped
1	onion, thinly sliced
1	tablespoon capers, rinsed and drained
1	teaspoon dried thyme
8	thin slices lime or lemon
4	tablespoons dry sherry or 2 teaspoons sherry extract
	Ground black pepper
	Salt (optional)

1 Preheat the oven to 200°C, Gas 6. Rinse the fish and pat dry with paper towels.

2 Place four 45 x 30 cm pieces of aluminium foil on a work surface. Tip the edges up slightly. Place 1 fillet in the centre of each foil piece. Sprinkle with the carrots, celery, onions, capers and thyme.

3 Top with the lime slices or lemon slices. Sprinkle with the sherry or sherry extract, pepper and salt (if using). Fold the edges of the foil tightly to seal, leaving some air space within each packet for steam to rise.

4 Bake for 20 minutes. Remove from the oven. Let stand for 2 to 3 minutes. Open 1 packet carefully, pointing it away from you to vent the hot steam. Check for doneness by inserting the tip of a sharp knife in the centre of the fillet.

5 If the fish is still translucent, close up the opened packet and return all the packets to the oven to bake for 2 to 3 minutes more. Carefully unwrap the packets. Slide the fish and vegetables onto dinner plates to serve.

Makes **4** servings.

Lynn's Fun Food Fact

Young cod are also known as scrod in the US. They swim in both the Atlantic and Pacific Oceans. Members of the cod family include hake, haddock, and pollack. All are white-fleshed, mild-tasting, and quite low in fat.

nutrition at a glance
per serving
0.6 g. total fat
0.1 g. saturated fat
101 calories
30 mg. cholesterol
146 mg. sodium
13.1 g. protein
6.9 g. carbohydrates
1.9 g. dietary fibre

Herb-Breaded Orange Roughy

quick and easy

The orange roughy stays exceptionally moist inside a garlicky herb and breadcrumb coating. Serve with a green vegetable and wild rice, spaetzle or oven-fried potatoes. Red snapper is also a good choice for the fish.

4	orange roughy fillets (75 g each)
80	ml fat-free mayonnaise
4	tablespoons fat-free Parmesan topping
1	teaspoon dried basil
1	teaspoon dried oregano
1	teaspoon freshly squeezed lemon juice
2	cloves garlic, minced
4	tablespoons fine dried breadcrumbs
	Ground black pepper
2	teaspoons chopped fresh parsley

1 Preheat the oven to 180°C, Gas 4. Rinse the fish and pat dry with paper towels.

2 In a small bowl, combine the mayonnaise, Parmesan, basil, oregano, lemon juice and garlic. Stir well to combine. Place the breadcrumbs on a dinner plate.

3 Spread both sides of the fish with the mayonnaise mixture, then coat with the breadcrumbs. Place in a 32 x 23 cm baking dish. Season to taste with the pepper. Bake for 20 to 25 minutes, or until the fish is opaque in the centre. (Check by inserting the tip of a sharp knife in the centre of 1 fillet.) Sprinkle with the parsley.

Makes **4** servings.

Lynn's Kitchen Tip

It is easy to make breadcrumbs instantly with a hand blender. You can use stale or fresh bread even bagels. First, break the bread or bagels into chunks. Place in a medium mixing bowl. Lift the hand blender up and down into the bowl. In a few seconds, it will be crumbs. Season with ¼ teaspoon dried oregano, dried basil, dried tarragon, dried thyme or garlic salt.

nutrition at a glance
per serving

0.9 g.	total fat
0.2 g.	saturated fat
126	calories
16 mg.	cholesterol
391 mg.	sodium
15.7 g.	protein
13.2 g.	carbohydrates
0.3 g.	dietary fibre

Crispy Fish with Tartare Sauce

quick and easy

Satisfy cravings for fried fish with this heart-healthy baked version. For a bit more colour in the crust, add ¼ teaspoon paprika. To vary the tartare sauce, you can substitute cornichons for the gherkins.

Fish

4	flounder or cod fillets (90 g each)
	Salt (optional)
1	egg white
45	g grated onions
45	g dried herbed breadcrumbs

Tartar Sauce

250	ml fat-free mayonnaise
2	tablespoons chopped gherkins
2	tablespoons chopped onions
1	teaspoon freshly squeezed lemon juice
½	teaspoon capers, rinsed, drained and finely chopped (optional)

1 *To make the fish:* Preheat the oven to 200°C, Gas 6. Rinse the fish and pat dry with paper towels.

2 Season the fish lightly with the salt (if using). Place the egg white in a wide shallow bowl and beat lightly with a fork. Add the onions and mix well. Place the breadcrumbs on a piece of greaseproof paper or foil. Dip the fish into the egg mixture, then the crumbs, to coat evenly on both sides.

3 Set the fish in an ovenproof grill pan or on a baking tray topped with a wire rack. Place in the oven and reduce the heat to 190°C, Gas 5. Bake for 10 minutes, or until the fish is opaque in the centre. (Check by inserting the tip of a sharp knife in the centre of 1 fillet.)

4 *To make the tartare sauce:* While the fish is baking, in a small bowl, mix the mayonnaise, gherkins, onions and lemon juice. Add the capers (if using) to the bowl. Mix well. Serve with the fish.

Makes **4** servings.

Lynn's Kitchen Tip

Tartare sauce is most often served with fried fish, but it also makes a terrific dip for raw vegetables. Thinned with a bit of water, it's a wonderful salad dressing.

nutrition at a glance
per serving

0.8 g.	total fat
0.2 g.	saturated fat
144	calories
23 mg.	cholesterol
877 mg.	sodium
12.5 g.	protein
19.3 g.	carbohydrates
0.3 g.	dietary fibre

Hawaiian Mahimahi-Prawn Kebabs

You can substitute scallops, turbot or monkfish for the mahimahi without changing the fat content of this spicy island dish. Serve the kebabs over steamed rice, with green beans, sliced bananas and a green salad containing tiny yellow plum tomatoes. You'll need some long metal or bamboo skewers for this dish.

1	mahimahi fillet (440 g), 2.5 cm thick
2	tablespoons freshly squeezed lemon juice
4	cloves garlic, minced
2	teaspoons chilli powder
½	teaspoon ground cumin
¼	teaspoon cayenne pepper or several drops hot-pepper sauce
¼	teaspoon ground cinnamon
	Pinch of ground cloves
90	g peeled medium prawns
½	pineapple, peeled, cut in half lengthwise and cut into 24 (2.5 cm) cubes
1	large green pepper, cut into 24 (2.5 cm) squares
1	large sweet red pepper, cut into 24 (2.5 cm) squares
1	large Spanish onion, cut into 24 (2.5 cm) wedges

1   If using bamboo skewers, submerge 6 long ones in cold water for 30 minutes (to prevent burning during cooking).

2   Meanwhile, rinse the fish and pat dry with paper towels. Cut into 12 (2.5 cm) cubes.

3   In a resealable plastic bag, combine the lemon juice, garlic, chilli powder, cumin, cayenne pepper, cinnamon and cloves. Seal the bag and knead until blended.

4   Add the fish and prawns to the bag; seal, then turn gently to coat the fish and prawns with the marinade. Refrigerate for 30 minutes.

5   Preheat the grill or prepare a barbecue. Coat a grill pan or barbecue rack with non-stick spray.

6   Remove the fish and prawns from the marinade; set the marinade aside. Thread the fish and prawns alternately on the skewers with the pineapple, green peppers, red peppers and onions.

Mahimahi means "strong strong" in Hawaiian. Although this extremely low fat fish is sometimes called dolphinfish, it is not related to the dolphin, which is a mammal.

7   Grill the kebabs 10 cm from the heat, basting several times with the reserved marinade, for 7 minutes. Turn and cook, basting several times, for 2 to 3 minutes, or until the fish is opaque. (Check by inserting the tip of a sharp knife in the centre of 1 cube.) Discard any remaining marinade. Serve hot, on or off the skewers.

Makes **6** kebabs.

Spicy Prawns

quick and **easy**

To use this dish as an appetiser, peel the prawns and serve with a dip (leave the tip of the tail attached as a handle) or as part of a crudité tray. For a casual meal, serve with other finger foods, such as grilled chunks of corn on the cob, baked courgettes and carrot sticks.

500	ml water
125	ml white wine or non-alcoholic white wine
2	tablespoons tomato paste
1	teaspoon crushed fennel seeds
1	teaspoon dried basil
½	teaspoon crushed chillies
½	teaspoon dried oregano
½	teaspoon dried thyme
¼	teaspoon hot-pepper sauce
¼	teaspoon onion salt
375	g unpeeled prawns
2	tablespoons chilli powder

Lynn's Fat-Free Flavour

Five-spice powder is a delightfully aromatic Chinese spice mixture usually made up of ground cinnamon, cloves, fennel, star anise and Szechuan peppercorns. It's sold in most supermarkets. Try a pinch on carrots, sweet potatoes, or courgettes for a flavour boost.

1   In a large non-stick saucepan, combine the water, wine, tomato paste, fennel seeds, basil, crushed chillies, oregano, thyme, hot-pepper sauce and onion salt. Whisk to combine.

2   Bring to a boil over medium-high heat. Add the prawns. Reduce the heat to medium, cover and cook for 2 minutes. Add the chilli powder and stir to combine. Cover and cook for 1 to 1½ minutes, or until all the prawns are bright pink. Remove from the heat and drain. Serve hot or chilled.

Makes **4** servings.

Photograph on page 146

Prawns with Shiitakes in Orange Sauce

quick and easy

This rich-looking dish of earthy mushrooms dotted with tender pink prawns will please the most discerning palate. Scallops or chunks of flounder, cod or halibut can replace the prawns.

2	tablespoons low-sodium soy sauce
1	teaspoon Worcestershire sauce
2	cloves garlic, minced
180	ml freshly squeezed orange juice
315	g shiitake mushroom caps, thinly sliced
1	large onion, thinly sliced
1	tablespoon cornflour
375	g medium peeled prawns
2	spring onions, sliced into 5 cm thin shreds

1   In a large non-stick saucepan, combine the soy sauce, Worcestershire sauce, garlic, and 125 ml of the orange juice. Add the mushrooms and onions. Cook over medium heat, stirring often, for 10 to 12 minutes, or until the mushrooms and onions are nearly cooked.

2   Place the cornflour in a small bowl. Add the remaining orange juice and stir to dissolve the cornflour. Add to the saucepan. Stir over medium-high heat for 1 minute, or until the mixture thickens.

3   Add the prawns. Cook, stirring, for 3 minutes, or until the prawns are bright pink. Serve sprinkled with the spring onions.

Makes **4** servings.

nutrition at a glance
per serving

0.9 g.	total fat
0.2 g.	saturated fat
153	calories
121 mg.	cholesterol
458 mg.	sodium
15.4 g.	protein
22.1 g.	carbohydrates
2.2 g.	dietary fibre

Braised Rice with Mushrooms and Prawns

quick and easy

Sweet prawns and meaty mushrooms complement each other in this satisfying main-course rice dish. It also makes an excellent appetiser that will serve 8.

1	large onion, chopped
185	g large flat mushrooms, sliced
4	shiitake mushroom caps, sliced
250	g short-grain white rice
300-375	ml skimmed chicken stock (page 94) or water
220	g peeled prawns, cut in half lengthwise
	Salt (optional)
2	spring onions, chopped
2	tablespoons chopped fresh coriander

1 Coat a large non-stick frying pan with non-stick spray. Add the onions and cook over medium-high heat, stirring, for 3 minutes. Add the flat mushrooms and shiitake mushrooms. Cook, stirring, for 3 minutes.

2 Add the rice, mixing well. Add 125 ml of the stock or water. Cook, stirring, for 4 minutes, or until the liquid is absorbed. Add an additional 125 ml stock or water. Cook, stirring occasionally, for 4 minutes, or until the liquid is absorbed.

3 Add the prawns and 60 ml of the remaining stock or water. Cook, stirring occasionally, for 4 minutes, or until the rice is tender and the liquid is absorbed. (If the rice isn't cooked, add the remaining stock or water and continue cooking until tender.) Season to taste with the salt (if using). Stir in the spring onions and coriander.

Makes **4** servings.

nutrition at a glance

per serving

0.9 g.	total fat
0.2 g.	saturated fat
207	calories
71 mg.	cholesterol
92 mg.	sodium
11.8 g.	protein
38 g.	carbohydrates
2.2 g.	dietary fibre

Scallop Risotto Primavera

Arborio rice, a type of rounded, starchy rice, is essential for an authentic Italian risotto. Risotto takes a little bit of tending to make, but it is not difficult. The key to success is to add the liquid gradually, cooking at a medium simmer, so the rice grains can absorb the liquid. A perfect risotto will have distinct tender grains suspended in a creamy sauce.

250	g button mushrooms, sliced
125	g baby carrots, cut in half lengthwise
1	onion, chopped
1	clove garlic, minced
185	g Arborio rice
1	chicken or vegetable bouillon cube
560-680	ml skimmed chicken stock (page 94)
125	g mangetout or sugar snap peas, cut in half crosswise
30	g chopped spinach leaves
1	jarred roasted red pepper, thinly sliced
125	g scallops
125	ml dry white wine or non-alcoholic white wine
	Dash of Cajun spice blend
4	tablespoons fat-free Parmesan topping
2	tablespoons chopped fresh parsley
3	dry sun-dried tomato halves, finely chopped

1 Coat a large non-stick frying pan with non-stick spray. In the pan, combine the mushrooms, carrots, onions and garlic. Cover and cook over medium-high heat, stirring occasionally, for 3 to 4 minutes, or until the mushrooms release some liquid. Uncover and cook over medium heat, stirring occasionally, for 2 to 3 minutes, or until the liquid evaporates.

2 Stir in the rice, bouillon cube, and 60 ml of the stock. Reduce the heat slightly, if necessary; the liquid should be absorbed by the rice, not just evaporate. When the rice has absorbed the liquid, continue adding the stock in 60-125 ml increments.

3 Cook, stirring after each addition, for a total of 20 minutes, or until the rice is tender but firm. Add the mangetout or sugar snap peas, spinach and peppers.

4 Meanwhile, in a small non-stick frying pan, combine the scallops, wine and Cajun spice blend. Cook over medium-high heat for 3 minutes, or until the scallops barely turn opaque. Drain the liquid into the risotto, stirring lightly to mix. Cook for 2 to 3 minutes.

5 Stir in the scallops, Parmesan, parsley and tomatoes. Remove from the heat; cover and set aside for 2 minutes to steam.

Makes **8** servings.

Photograph on page 148

Malaysian Prawn Fried Rice

quick and easy

Malaysian fried rice is usually served with a red-pepper sauce and sliced cucumbers with hot chilli peppers, according to Indian cooking authority Madhur Jaffrey, whose recipe inspired this dish. For authentic Malaysian flavour, add part of a stalk of fresh or dried lemongrass – which is available in some supermarkets or Asian food shops – to the rice as you cook it. Discard the stalk after cooking.

90	g finely shredded bok choy
½	sweet red pepper, chopped
4	tablespoons water
3	cloves garlic, minced
	Pinch of five-spice powder (optional)
125	g hot cooked long-grain white rice
5	spring onions
2	tablespoons low-sodium soy sauce
2	tablespoons chopped fresh coriander
1	tablespoon chopped fresh parsley
180	ml fat-free egg substitute
75	g frozen peas, thawed
125	g tiny shrimp or large prawns, shelled and cut into 6 mm slices
½–1	teaspoon Chinese chilli paste
¼	teaspoon dark sesame oil

Lynn's Lore

In rice-eating cultures, this ingredient is treated with great care. The Japanese often rinse their rice 10 times or more, placing the rice in the bottom of a pan filled with water and rubbing the kernels together by hand to get rid of all the starchy coating. The rice is rinsed and drained until the water is clear.

1   Coat a large non-stick frying pan with non-stick spray. Add the bok choy, peppers, water, garlic and five-spice powder (if using). Stir to mix. Cover and cook over medium heat for 5 minutes, or until the bok choy wilts. If necessary, add additional water, 1 tablespoon at a time, to keep the bok choy from sticking.

2   Stir in the rice. Cook over medium heat for 4 minutes, or until hot, adding a few tablespoons water to moisten if necessary.

3   Slice 4 of the spring onions and add to the frying pan. Stir in the soy sauce, coriander and parsley. Cook for 1 minute, or until hot, adding 1 tablespoon water if necessary to keep moist.

4   When the mixture is hot, drizzle half of the egg substitute into the frying pan in a thin stream, stirring the rice constantly. Make a shallow well in the centre of the rice mixture; pour the rest of the egg substitute into the well. Reduce the heat to low and cover the frying pan.

5   Cook for 4 minutes, or until the egg substitute in the centre is firm. Dice the egg with the tip of a sharp knife. Add the peas, prawns, chilli paste and oil, stirring gently. Cover and let stand for 3 minutes on very low heat.

6   Chop the remaining spring onion and sprinkle over the rice.

Makes **4** servings.

nutrition at a glance	
per serving	
0.8 g.	total fat
0.2 g.	saturated fat
148	calories
46 mg.	cholesterol
460 mg.	sodium
13 g.	protein
21.5 g.	carbohydrates
2.1 g.	dietary fibre

Golden Rice with Prawns and Shiitakes

Serve with steamed green beans or broccoli. For dessert, serve fresh berries over angel food cake slices and top with fat-free whipped topping or fat-free frozen yogurt.

1	medium onion, coarsely chopped
125	g sliced shiitake mushroom caps
315	g basmati or long-grain white rice
750	ml water or skimmed chicken stock (page 94)
1	package (375 g) frozen cooked courgettes, thawed
⅛	teaspoon ground nutmeg
	Salt (optional)
125	g peeled medium prawns, cut in half lengthwise
1	tablespoon chopped fresh parsley (optional)

1   Coat a non-stick oven-proof casserole with non-stick spray. Warm the pan over medium heat. Add the onions and mushrooms; mist with non-stick spray. Cook, stirring, for 4 to 5 minutes.

2   Add the rice. Cook, stirring, for 2 minutes. Add the water or stock. Increase the heat to high and bring to a boil. Reduce the heat to medium, cover and cook for 10 minutes.

3   Add the courgettes and nutmeg. Season to taste with the salt (if using). Reduce the heat to low, cover and cook for 5 minutes. Check to make sure that the rice is not sticking.

4   Top with the prawns; cover and cook for 4 minutes, or until the prawns turn pink. Set aside a few prawns for a garnish. Stir to mix the ingredients. Let stand for 3 minutes, or until the mixture thickens somewhat. Garnish with the reserved prawns. Sprinkle with the parsley (if using).

Makes **4** servings.

Lynn's Kitchen Tip

The stems of shiitake mushrooms are much tougher than the caps, but they can still add a lot of flavour to many dishes. Wash and dry the stems and store them in a heavy plastic bag in the freezer. When you accumulate a cupful of stems, add them to vegetable stock (the stems will be strained and thrown away after thorough cooking) or mince and add to a pot of vegetable soup.

---

nutrition at a glance

per serving

0.9 g.	total fat
0.3 g.	saturated fat
316	calories
40 mg.	cholesterol
57 mg.	sodium
11.1 g.	protein
66.4 g.	carbohydrates
4.5 g.	dietary fibre

Prawns Creole

This fine old New Orleans dish never tasted so good – or was quite so low in fat. Serve with 125 g cooked rice per portion. It's a great dish for entertaining because you can double it and make it in advance. (Don't stir in the prawns until after reheating, or they will toughen.) On the side, I like okra or spring greens.

125	ml skimmed chicken stock (page 94)
1	small onion, chopped
½	green pepper, chopped
1	stalk celery, chopped
2	cloves garlic, minced
1	can (500 g) tomatoes, chopped (with juice)
180	ml tomato sauce
2	teaspoons Worcestershire sauce
2	teaspoons chopped fresh thyme or 1 teaspoon dried
1	teaspoon chopped fresh oregano or ½ teaspoon dried
1	bay leaf
2	teaspoons hot-pepper sauce
1	teaspoon cornflour
1	tablespoon water
250	g peeled medium prawns, cut in half lengthwise

1 In a large non-stick frying pan over medium-high heat, bring the stock to a boil. Reduce the heat to medium. Add the onions, peppers, celery and garlic. Cook for 3 minutes, or until the onions begin to turn translucent.

2 Add the tomatoes (with juice), tomato sauce, Worcestershire sauce, thyme, oregano, bay leaf and 1 teaspoon of the hot-pepper sauce. Bring to a boil. Reduce the heat to medium-low and simmer, stirring occasionally, for 20 minutes.

3 Place the cornflour in a cup. Add the water and stir to dissolve the cornflour. Add to the frying pan. Stir for 1 to 2 minutes, or until the sauce thickens slightly.

4 Add the prawns; cook for 2 to 3 minutes, or until pink. Taste and add the remaining hot-pepper sauce if needed.

Makes **4** servings.

Creole is the city cousin of rustic Cajun cooking. Historically, it is a vivid blend of French, Spanish and African, with a smidgen of Italian, Hispanic and Native American. Seafood and luxurious sauces have traditionally been emphasised. Both cuisines rely on the "holy trinity" of chopped green peppers, onions and celery.

nutrition at a glance
per serving

0.9 g.	total fat
0.2 g.	saturated fat
101	calories
81 mg.	cholesterol
596 mg.	sodium
11.3 g.	protein
13 g.	carbohydrates
2.3 g.	dietary fibre

Dungeness Crab Cakes

quick and easy

Sweet Dungeness crab inspired these luscious morsels, but any good-quality lump crabmeat is fine for the recipe. Try them with Rémoulade Sauce (page 300). If you serve them on an toasted muffin or bun, it will boost the fat content only slightly.

90	g sweetcorn kernels
500	g backfin or lump crabmeat, flaked
125	g cold cooked rice
2	tablespoons finely chopped spring onions
2	tablespoons finely chopped celery
2	tablespoons chopped fresh parsley
2	tablespoons + 40 g dried breadcrumbs
125	ml fat-free egg substitute
3	tablespoons fat-free mayonnaise
2	teaspoons freshly squeezed lemon juice
1	teaspoon Worcestershire sauce
½	teaspoon dry mustard
4	dashes hot-pepper sauce
	Pinch of ground black pepper
	Pinch of salt (optional)

1 In a blender or food processor, process the corn until finely chopped. Place in a medium bowl. Add the crab, rice, spring onions, celery, parsley and 2 tablespoons of the breadcrumbs.

2 In a small bowl, combine the egg substitute, mayonnaise, lemon juice, Worcestershire sauce, mustard, hot-pepper sauce, black pepper and salt (if using). Add to the crab mixture and stir to combine. Form the mixture into 8 cakes.

3 Place the remaining breadcrumbs in a shallow bowl. Dredge the cakes in the breadcrumbs to coat, gently shaking off the excess.

4 Coat a large non-stick frying pan with non-stick spray. Warm the pan over medium heat. Add the cakes and cook for 3 minutes on each side, or until golden brown.

Makes **8** crab cakes.

nutrition at a glance

per crab cake

0.8 g.	total fat
0.2 g.	saturated fat
105	calories
13 mg.	cholesterol
201 mg.	sodium
7.4 g.	protein
16.6 g.	carbohydrates
0.8 g.	dietary fibre

Fisherman's Casserole

This is pure comfort food and quite easy to make. Vary the dish, if you like, by adding a bit of peas, sweetcorn or diced carrots, potatoes or tomatoes.

4	large stalks celery, chopped
155	g button mushrooms, sliced
1	large green pepper, chopped
1	small onion, chopped
4	tablespoons dry sherry or 2 teaspoons sherry extract
250	ml skimmed milk
4	tablespoons plain flour
125	ml water
125	g drained sliced canned water chestnuts
1½	teaspoons Dijon mustard
½	teaspoon Old Bay seasoning
	Several dashes of hot-pepper sauce
	Ground black pepper
	Salt (optional)
185	g flounder fillets, cut into 1 cm chunks
125	g peeled medium prawns
3	tablespoons fat-free Parmesan topping
1	tablespoon chopped fresh parsley

1 Preheat the oven to 180°C, Gas 4. Coat a 2-litre baking dish with non-stick spray.

2 Coat a large non-stick frying pan with non-stick spray. Add the celery, mushrooms, green peppers and onions. Mist with non-stick spray. Cover and cook over medium heat, stirring often, for 5 minutes, or until the onions are golden.

3 Add the sherry or sherry extract and bring to a boil over medium-high heat. Cook for 2 minutes. Add the milk. Reduce the heat to medium and bring almost to a boil.

4   Place the flour in a small bowl. Gradually whisk in the water until smooth. Stir into the frying pan. Cook, whisking constantly, for 3 to 4 minutes, or until the sauce thickens.

5   Add the water chestnuts, mustard, Old Bay seasoning and hot-pepper sauce. Season to taste with the black pepper and salt (if using). Reduce the heat to low, cover and cook for 2 minutes.

6   Remove from the heat. Stir in the fish, prawns and 2 tablespoons of the Parmesan. Pour the mixture into the prepared baking dish. Dust the top with the remaining 1 tablespoon Parmesan.

7   Bake for 25 minutes, or until hot and bubbly. Sprinkle with the parsley.

Makes **6** servings.

nutrition at a glance	
per serving	
0.9 g.	total fat
0.2 g.	saturated fat
128	calories
43 mg.	cholesterol
402 mg.	sodium
13.4 g.	protein
16 g.	carbohydrates
2.7 g.	dietary fibre

Breton Seafood Stew

quick and easy

This seafood stew is quick to make but special enough to serve to guests. Serve it over tiny new potatoes, rice, quinoa or orzo and accompany it with bread, salad and a steamed green vegetable.

125	ml water
2	stalks celery, thinly sliced
2	medium carrots, thinly sliced
1	leek, white part only, thinly sliced
680	ml skimmed fish stock or vegetable stock (page 93)
2	tablespoons plain flour
4	tablespoons dry vermouth or cider
3	plum tomatoes, diced
1	tablespoon freshly squeezed lemon juice
1	teaspoon grated lemon rind
1	teaspoon grated orange rind
3	cloves garlic, minced
1	sprig fresh thyme
¼	teaspoon saffron threads
250	g cod fillet, cut into 2.5 cm cubes
90	g squid rings or small peeled prawns

1   In a non-stick flameproof casserole over medium-high heat, bring the water to a boil. Add the celery, carrots and leeks. Reduce the heat to medium, partially cover and cook, stirring occasionally, for 5 minutes. Add the stock.

2   Place the flour in a small bowl. Gradually whisk in the vermouth or cider until smooth. Stir into the pan. Cook, stirring, until thickened.

3   Add the tomatoes, lemon juice, lemon rind, orange rind, garlic, thyme and saffron. Simmer, stirring occasionally, for 15 minutes. Add the cod and squid or prawns. Simmer for 5 minutes, or until the cod is cooked. (Check by inserting the tip of a sharp knife in the centre.)

Makes **4** servings.

Photograph on page 147

Photograph on page 147

Lynn's Lore

Cut into rings or strips, squid is often fried, which adds an enormous amount of fat. Better to enjoy its mild flavour in fat-free soups or salads. When cooked quickly, as it is here, squid remains tender.

nutrition at a glance
per serving

0.9 g.	total fat
0.2 g.	saturated fat
141	calories
64 mg.	cholesterol
83 mg.	sodium
11.8 g.	protein
18.4 g.	carbohydrates
3 g.	dietary fibre

Greek Salad (page 104)

Asian Coleslaw (page 107)

Mexicali Pasta Salad (page 98)

Spicy Prawns (page 131)

Breton Seafood Stew (page 142)

Scallop Risotto Primavera (page 134)

Cod with Ginger-Orange Sauce (page 124)

Fiesta Chilli (page 186)

Garden Pita Pizza (page 177)

Couscous-Stuffed Peppers (page 188)

Moroccan Vegetable Medley (page 190)

Spaghetti with Sun-Dried Tomato Sauce (page 176)

Southwestern Polenta (page 33)

Turkey Cutlets Tarragon (page 165)

Italian Stuffed Artichokes (page 191)

Wild Mushroom Moussaka (page 194)

Main Dishes

Not long ago, a meal without a huge piece of meat
anchoring the plate seemed incomplete. Today,
nutrient-dense low-fat grains, legumes and
vegetables are the stars of the plate, alongside
moderate portions of lean poultry and meat.

Meat and skin-on poultry are two of the highest
sources of fat, particularly saturated fat, in the
Western diet. Because a diet that is too high in saturated fat is linked to heart disease, diabetes

and some forms of cancer, it makes perfect sense to reduce the amounts of these foods. Notice that I said *reduce*, not eliminate.

Meals with Meat

I have developed wonderful main dishes using boneless, skinless turkey breast. In addition to being the leanest animal protein around (at 1 gramme of fat per 90-g cooked portion), turkey breast never met a seasoning that it didn't like. Prepared so many different ways, it's like eating a different meat each time.

Turkey Cutlets Tarragon, for instance, are delicate, in contrast to the vibrant seasonings in Turkey and Black Bean Stew. And exotic Sweet-and-Sour Turkey is worlds away from the American classic Turkey-Broccoli Divan.

Lean beef topside, trimmed of all visible fat, is also a reasonable meat choice (at 3.4 grammes of fat per 90-g cooked portion). Try my Beef and Mushroom Fajitas and Vegetable Stew with Beef to see how flavourful this cut really is.

Meat-Free Meals

Main dishes made from fibre-filled vegetables, fruits and grains are earthy, simple and inexpensive. You'll feel good – and energetic – after you eat them.

Garden Pita Pizza, Spaghetti with Sun-Dried Tomato Sauce, Couscous-Stuffed Peppers and Wild Mushroom Moussaka won't leave anyone in your family asking, "Where's the beef?"

Soybean meat substitutes such as texturised vegetable protein mimic the texture and appearance of minced beef but are low in saturated fat and contain no cholesterol. Try my White Chilli and Fiesta Chilli to see what I mean. Look for texturised vegetable protein (TVP) in health food shops and some supermarkets.

Tofu – pressed soybean curd – is also versatile, easy to use and very low in saturated fat. It's renowned as a carrier of spicy flavours.

Every serving of my main dishes contains less than 1 gramme of fat. Of course, the number of servings that you'll eat may vary. If you're a petite woman, you might choose one serving and accompany it with several fat-free or low-fat side dishes to round out the meal. If you're a six-foot-plus man with greater calorie needs, you may need to eat two or even three servings. But these dishes are so lean that your total fat intake will still be extremely low – so eat hearty!

Turkey Teriyaki Kebabs

For this Japanese-style dish, you use long wooden or metal skewers. Serve with rice and crisp steamed asparagus or broccoli.

500 g boneless, skinless turkey breast, trimmed of all visible fat
2 tablespoons low-sodium soy sauce
2 teaspoons grated fresh ginger
2 teaspoons sugar
1 large clove garlic, minced
8 closed cap mushrooms
1 medium aubergine, cut into 16 cubes
16 mangetout
4 spring onions, cut into 4 pieces each
16 yellow pear tomatoes or cherry tomatoes

1 If using wooden skewers, submerge 8 long ones in cold water for 30 minutes.

2 Cut the turkey into 2.5 cm cubes. In a medium bowl, combine the soy sauce, ginger, sugar and garlic. Add the turkey and mushrooms. Cover and refrigerate for 20 minutes, stirring occasionally.

3 Bring a medium saucepan of water to a boil. Add the aubergine; cook for 2 minutes. Add the mangetout and spring onions; cook for 1 minute. Drain, then plunge the vegetables into a big bowl of iced water. Let stand for 30 seconds; drain and pat dry.

4 Preheat the oven grill or prepare a barbecue grill.

5 Divide the turkey, mushrooms, aubergine, mangetout, spring onions and tomatoes among 8 skewers. Brush well with the marinade; reserve the marinade.

6 Grill or barbecue 10 cm from the heat for 2 to 3 minutes. Turn the skewers and brush with the marinade. Cook for 2 to 3 minutes, or until the turkey cubes are no longer pink in the centre when tested with the point of a sharp knife. Discard the remaining marinade.

Makes **8** kebabs.

nutrition at a glance

per kebab

0.8 g.	total fat
0.2 g.	saturated fat
96	calories
39 mg.	cholesterol
181 mg.	sodium
15 g.	protein
7.3 g.	carbohydrates
1.9 g.	dietary fibre

Orange-Rosemary Turkey

For a tasty variation, substitute dried sage for the rosemary and 1 tablespoon lemon juice for the orange juice. Sprinkle with fat-free Parmesan topping before serving.

4   boneless, skinless turkey breast cutlets (90 g each)
4   tablespoons orange juice
2   teaspoons dried rosemary, crumbled
1   large clove garlic, minced
    Ground black pepper
    Salt (optional)
1   teaspoon finely chopped fresh parsley

1   Use a meat mallet to flatten the turkey cutlets to 6 mm thickness.

2   In a non-aluminium 30 x 20 cm baking dish, combine the orange juice, rosemary and garlic. Add the turkey and turn to coat both sides. Cover and refrigerate for 1 hour, turning the turkey once during this time.

3   Preheat the grill or prepare a barbecue. Coat a grill pan or barbecue rack with non-stick spray.

4   Remove the turkey from the marinade; reserve the marinade. Grill or barbecue the turkey 10 cm from the heat, basting once with the reserved marinade, for 2 minutes, or until lightly browned at the edges. Turn and cook, basting once with the reserved marinade, for 2 minutes, or until the turkey is no longer pink in the centre when tested with the point of a sharp knife. Discard any remaining marinade.

5   Season the turkey to taste with the pepper and salt (if using). Sprinkle with the parsley.

Makes **4** servings.

nutrition at a glance

per serving
0.9 g. total fat
0.3 g. saturated fat
102 calories
58 mg. cholesterol
38 mg. sodium
20 g. protein
1.6 g. carbohydrates
0.2 g. dietary fibre

20 Fast and Tasty Turkey Cutlets

Sprinkled with fresh herbs or spices, splashed with flavoured vinegar or citrus juice or topped with a dollop of a savoury condiment, boneless, skinless turkey breast cutlets are the fastest fat-free dish in town. To make, coat a large non-stick frying pan with non-stick spray. Warm the pan over medium heat. Add 6 mm-thick turkey cutlets and cook for 2 minutes, or until browned on the bottom. Flip and cook for 2 to 3 minutes, or until the cutlets are no longer pink in the centre when tested with the point of a sharp knife. Top as desired. Here are some tasty fat-free suggestions.

* Balsamic vinegar
* Cajun spice blend
* Caramelised Onion Compote (page 301)
* Chicken Gravy (page 293)
* Chopped fresh dill
* Chutney
* Cranberry sauce
* Curry powder
* Dijon mustard
* Finely chopped spring onions
* Ground cumin
* Hoisin sauce
* Horseradish
* Orange juice
* Rémoulade Sauce (page 300)
* Roasted Garlic (page 304)
* Salsa
* Thinly sliced fresh basil
* Teriyaki sauce
* White-wine Worcestershire sauce

Sweet-and-Sour Turkey

quick and easy

For a bit of spicy heat, stir in ¼ teaspoon crushed chillies just before serving. Serve with cooked white or brown rice. Increasing the turkey in the recipe to 500 g will increase the fat only slightly – to 1.4 grammes per serving.

1	large onion, coarsely chopped
1	green pepper, cut into 2.5 cm pieces
2	carrots, sliced
1	clove garlic, minced
315	g boneless, skinless turkey breast, trimmed of all visible fat and cut into 1 cm cubes
1½	tablespoons cornflour
3	tablespoons white-wine vinegar or cider vinegar
3	tablespoons brown sugar
2	tablespoons water
2	teaspoons low-sodium soy sauce
1	can (630 g) pineapple chunks (packed in juice)

1 Coat a large non-stick frying pan with non-stick spray. Warm over medium heat. Add the onions, peppers, carrots and garlic. Cover and cook, stirring occasionally, for 6 to 8 minutes, or until the onions are golden. If necessary, add 1 to 2 teaspoons water to prevent sticking. Remove from the pan.

2 Add the turkey to the frying pan. Cook over medium heat, stirring occasionally, for 3 to 4 minutes, or until no longer pink.

3 Place the cornflour in a medium bowl. Add the vinegar and stir to dissolve the cornflour. Add the brown sugar, water and soy sauce; stir to dissolve the brown sugar.

4 Drain the pineapple, reserving 180 ml of the juice. Set aside the pineapple. Add the juice to the bowl and stir the mixture into the frying pan. Cook, stirring, for 1 to 2 minutes, or until the mixture thickens. Stir in the pineapple and the reserved onion mixture. Cook for 1 minute to heat.

Makes **4** servings.

Opposites do attract. At least in cooking. Sweet-and-sour combinations are very popular, not only in China but in Europe as well. The French term for sweet-and-sour is *aigre-doux*. The Italian is *agrodolce*.

nutrition at a glance

per serving

0.9 g.	total fat
0.2 g.	saturated fat
269	calories
48 mg.	cholesterol
153 mg.	sodium
18.7 g.	protein
48.1 g.	carbohydrates
2.7 g.	dietary fibre

Turkey Cutlets Tarragon

quick and easy

If your butcher doesn't sell turkey breast cutlets, buy a skinless turkey breast half and ask him to thinly slice it.

4   boneless, skinless turkey breast cutlets (90 g each)
4   tablespoons fat-free mayonnaise
2   teaspoons dried tarragon
½   teaspoon Dijon mustard

1   Use a meat mallet to flatten the turkey cutlets to 6 mm thickness.

2   In a small bowl, mix the mayonnaise, tarragon and mustard. Divide half of the mixture among the cutlets and spread evenly over the top side of each.

3   Coat a large non-stick frying pan with non-stick spray. Warm the pan over medium heat. Add the turkey, seasoned side down, and cook for 2 minutes, or until browned on the bottom. Flip the cutlets over.

4   Spread with the remaining mayonnaise mixture. Cover and cook for 2 to 3 minutes, or until the turkey is no longer pink in the centre when tested with the point of a sharp knife.

Makes **4** servings.

Photograph on page 156

Photograph on page 156

nutrition at a glance

per serving
0.9 g.	total fat
0.3 g.	saturated fat
106	calories
58 mg.	cholesterol
147 mg.	sodium
20.5 g.	protein
2.2 g.	carbohydrates
0 g.	dietary fibre

Peking Turkey and Vegetables

quick and easy

This colourful wok dish is quick to get on the table. The secret to success in Chinese stir-frying is having all the ingredients cut and measured before you turn on the hob. Doubling the amount of turkey in the recipe to 375 g will increase the total fat to only 1.3 grammes per serving. Serve with basmati, long-grain white or brown rice.

2	teaspoons cornflour
1	tablespoon rice vinegar
80	ml hoisin sauce
1	tablespoon grated fresh ginger
2	teaspoons sugar
250	ml water or skimmed chicken stock (page 94)
185	g boneless, skinless turkey breast, trimmed of all visible fat and cut into 6 mm strips
185	g chopped onions
½	sweet red pepper, cut into thin strips
2	cloves garlic, minced
125	g diagonally sliced carrots
125	g broccoli florets
45	g mangetout
90	g sliced water chestnuts
1	tablespoon chopped fresh coriander

1 Place the cornflour in a small bowl. Add the vinegar and stir to dissolve the cornflour. Stir in the hoisin sauce, ginger, sugar and 125 ml of the water or stock. Set aside.

2 Coat a non-stick wok or large non-stick frying pan with non-stick spray. Warm over medium-high heat. Add the turkey and cook, tossing frequently, for 2 minutes, or until no longer pink. Transfer to a bowl and set aside.

3 Add the onions, peppers and garlic to the pan. Remove the pan from the heat and mist the vegetables with non-stick spray. Cover and cook over medium-high heat, stirring occasionally, for 3 to 4 minutes, or until the onions are golden. Add to the turkey and set aside.

4 Add the remaining 125 ml water or stock to the pan; bring to a simmer. Add the carrots; cook for 2 minutes. Add the broccoli; cook for 4 minutes, stirring occasionally. Add the mangetout; cook for 1 to 2 minutes, or until the broccoli is barely tender.

5 Add the water chestnuts and coriander. Add the reserved hoisin-sauce mixture and turkey mixture. Cook, stirring, for 2 to 3 minutes, or until the sauce thickens.

Makes **4** servings.

Photograph on page 241

nutrition at a glance
per serving
0.9 g.	total fat
0.2 g.	saturated fat
153	calories
29 mg.	cholesterol
390 mg.	sodium
14 g.	protein
23.3 g.	carbohydrates
3.9 g.	dietary fibre

Turkey-Broccoli Divan

Our male taste testers were crazy about this dish. You can serve it over fat-free crumpets, toast, muffins, pasta, rice or potatoes. Or just enjoy it on its own, as our tasters did.

185	g broccoli florets cut into 4 cm lengths
250	g closed cap mushrooms, cut in half
1	large onion, coarsely chopped
220	g diced cooked turkey breast
2½	tablespoons plain flour
125	ml fat-free liquid creamer
250	ml skimmed vegetable stock (page 93) or chicken stock (page 94)
2	tablespoons dry white wine or non-alcoholic white wine (optional)
¼	teaspoon ground black pepper
	Salt (optional)
3	tablespoons fat-free Parmesan topping

1 Preheat the oven to 180°C, 350°F, Gas 4.

2 In a large non-stick frying pan over medium-high heat, bring 6 mm water to a boil. Add the broccoli. Cover and return to a boil. Cook for 2 minutes, or until the broccoli is bright green. Drain and place in a 30 x 20 cm baking dish.

Lynn's Lore
Turkey is native to the Americas and was domesticated by the Aztecs. Today, most American turkeys come from a Dutch breed that's prized for its plumpness.

(continued)

3 Coat the frying pan with non-stick spray. Add the mushrooms and onions. Cover and cook over medium-high heat for 1 to 2 minutes, or until the mushrooms start to release some liquid. Uncover and cook, stirring often, for 1 to 2 minutes, or until the onions are softened. Spread over the broccoli. Cover with the turkey.

4 Place the flour in a small saucepan. Gradually whisk in the creamer until smooth. Add the stock, wine (if using) and pepper. Cook over medium heat, whisking constantly, for 4 minutes, or until thickened. Season to taste with the salt (if using). Pour over the turkey. Sprinkle with the Parmesan.

5 Cover with foil and bake for 15 minutes. Uncover and bake for 15 minutes, or until bubbly and golden. Let stand for 10 minutes.

Makes **6** servings.

Photograph on page 242

Turkey and Black Bean Stew

Increasing the turkey to 500 g will raise the fat per serving to a mere 1.2 grammes. Serve with cooked rice and chopped spring onions and lime wedges for garnish.

185	g dry black beans
1	medium onion, chopped
1	carrot, grated
½	green pepper, cut into 2.5 cm squares
½	sweet red pepper, cut into 2.5 cm squares
2	teaspoons ground oregano
1½	teaspoons ground cumin
4	cloves garlic, minced
1	litre water or skimmed chicken stock (page 94)
250	g boneless, skinless turkey breast, trimmed of all visible fat and cut into 2.5 cm cubes
2	plum tomatoes, coarsely chopped
2	jalapeño peppers, minced (wear rubber gloves when handling)
1	tablespoon vinegar
½	teaspoon salt (optional)
2	tablespoons thinly sliced fresh basil

Lynn's Lore

A bag of beans (*fagiole*) was added to Florentine noble-woman Catherine de Médicis' dowry, tucked among her pearls and lace, when she wed Henry II of France.

1 Place the beans in a large saucepan and cover with cold water. Bring to a boil over medium-high heat. Remove from the heat and set aside for 1 hour.

2 Meanwhile, coat a non-stick flameproof casserole with non-stick spray. Warm over medium-high heat. Add the onions, carrots, green peppers, sweet red peppers, oregano, cumin and garlic.

3 Reduce the heat to medium. Cook, stirring, for 4 to 6 minutes, or until the onions start to soften. Remove the vegetables and set aside.

4 Drain and rinse the beans. Add the beans to the casserole. Add the water or stock. Bring to a boil over medium-high heat. Reduce the heat to medium-low. Partially cover and simmer, stirring occasionally, for 1½ hours, or until the beans are nearly tender.

5 Add the reserved vegetables. Simmer for 30 minutes, or until the beans are tender.

6 Add the turkey, tomatoes, jalapeño peppers, vinegar and salt (if using). Simmer for 5 minutes, or until the turkey is cooked. Remove from the heat and stir in the basil. Let stand for 5 minutes to allow the flavours to blend.

Makes **8** servings.

nutrition at a glance
per serving
0.9 g.	total fat
0.2 g.	saturated fat
144	calories
19 mg.	cholesterol
26 mg.	sodium
13.5 g.	protein
21.3 g.	carbohydrates
7 g.	dietary fibre

Turkey and Potato Curry

Serve with rice, a steamed vegetable, and Cuke and Zuke Raita (page 105). Doubling the amount of turkey to 375 g will increase the total fat to only 1.2 grammes per serving.

1	large onion, chopped
3	cloves garlic, minced
½	teaspoon curry powder
2	large potatoes, cut into 1 cm cubes
185	g boneless, skinless turkey breast, trimmed of all visible fat and cut into 1 cm cubes
60	g raisins
1	tablespoon minced fresh ginger
1	tablespoon cornflour
1	teaspoon freshly squeezed lemon juice or lime juice
185	ml fat-free natural yogurt
250	ml skimmed chicken stock (page 94)
75	g thawed frozen peas
1	tablespoon chopped fresh coriander

1   Preheat the oven to 180°C, Gas 4.

2   Coat a large ovenproof non-stick frying pan with non-stick spray. Add the onions, garlic and curry powder. Cover and cook over medium heat, stirring occasionally, for 4 to 5 minutes, or until the onions start to soften. If necessary, add 1 to 2 teaspoons water to prevent sticking.

3   Add the potatoes, turkey, raisins and ginger. Remove from the heat.

4   Place the cornflour in a small bowl. Add the lemon juice and stir to dissolve the cornflour. Whisk in the yogurt. Gradually whisk in the stock. Add to the frying pan. Stir gently to combine.

5   Cover and bake for 45 to 50 minutes, or until the potatoes are tender when pierced with a knife. Remove from the oven.

6   Sprinkle with the peas. Cover and let stand for 2 minutes to heat the peas. Sprinkle with the coriander.

Makes **4** servings.

Lynn's Fat-Free Flavour

Fat-free natural yogurt adds tangy flavour and creamy texture to dishes without contributing fat. And you can make a marvellous soft cheese from yogurt (page 304) that requires virtually no work.

nutrition at a glance

per serving
0.8 g.	total fat
0.2 g.	saturated fat
225	calories
30 mg.	cholesterol
85 mg.	sodium
16.4 g.	protein
39.3 g.	carbohydrates
3.4 g.	dietary fibre

Beef and Mushroom Fajitas

Starting in the American Southwest and spreading far and wide, fajitas are on more and more dinner tables. This delightful fat-free version is sure to become a family favourite. Doubling the amount of beef in this recipe to 500 g raises the total fat to only 1.8 grammes per fajita. Garnish each fajita with chopped fresh coriander, fat-free soured cream and hot-pepper sauce to taste.

4	tablespoons lime juice
1½	teaspoons chilli powder
1	teaspoon dried oregano
1	teaspoon sugar
3	cloves garlic, minced
250	g lean beef topside, trimmed of all visible fat and cut into thin strips
125	g large flat mushrooms or shiitake mushroom caps, cut into 1 cm slices
½	Spanish onion, cut into 1 cm slices
½	sweet red pepper, cut into 1 cm strips
½	yellow pepper, cut into 1 cm strips
	Ground black pepper
	Salt (optional)
8	fat-free flour tortillas (18 cm diameter), heated

1 In a resealable plastic bag, mix the lime juice, chilli powder, oregano, sugar and garlic. Add the meat and mushrooms, seal the bag, and press gently to coat the meat with the marinade. Place in the refrigerator and marinate for 30 minutes.

2 Coat a large non-stick frying pan with non-stick spray. Warm over medium-high heat. Add the meat, mushrooms and 2 tablespoons of the marinade. Cook, stirring frequently, for 4 to 5 minutes, or until the meat is cooked. Remove and set aside.

3 Wash and dry the frying pan. Coat with non-stick spray. Warm over medium-high heat. Add the onions, red peppers and yellow peppers.

(continued)

Cover and cook for 1 to 2 minutes, or until the onions start to release moisture. Uncover and cook, stirring frequently, for 4 to 5 minutes, or until the onions are golden. If necessary, add 1 to 2 teaspoons water to prevent sticking. Season to taste with the black pepper and salt (if using).

4 Place the tortillas on a work surface. Divide the beef mixture among them, spooning it down the middle. Top with the onions and peppers. Fold the tortillas to enclose the filling.

Makes **8** fajitas.

Photograph on page 240

Vegetable Stew with Beef

This stew tastes so meaty that no one would ever guess it has only 125 g lean beef – and less than 1 gramme of fat per serving. Doubling the amount of beef to 250 g increases the fat to only 1.5 grammes per serving.

125	g lean beef topside, trimmed of all visible fat
1	medium potato, cut into 2.5 x 1 cm strips
1	medium onion, coarsely chopped
185	g sliced carrots
125	g sliced mushrooms
2	stalks celery, cut into 2.5 cm pieces
75	g plain flour
250	ml apple juice
250	ml water
4	tablespoons chopped fresh parsley
1	teaspoon dried rosemary, crumbled
1	teaspoon dried thyme
1	teaspoon dried basil
¼	teaspoon dried tarragon
3	cloves garlic, thinly sliced
¼	teaspoon ground black pepper
1	beef bouillon cube
1	vegetable bouillon cube
	Salt (optional)

Lynn's Kitchen Tip

When buying beef, use your eyes to gauge the amount of visible fat. Even if meat is labelled lean, judge for yourself. For a stew, select the leanest topside with no marbling. Trim away all visible fat before cooking.

1   Preheat the oven to 180°C, Gas 4.

2   Cut the beef into 6 cm-thick slices, then into 2.5 x 1 cm strips. Place in a 3-litre baking dish. Scatter the potatoes, onions, carrots, mushrooms and celery over the meat.

3   Place the flour in a medium bowl. Gradually whisk in the apple juice and water until smooth. Add the parsley, rosemary, thyme, basil, tarragon, garlic and pepper. Pour over the vegetables. Add the beef bouillon cube and the vegetable bouillon cube.

4   Cover and bake for 1½ hours, or until the meat and vegetables are tender. Season to taste with the salt (if using). Stir gently before serving.

Makes **6** servings.

Photograph on page 239

nutrition at a glance	
per serving	
0.9 g.	total fat
0.3 g.	saturated fat
132	calories
12 mg.	cholesterol
218 mg.	sodium
7.3 g.	protein
24 g.	carbohydrates
2.3 g.	dietary fibre

Soufflé Primavera

This soufflé is delightful for brunch or lunch or as part of a light dinner. For a formal meal, it's smashing served as a side dish with fish. Don't be intimidated by this French classic – I've included several tips to ensure that your soufflé gets a great liftoff.

1	litre water
280	g finely chopped carrots
375	g finely chopped broccoli florets
250	ml skimmed milk
125	g chopped leeks
90	g finely chopped onions
3	tablespoons plain flour
125	ml fat-free egg substitute
½	teaspoon ground black pepper
⅛	teaspoon ground nutmeg
	Pinch of salt (optional)
9	tablespoons fat-free Parmesan topping
5	egg whites, at room temperature
	Dash of freshly squeezed lemon juice or cream of tartar

Lynn's Kitchen Tip

To clean a leek, cut off the dark leaves and the root end. Make a lengthwise cut through the leek, starting in the white area and going up through the light-green stem. Rinse completely under cold running water, lifting layers to release trapped dirt. After cleaning, chop the leek.

1 Preheat the oven to 220°C, Gas 7.

2 Place the water in a large saucepan and bring to a boil over medium-high heat. Add the carrots and broccoli. Reduce the heat to low and simmer for 5 minutes, or until the carrots are crisp-tender. Drain, reserving the cooking liquid. Transfer the vegetables to a medium bowl and set aside.

3 Add the milk to the saucepan. Bring almost to a boil, stirring occasionally, over medium heat. Pour into a small heatproof bowl and set aside.

4 Add 250 ml of the reserved cooking liquid to the saucepan; bring to a boil over medium-high heat. Add the leeks and onions; cook for 5 to 7 minutes.

5 Sprinkle the flour over the leek mixture. Whisk constantly for 3 minutes. Pour in the milk and cook, whisking constantly, for 3 minutes, or until thickened. Remove from the heat.

6   Gradually whisk in the egg substitute. Stir in the pepper, nutmeg, salt (if using), the reserved vegetables and 4 tablespoons of the Parmesan.

7   Place the egg whites in a large bowl. Beat with an electric mixer until foamy. Add the lemon juice or cream of tartar. Beat until stiff peaks form.

8   Add about one-third of the whites to the vegetable mixture. Carefully fold in with a rubber spatula. Do not overmix; some streaks of white can remain. Add the remaining whites and fold them in until just incorporated.

9   Coat a 1.5-litre soufflé dish with non-stick spray. Add 4 tablespoons of the remaining Parmesan to the dish and coat the bottom and sides of the dish with the Parmesan. Spoon the soufflé mixture into the dish. Sprinkle with the remaining 1 tablespoon Parmesan.

10   Place the dish in the oven. Reduce the heat to 190°C, Gas 5. Bake for 20 minutes without opening the oven. Bake an additional 10 minutes, or until the soufflé jiggles slightly in the centre when gently shaken. Bake for 5 minutes more, if desired, to cook until firm.

Makes **4** servings.

nutrition at a glance

per serving

0.7 g.	total fat
0.2 g.	saturated fat
222	calories
1 mg.	cholesterol
478 mg.	sodium
23.8 g.	protein
32.7 g.	carbohydrates
5.6 g.	dietary fibre

Spaghetti with Sun-Dried Tomato Sauce

This satisfying spaghetti was one of our tasters' top picks. Serve it with Artichoke Salad (page 103) and Italian bread spread with Roasted Garlic (page 304).

125	ml hot water
1	teaspoon chopped dry-pack sun-dried tomatoes
½	medium onion, sliced
1	large clove garlic, minced
1	can (500 ml) tomato juice
4	large cherry tomatoes, chopped
4	tablespoons thinly sliced fresh basil
2	teaspoons dried oregano
	Pinch of sugar
	Ground black pepper
	Salt (optional)
250	g low-fat spaghetti (0.5 g. fat per 90-g serving)
4	tablespoons fat-free Parmesan topping

1 In a small bowl, combine the water and sun-dried tomatoes. Let stand for 10 minutes, or until the tomatoes are softened. Transfer the tomatoes and water to a large non-stick frying pan.

2 Add the onions and garlic. Cook over medium heat, stirring occasionally, for 8 minutes. Stir in the tomato juice, cherry tomatoes, basil, oregano and sugar. Cover and simmer over low heat, stirring occasionally, for 20 minutes. Season to taste with the pepper and salt (if using).

3 Meanwhile, cook the spaghetti according to the package directions. Drain and serve topped with the sauce. Sprinkle with the Parmesan.

Makes **4** servings.

Photograph on page 154

Lynn's Kitchen Tip

Choose sun-dried tomatoes that are dry-packed in plastic. They have barely any fat, as opposed to sun-dried tomatoes packed in olive oil.

nutrition at a glance
per serving

0.8 g.	total fat
0 g.	saturated fat
290	calories
0 mg.	cholesterol
634 mg.	sodium
14.2 g.	protein
56.4 g.	carbohydrates
3 g.	dietary fibre

Garden Pita Pizza

quick and easy

Pita pizzas are so easy and so satisfying. For terrific flavour, I sauté the vegetables before they go on the pizza. It takes just a few minutes and makes a huge difference in the taste. This recipe multiplies perfectly, so you can make it for one or a party of ten. Garnish with crushed chillies.

45	g thinly sliced mushrooms
45	g thinly sliced courgette
⅛	teaspoon garlic powder
4	tablespoons tomato sauce
1	fat-free whole-wheat or white pita (15 cm diameter)
2	tablespoons finely chopped spring onions
1	tablespoon slivered fresh basil
¼	teaspoon dried oregano
1	large stoned black olive, chopped
2	tablespoons grated fat-free mozzarella cheese
1	tablespoon fat-free Parmesan topping

1 Preheat the oven to 220°C, Gas 7.

2 Place the mushrooms and courgette in a large non-stick frying pan. Coat with non-stick spray. Cover and cook over medium-high heat for 2 to 3 minutes, or until the mushrooms start to release their juice. Remove the cover and cook, stirring occasionally, for 1 to 2 minutes, or until the mushrooms and courgette are golden. Stir in the garlic powder and 2 tablespoons of the tomato sauce. Set aside.

3 Place the pita bread on a baking tray. Bake for 1 minute to crisp. Remove from the oven and spread with the remaining 2 tablespoons tomato sauce. Spoon on the mushroom mixture. Sprinkle with the spring onions, basil, oregano, olives, mozzarella and Parmesan.

4 Bake for 8 to 10 minutes, or until the cheese melts and is golden.

Makes **1** pita pizza.

Photograph on page 151

Photograph on page 151

Lynn's Fun Food Fact

Pizza – the formerly humble concoction of bread dough, tomato sauce and cheese – can now often be found topped with smoked salmon, figs, goat cheese, herring, papaya, tart cherries, lime-marinated chicken breast, duck breast, caviar and other exotica.

---

nutrition at a glance

per pita pizza

0.9 g.	total fat
0.1 g.	saturated fat
183	calories
1 mg.	cholesterol
414 mg.	sodium
15.4 g.	protein
32 g.	carbohydrates
3.4 g.	dietary fibre

Polenta Italiana

**This open-faced polenta and vegetable sandwich is really a
stacked tower of vegetable power. Serve with ripe melon, a
couple strips of fat-free ham, roasted sweet red peppers and a
tossed salad with Creamy Italian Dressing (page 115).**

Polenta

375	ml vegetable stock (page 93)
60	g yellow cornmeal
1	small onion, finely chopped
2	cloves garlic, minced
	Pinch of salt
4	tablespoons fat-free Parmesan topping

Sun-Dried Tomato Sauce

4	teaspoons cornflour
250	ml vegetable stock (page 93)
8	dry-packed sun-dried tomato halves, cut into small pieces
125	ml dry red wine or apple juice
2	tablespoons balsamic vinegar
1	teaspoon finely chopped fresh rosemary
2	cloves garlic, minced
	Ground black pepper
	Salt (optional)

Vegetable Filling

4	round aubergine slices (2.5 cm thick)
4	tomato slices (2 cm thick)
	Ground black pepper
	Salt (optional)

1 *To make the polenta:* Line a
baking tray with foil and coat it with non-stick spray. Set
aside.

2 In a medium saucepan, combine the stock, cornmeal, onions, garlic and salt. Bring
to a boil over medium-high heat, stirring constantly. Reduce the heat to medium and cook, stirring occasionally, for 12 to 15 minutes, or until the polenta is thick
enough to hold a spoon upright.

3 Pour the polenta onto the
baking tray; spread it evenly into an 20 x 20 cm
square, about 2 cm thick.

4 Cover loosely with cling film and place in the refrigerator to chill for at least 4 hours, or until firm. Cut diagonally from corner to corner to make 4 triangles. Sprinkle with the Parmesan.

5 *To make the sun-dried tomato sauce:* Place the cornflour in a small saucepan. Gradually whisk in the stock to dissolve the cornflour. Add the tomatoes, wine or apple juice, vinegar, rosemary and garlic. Stir over medium-high heat for 2 to 3 minutes, or until thickened. Season to taste with the pepper and salt (if using). Cover and keep warm.

6 *To make the vegetable filling:* Preheat the oven to 220°C, Gas 7. Coat a large baking tray with non-stick spray.

7 Place the aubergine and tomatoes on the baking tray and mist with non-stick spray. Sprinkle with the pepper and salt (if using). Cover loosely with foil and bake for 10 minutes. Remove the foil.

8 Place the polenta in a single layer on the baking tray with the aubergine and tomatoes. Bake for 10 minutes, or until the aubergine and tomatoes are tender and the polenta is crisp.

9 Top each polenta triangle with 1 aubergine slice and 1 tomato slice. Reheat the sun-dried tomato sauce if needed. Spoon over the sandwiches.

Makes **4** servings.

nutrition at a glance	
per serving	
0.9 g.	total fat
0.1 g.	saturated fat
180	calories
0 mg.	cholesterol
570 mg.	sodium
6.6 g.	protein
33.2 g.	carbohydrates
3.6 g.	dietary fibre

Sicilian Calzone

quick and easy

This savoury pizza turnover makes a terrific dinner with my Tossed Antipasto Salad (page 97).

125	g thawed frozen French bread dough
155	g chopped spinach leaves, blanched, drained and squeezed dry
2	plum tomatoes, diced
250	g fat-free ricotta cheese
4	tablespoons finely chopped spring onions
1	tablespoon finely chopped fresh basil
½	teaspoon dried oregano
1	clove garlic, minced
¼	teaspoon ground black pepper
	Pinch of salt (optional)
1	tablespoon grated fat-free mozzarella cheese
125	ml tomato sauce with Italian seasonings

1 Position the oven rack in the lower third of the oven. If desired, place a baking stone on the rack. Preheat the oven to 220°C, Gas 7.

2 On a lightly floured work surface, roll the dough into a 25 cm circle. Cover and let rest while making the filling.

3 In a medium bowl, combine the spinach, tomatoes, ricotta, spring onions, basil, oregano, garlic, pepper and salt (if using). Spoon the mixture over half of the dough circle to within 1 cm of the edge. Fold the dough over the filling to enclose. Crimp the edges to seal.

4 With a large spatula, transfer the calzone to a baking tray or to the baking stone in the oven. Sprinkle the top with the mozzarella. Bake for 20 to 25 minutes, or until the crust browns. Cut in half.

5 Heat the tomato sauce in a small saucepan. Serve with the calzone.

Makes **2** servings.

nutrition at a glance

per serving

0.9 g.	total fat
0.1 g.	saturated fat
264	calories
10 mg.	cholesterol
852 mg.	sodium
21.5 g.	protein
39.5 g.	carbohydrates
4 g.	dietary fibre

Black Bean and Rice Cakes

Serve with Tomato Relish (page 299) or, if you're pressed for time, with jarred salsa spiked with a bit of freshly squeezed lime juice and chopped fresh basil.

250	ml water
125	ml white rice
	Pinch of salt (optional)
1	can (470 g) black beans, rinsed and drained
40	g fresh breadcrumbs (from 40-calorie-per-slice bread)
1	stalk celery, finely chopped
4	tablespoons finely chopped sweet red peppers
4	tablespoons fat-free egg substitute
¼	teaspoon ground black pepper

Lynn's Kitchen Tip

When preparing cooked beans, make a double or triple batch. Freeze the extra in resealable storage bags for stews, soups and bean cakes. You'll have the convenience of canned beans without the excess sodium.

1 Preheat the oven to 190°C, Gas 5. Coat a baking tray with non-stick spray and set aside.

2 In a medium non-stick saucepan, combine the water, rice and salt (if using). Bring to a boil over medium-high heat. Reduce the heat to low. Cover and cook for 20 minutes, or until the rice is tender and the water has been absorbed.

3 Remove from the heat. Stir in the beans, breadcrumbs, celery, red peppers, egg substitute and black pepper.

4 Coat a 125-ml metal or plastic measuring cup with non-stick spray. Pat one quarter of the rice mixture firmly into the cup and then turn it out onto the baking tray by rapping the cup lightly on the tray. Press to flatten to a 2 cm-thick cake. Repeat with remaining mixture to form 4 cakes.

5 Bake for 20 minutes, or until heated through.

Makes **4** cakes.

Photograph on page 320

nutrition at a glance

per cake

0.7 g.	total fat
0.2 g.	saturated fat
213	calories
0 mg.	cholesterol
232 mg.	sodium
10.1 g.	protein
42 g.	carbohydrates
5.2 g.	dietary fibre

Garden and Grain Loaf

This moist, satisfying loaf – delicately seasoned with an herb mixture from the south of France – can be served with Roasted Pepper Sauce (page 291), Chicken Gravy (page 293), Marinara Sauce (page 288) or Mushroom Sauce (page 294). Paper-thin carrot curls, cut with a vegetable peeler, make a pretty garnish.

Lynn's Fat-Free Flavour

Herbes de Provence is an herb mixture sold in most supermarkets. If unavailable, use equal amounts of crumbled dried rosemary, dried sage and dried thyme.

45	g quick-cooking rolled oats
5	tablespoons Grape-Nuts cereal
375	g closed cap mushrooms, finely chopped
1	large onion, finely chopped
1	large carrot, finely grated
1	medium courgette, grated
3	cloves garlic, minced
185	g fresh whole-grain breadcrumbs (from 40-calorie-per-slice bread)
4	tablespoons fat-free egg substitute
1	tablespoon Dijon mustard
1	tablespoon tomato paste
1½	teaspoons dried herbes de Provence
1	teaspoon low-sodium Worcestershire sauce
¼	teaspoon ground black pepper
	Pinch of salt (optional)

1 Preheat the oven to 180°C, Gas 4. Coat an 20 x 10 cm loaf tin with non-stick spray.

2 Line a baking tray with foil. Place the oats and Grape-Nuts in separate piles on the sheet; spread each pile into a thin layer. Bake for 12 to 15 minutes, or until golden; stir occasionally and keep the oats and cereal separate. Let cool for a few minutes. Transfer the Grape-Nuts to a blender or food processor and grind coarsely; set aside. Do not turn off the oven.

3 Coat a large non-stick frying pan with non-stick spray. Add the mushrooms, onions, carrots, courgette and garlic. Mist the vegetables with non-stick spray. Stir-fry over medium-high heat for 5 minutes. Remove from the heat. Stir in the breadcrumbs and the reserved oats and Grape-Nuts.

4 In a small bowl, combine the egg substitute, mustard, tomato paste, herbes de Provence, Worcestershire sauce, pepper and salt (if using). Whisk to combine. Add to the frying pan and mix well.

5 Spoon the mixture into the prepared loaf tin. Smooth the top with the back of a spoon.

6 Bake for 40 to 45 minutes, or until browned on top and firm to the touch. Remove from the oven and let stand for 10 minutes. Run a knife around the edge. Unmould and slice.

Makes **8** servings.

nutrition at a glance

per serving
0.9 g.	total fat
0.1 g.	saturated fat
99	calories
0 mg.	cholesterol
167 mg.	sodium
5 g.	protein
21.2 g.	carbohydrates
4.5 g.	dietary fibre

Black Bean Tamale Pie

This hearty American Southwestern-style casserole is a perfect buffet dish. Everything but the topping can be made ahead of time and stored in the refrigerator. Serve with a green vegetable, a salad and fat-free vanilla ice cream topped with orange slices.

Black Beans

1	dried chipotle pepper (wear rubber gloves when handling)
125	ml hot water
500	ml vegetable stock (page 93)
470	g chopped onions
375	ml tomato sauce
4	cloves garlic, minced
1	tablespoon chilli powder
1	tablespoon tomato paste
2	teaspoons dried oregano
1	teaspoon ground cumin
1	teaspoon sugar
	Pinch of salt (optional)
375	g cooked black beans
4	tablespoons chopped fresh coriander

Cornbread Topping

75	g plain flour
4	tablespoons yellow cornmeal
1½	teaspoons baking powder
	Pinch of salt (optional)
80	ml canned creamed-style sweetcorn
5	tablespoons canned chopped mild green chilli peppers
2	tablespoons skimmed milk
½	tablespoon sugar
1	egg white

1 *To make the black beans:* In a small bowl, combine the pepper and the water. Let soak for 30 minutes, or until softened. Split the pepper and discard the seeds and stem. Purée the pepper and the liquid in a blender or food processor. Set aside.

2   Meanwhile, in a large saucepan over medium-high heat, bring the stock to a boil. Add the onions, tomato sauce, garlic, chilli powder, tomato paste, oregano, cumin, sugar and salt (if using). Reduce the heat to medium-low and simmer for 1 hour, or until the mixture thickens.

3   Add the beans and 1 to 2 teaspoons of the chipotle purée (reserve the remainder for another use). Simmer for 15 minutes. Remove from the heat and stir in the coriander.

4   Pour into a 30 x 20 cm baking dish. Set aside.

5   *To make the cornbread topping:* Preheat the oven to 200°C, Gas 6.

6   In a small bowl, mix the flour, cornmeal, baking powder and salt (if using).

7   In a large bowl, combine the sweetcorn, peppers, milk and sugar.

8   Place the egg white in a medium bowl. Beat with an electric mixer until soft peaks form. Fold into the sweetcorn mixture. Stir in half of the flour mixture just until incorporated, then add the remaining flour mixture and stir just until the dry ingredients are moistened.

9   Spoon over the bean mixture; spread with the back of a spoon to cover. Bake for 20 minutes, or until a cocktail stick inserted in the centre of the cornbread topping comes out clean.

Makes **8** servings.

nutrition at a glance	
per serving	
0.9 g.	total fat
0.2 g.	saturated fat
168	calories
0 mg.	cholesterol
756 mg.	sodium
7.6 g.	protein
34.1 g.	carbohydrates
6.7 g.	dietary fibre

Fiesta Chilli

I like to use chipotle peppers (dried smoked jalapeños) to add a complex smoky note to this chilli, but a fresh jalapeño pepper works fine, too.

185	g dry red beans
1	can (500 g) tomatoes, chopped (with juice)
500	ml tomato juice
1	large tomato, coarsely chopped
250	ml orange juice
1	large onion, coarsely chopped
1	sweet red pepper, cut into 2.5 cm cubes
250	g granulated texturised vegetable protein (optional)
½	carrot, grated or finely diced
1	dried chipotle pepper, cut into small pieces (wear rubber gloves when handling)
3	cloves garlic, minced
2	tablespoons chilli powder
1	tablespoon dried basil
2	teaspoons grated orange rind
2	teaspoons vinegar
1	teaspoon ground cumin
1	teaspoon dried oregano
1	teaspoon brown sugar or 2 tablespoons raisins
	Ground black pepper
	Salt (optional)
125	g grated fat-free mozzarella cheese

1 Place the beans in a large non-stick flameproof casserole. Cover generously with cold water. Bring to a boil over medium-high heat. Remove from the heat, cover and allow to stand for 1 hour. Discard the soaking water. Rinse the beans and return to the pot.

2 Add the canned tomatoes, tomato juice, chopped tomatoes, orange juice, onions, red peppers, texturised vegetable protein (if using), carrots, chipotle peppers, garlic, chilli powder, basil, orange rind, vinegar, cumin, oregano and brown sugar or raisins. Mix well.

3 Simmer over medium heat, stirring occasionally, for 1½ hours, or until the beans are tender. Season to taste with the black pepper and salt (if using). Serve sprinkled with the mozzarella.

Makes **8** servings.

Photograph on page 150

White Chilli

quick and easy

Sometimes just the aroma of cooking chilli tickles the nose and starts the hunger pangs. I guarantee that you will love this unique stew. You can easily add 250 g granulated texturised vegetable protein with the amount of water called for on the package directions to make the chilli seem meaty.

1	Spanish onion, chopped
140	g diced yellow peppers
2	cloves garlic, minced
625	ml water
1	can (470 g) navy beans or cannellini beans, rinsed and drained
185	g diced tomatoes
60	g white sweetcorn kernels
2	tablespoons diced canned mild green chilli peppers
½	teaspoon chopped jalapeño peppers (wear rubber gloves when handling)
½	teaspoon ground cumin
½	teaspoon chilli powder
½	teaspoon vinegar
⅛	teaspoon ground red pepper (optional)
	Salt (optional)
45	g grated fat-free Swiss cheese

1 In a large non-stick pan, combine the onions, yellow peppers, garlic and 125 ml of the water. Stir over medium-high heat for 5 minutes, or until the peppers are nearly cooked and the water has evaporated.

Lynn's Fat-Free Flavour

Instead of complaining that winter tomatoes don't taste as sweet and juicy as summer's red beauties, I developed this chilli recipe to take advantage of pale varieties. When cooked, they add a delightful tart sweetness to this unusual dish. Green tomatoes or tomatillos also work beautifully, as do slightly underripe yellow tomatoes.

(continued)

2 Add the beans, tomatoes, sweetcorn, mild chilli peppers, jalapeño peppers, cumin, chilli powder, vinegar, ground red pepper (if using) and the remaining 500 ml water. Cover and cook over medium-low heat, stirring occasionally, for 15 minutes. Season to taste with the salt (if using). Serve sprinkled with the cheese.

Makes **4** servings.

Couscous-Stuffed Peppers

For this very colourful dish, you can use a mixture of coloured peppers. The varieties most often available are purple, green, red, orange, yellow and white. Garnish with slivers of orange rind.

375	g canned chopped plum tomatoes
2	cloves garlic, minced
4	yellow peppers
4	tablespoons chopped onions
2	dried apricot halves, slivered
2	dates, chopped
2	tablespoons raisins
2	vegetable bouillon cubes
½	teaspoon dried thyme
¼	teaspoon grated orange rind
200	g couscous
2	tablespoons chopped fresh parsley
2	tablespoons thinly sliced fresh basil
	Ground black pepper
	Salt (optional)

1 In a small non-stick saucepan, combine the tomatoes and garlic. Cover and simmer over medium heat for 10 minutes. Coat an 20 x 20 cm baking dish with non-stick spray. Cover the bottom of the dish with the tomatoes and garlic. Set aside.

Lynn's Kitchen Tip

You don't need a citrus zester to make julienne slivers of orange rind. First, scrub the fruit with warm, soapy hot water. Rinse well, then dry. With a paring knife or vegetable peeler, take off 1 cm-wide strips of rind, with as little white pith attached as possible. Cut the strips into slivers.

2   Bring a large pan of water to a boil over high heat. Cut the tops off the yellow peppers; discard the membranes and seeds. Drop the peppers and the tops into the pan. Boil for 2 minutes. Using tongs, remove the tops and set aside to drain. Boil the peppers for 2 to 3 minutes more, or until partially cooked. Using tongs, remove the peppers and rinse under cold water. Drain upside down in a colander. Reserve 680 ml of the cooking water.

3   Pour 625 ml of the reserved cooking water into a medium saucepan. Bring to a boil over medium heat. Add the onions, apricots, dates, raisins, bouillon cubes, thyme and orange rind. Reduce the heat to low and simmer for 15 minutes.

4   Remove from the heat and stir in the couscous. Cover and let stand for 5 minutes. Fluff with a fork. Sprinkle with the parsley, basil, black pepper and salt (if using). Mix lightly.

5   Preheat the oven to 180°C, Gas 4.

6   Divide the couscous mixture among the peppers. Stand the peppers in the baking dish. Drizzle the remaining 60 ml cooking water over the peppers. Top with the reserved pepper tops.

7   Cover loosely with foil. Bake for 30 minutes, or until the peppers are tender.

Makes **4** servings.

Photograph on page 152

nutrition at a glance

per serving
0.8 g.	total fat
0.1 g.	saturated fat
279	calories
0 mg.	cholesterol
265 mg.	sodium
8.3 g.	protein
62.3 g.	carbohydrates
7.3 g.	dietary fibre

Moroccan Vegetable Medley

This beautifully spiced vegetable dish was a hit with our taste testers. Serve each portion over 200 g steamed couscous, which will raise the fat content by only 1 gramme.

(page 93)

1.5	litres water or vegetable stock (page 93)
4	sprigs fresh coriander
4	cloves garlic
1	tablespoon chopped fresh parsley
1	teaspoon curry powder
¾	teaspoon ground cumin
¼–½	teaspoon crumbled saffron threads
	Pinch of ground cinnamon
	Pinch of salt (optional)
3	carrots, halved lengthwise and cut into 2.5 cm pieces
2	small baking potatoes, cut into large pieces
½	medium onion, cut into quarters
1	medium courgette, quartered lengthwise and cut into 2.5 cm pieces
90	g canned chickpeas, rinsed and drained
4	tablespoons raisins
2	tablespoons chopped fresh coriander

1 In a large pan, combine the water or stock, coriander sprigs, garlic, parsley, curry powder, cumin, saffron, cinnamon and salt (if using). Bring to a boil over medium-high heat. Add the carrots, potatoes and onions. Return to a boil. Reduce the heat to medium. Partially cover and simmer for 25 to 30 minutes, or until the potatoes are almost tender.

2 Add the courgette, chickpeas and raisins; stir gently so the vegetables don't break up. Simmer for 10 to 12 minutes, or until the courgette is tender. Sprinkle with the chopped coriander.

Makes **4** servings.

Photograph on page 153

Lynn's Fat-Free Flavour

Only a few varieties of grapes are dried to make raisins. The Thompson seedless, the tiny Zante and the Muscat are the most common. Both dark and golden raisins can be made from Thompson seedless grapes. The dark raisins are sun-dried for several weeks. The golden are treated with sulphur dioxide to prevent them from darkening.

---

nutrition at a glance

per serving

0.9 g.	total fat
0.1 g.	saturated fat
140	calories
0 mg.	cholesterol
87 mg.	sodium
4.6 g.	protein
30.8 g.	carbohydrates
4.7 g.	dietary fibre

Italian Stuffed Artichokes

Artichoke lovers, this lush and elegant main course is for you. The savoury stuffing gives way to the tender artichoke heart.

4	medium artichokes, cleaned, bottom trimmed flat
125	g chopped mushrooms
1	small leek, white and some green stem, chopped
¼	yellow pepper, finely chopped
1	stalk celery, finely chopped
4	tablespoons water
125	g fresh breadcrumbs (from 40-calorie-per-slice bread)
4	tablespoons fat-free egg substitute
2	tablespoons chopped fresh parsley
1	clove garlic, minced
¼	teaspoon ground black pepper
3	tablespoons freshly squeezed lemon juice

1 Place the artichokes, stem side down, in a deep non-stick saucepan wide enough to hold them tightly in a single layer. Add 5 cm of water. Cover and bring to a boil over medium-high heat. Reduce the heat to medium-low and cook for 30 to 40 minutes, or until an outer leaf pulls off easily. Add more water to the pan, if necessary, during cooking.

2 Drain the artichokes and set aside to cool. Preheat oven to 190°C, Gas 5.

3 While the artichokes are cooling, coat a large non-stick frying pan with non-stick spray. Warm over medium-high heat. Add the mushrooms, leeks, yellow peppers, celery and water. Cook, stirring, for 4 minutes. Remove from the heat. Stir in the breadcrumbs, egg substitute, parsley, garlic, black pepper and 1 tablespoon of the lemon juice. Mix well.

4 Divide the stuffing among the artichokes, spooning it into the centre cavity and also between a few of the inner leaves.

5 Place in a single layer in an 20 x 20 cm baking dish. Add 6 mm of water and the re-maining 2 tablespoons lemon juice to the bottom of the dish. Bake for 30 minutes, or until the stuffing is hot.

Makes **4** servings.

Photograph on page 157

Lynn's Kitchen Tip

To clean an artichoke, cut off the stem right at the base, so the artichoke will sit upright. Invert and, with the pointed end resting on a work surface, press down with your palm to spread the leaves open. Run cold water liberally through the leaves. You can scoop the choke out of the centre before or after cooking.

nutrition at a glance
per serving
- 0.9 g. total fat
- 0.2 g. saturated fat
- 132 calories
- 0 mg. cholesterol
- 253 mg. sodium
- 8.5 g. protein
- 27.9 g. carbohydrates
- 9.6 g. dietary fibre

Gingered Vegetables with Bulgur

quick and easy

This colourful dish with crisp-cooked vegetables in a savoury sauce has plenty of variety and nutrients. Serve with Oriental Coleslaw (page 107) or a crisp salad with Ranch Dressing (page 118).

4	teaspoons cornflour
1	tablespoon apricot jam
250	ml vegetable stock (page 93)
1	tablespoon low-sodium soy sauce
2	teaspoons grated fresh ginger
2	cloves garlic, minced
125	g baby carrots, cut in quarters lengthwise
2	tablespoons chopped onions
250	g cauliflower cut into 2.5 cm pieces
125	g sliced mushrooms
1	small sweet red pepper, cut into strips
1	small yellow pepper, cut into strips
8	asparagus spears, cut into 2.5 cm lengths
45	g broccoli florets
200	g cooked bulgur
90	g cubed low-fat firm tofu
¼	teaspoon toasted sesame seeds

1 In a small bowl, whisk the cornflour and jam to mix. Whisk in the stock, soy sauce, ginger and garlic. Set aside.

2 Pour 6 mm water into a large non-stick frying pan. Add the carrots and onions. Cook over medium-high heat, stirring, for 3 minutes. Add the cauliflower and mushrooms; add a little more water if the pan is dry. Cover and cook for 2 minutes. Add the red peppers, yellow peppers, asparagus and broccoli; cover and cook for 2 minutes. Pour off any excess water.

3 Add the reserved stock mixture. Cook over medium-high heat, stirring constantly, for 2 minutes, or until thickened. Stir in the bulgur. Cook for 1 to 2 minutes, or until hot.

4 Remove from the heat. Gently stir in the tofu. Sprinkle with the sesame seeds.

Makes **4** servings.

Fresh unpeeled ginger can be frozen, tightly wrapped, for several months. To use, slice off a piece of the frozen root. Wrap and return the remaining root to the freezer.

nutrition at a glance

per serving

0.9 g.	total fat
0.1 g.	saturated fat
143	calories
0 mg.	cholesterol
400 mg.	sodium
7.2 g.	protein
28.9 g.	carbohydrates
6.8 g.	dietary fibre

Greek Stuffed Peppers

This simple old favourite, with an updated stuffing, is colourful and a breeze to make. Briefly microwaving the peppers before stuffing cuts down on the baking time.

3	sweet red, yellow, or green peppers
2	stalks celery, finely chopped
1	medium onion, finely chopped
2	cloves garlic, minced
1	tablespoon water
250	g cooked white or brown rice
280	g cooked navy beans or chickpeas, lightly mashed
1	tablespoon freshly squeezed lemon juice
1	teaspoon finely chopped fresh mint (optional)
½	teaspoon dried oregano
	Salt (optional)
	Hot-pepper sauce (optional)

1 Preheat the oven to 220°C, Gas 6.

2 Cut the peppers in half lengthwise. Remove and discard the stems, membranes and seeds. Place the peppers, cut side up, on a microwaveable tray. Microwave on high power for 5 minutes.

3 Transfer the peppers to a 30 x 20 cm baking dish, arranging them cut side up in a single layer. Set aside.

4 Coat a medium non-stick saucepan with non-stick spray. Add the celery, onions and garlic. Cover and cook over medium heat for 2 to 3 minutes, or until the onions start to brown. Add the water and cook, stirring, until the water evaporates.

5 Remove the saucepan from the heat. Add the rice, beans or chickpeas, lemon juice, mint (if using) and oregano. Season to taste with the salt (if using) and hot-pepper sauce (if using). Stir to combine. Spoon into the pepper cavities.

6 Cover with foil and bake for 40 to 45 minutes, or until the peppers are tender and the stuffing is hot.

Makes **6** servings.

nutrition at a glance

per serving

0.5 g.	total fat
0.1 g.	saturated fat
131	calories
0 mg.	cholesterol
121 mg.	sodium
5.6 g.	protein
26.8 g.	carbohydrates
5.3 g.	dietary fibre

Wild Mushroom Moussaka

Instead of minced lamb in this classic Greek aubergine casserole, I use a mixture of cultivated and wild mushrooms. They lighten the dish and add sophistication. You can prepare the mushroom-aubergine filling up to a day in advance. Cover tightly with cling film and store in the refrigerator. Prepare the luscious fat-free cheese sauce just before baking.

Mushroom-Aubergine Filling

250	ml hot water
15	g dried mushrooms
1	medium aubergine
	Salt (optional)
1	large onion, chopped
3	cloves garlic, minced
500	g closed cap mushrooms, sliced
4	tablespoons red wine or non-alcoholic red wine (optional)
250	g canned crushed tomatoes
2	tablespoons tomato paste
½	teaspoon dried oregano
⅛	teaspoon ground cinnamon
4	tablespoons chopped fresh parsley
1	teaspoon dried basil
	Ground black pepper
2	egg whites

Mornay Sauce

4	tablespoons plain flour
500	ml skimmed milk
125	ml fat-free egg substitute
125	ml fat-free soured cream
5	tablespoons fat-free Parmesan topping

1 *To make the mushroom-aubergine filling:* In a small bowl, combine the water and dried mushrooms; set aside to soak for 20 minutes. Drain through a fine sieve set over a measuring jug; set aside 125 ml of the liquid. Chop the mushrooms into small pieces and set aside. Preheat the oven to 180°C, Gas 4. Coat a baking tray with non-stick spray.

2 Cut the aubergine lengthwise into 6 cm-thick slices. Season lightly with the salt (if using) on both sides. Place the aubergine on the baking tray in a single layer. Coat with non-stick spray. Bake for 10 minutes. Turn the slices and bake for 10 minutes, or until tender. Remove from the oven.

3 Coat a large non-stick frying pan with non-stick spray. Warm over medium-high heat. Add the onions and garlic. Reduce the heat to medium, cover and cook stirring occasionally, for 2 to 3 minutes, or until golden.

4 Add the sliced mushrooms, the reserved chopped mushrooms, and the reserved mushroom liquid. Cover and cook over medium-high heat, stirring occasionally, for 5 minutes, or until the mushrooms are wilted.

5 Uncover and cook, stirring occasionally, for 5 to 6 minutes, or until most of the liquid evaporates. Add the wine (if using) and cook, stirring occasionally, for 5 minutes, or until most of the liquid evaporates.

6 Add the crushed tomatoes, tomato paste, oregano and cinnamon. Cover and cook over medium-low heat for 5 minutes. Stir in the parsley, basil and pepper to taste. Remove from the heat.

7 Place the egg whites in a medium bowl. Beat with an electric mixer until soft peaks form. Fold the egg whites into the mushroom mixture and set aside.

8 Place half of the aubergine slices in a 30 x 20 cm baking dish. Top with the mushroom mixture and remaining aubergine slices.

9 *To make the Mornay sauce:* Place the flour in a medium non-stick saucepan; whisk in 125 ml of the milk until smooth. Whisk in the remaining milk. Cook over medium heat, stirring constantly, for 5 to 6 minutes, or until thickened. Remove from the heat.

10 Whisk in the egg substitute, soured cream and Parmesan. Pour over the aubergine. Bake for 45 to 50 minutes, or until the mixture bubbles at the sides of the pan. Remove from the oven and let stand for 5 minutes before cutting.

Makes **8** servings.

Photograph on page 158

nutrition at a glance

per serving
0.8 g.	total fat
0.2 g.	saturated fat
155	calories
1 mg.	cholesterol
249 mg.	sodium
10.7 g.	protein
26.9 g.	carbohydrates
4 g.	dietary fibre

Ratatouille with Saffron Custard

Ratatouille is a rustic Mediterranean vegetable stew that simmers the best of the summer garden – courgettes, aubergine, onions and tomatoes – into a savoury mélange. I've added a rich saffron-scented custard to make it even more special.

Ratatouille

1	green pepper
1	sweet red pepper
1	can (500 g) stewed tomatoes, chopped (with juice)
1	medium onion, chopped
4	cloves garlic, minced
1	small aubergine, cubed
1	small courgette, cubed
1	small yellow squash, cubed
2	tablespoons dry red wine or non-alcoholic red wine (optional)
125	ml tomato sauce
1	tablespoon tomato paste
½	teaspoon dried oregano
¼	teaspoon dried rosemary, crumbled
¼	teaspoon ground black pepper
	Pinch of salt (optional)
1	tablespoon thinly sliced fresh basil
2	teaspoons chopped fresh parsley

Saffron Custard

⅛	teaspoon saffron threads
3	tablespoons hot water
250	g fat-free ricotta cheese
125	ml fat-free egg substitute
5	tablespoons fat-free Parmesan topping
4	tablespoons skimmed milk
¼	teaspoon ground black pepper

1 *To make the ratatouille:*
Line a baking tray with foil. Cut the green pepper and red pepper in half lengthwise; discard the stems, mem-

Smooth, sweet ricotta cheese isn't a cheese at all. It's a cheese by-product. In Italy, it is traditionally made from whey, the liquid drained from cow's-milk curds during the production of mozzarella or provolone. Here milk is usually mixed with the whey. Fat-free ricotta is made with skimmed milk.

branes and seeds. Place the peppers, cut side down, on the baking tray and flatten with the palm of your hand. Grill 10 cm from the heat for 10 to 12 minutes, or until the peppers are blackened. Remove from the oven and wrap the foil tightly around the peppers. Set aside for 10 minutes. Peel off and discard the skin. Cut into 6 mm strips.

2 Pour the stewed tomatoes into a sieve placed over a medium bowl. Pour the juice from the bowl into a large non-stick frying pan; reserve the tomatoes. Bring the juice to a boil over medium-high heat. Add the onions and garlic; cook for 2 minutes.

3 Add the aubergine, courgette, squash, wine (if using), tomato sauce, tomato paste, oregano, rosemary, black pepper, salt (if using) and the reserved tomatoes. Bring to a boil.

4 Reduce the heat to medium-low and simmer, stirring occasionally, for 20 minutes. Add the roasted peppers and simmer for 10 minutes, or until all the vegetables are tender and excess liquid evaporates. Stir in the basil and parsley.

5 Coat a 30 x 20 cm baking dish with non-stick spray. Pour the mixture into the dish; set aside.

6 *To make the saffron custard:* Preheat the oven to 180°C, Gas 4.

7 Combine the saffron and water in a medium bowl. Set aside to soak for 5 minutes.

8 Whisk in the ricotta, egg substitute, Parmesan, milk and pepper. Pour over the vegetables.

9 Bake for 40 minutes, or until lightly browned. Remove from the oven and let stand for 5 minutes before serving.

Makes **6** servings.

nutrition at a glance	
per serving	
0.6 g.	total fat
0.1 g.	saturated fat
144	calories
4 mg.	cholesterol
580 mg.	sodium
12.3 g.	protein
23.1 g.	carbohydrates
4.8 g.	dietary fibre

Grain Casserole with Green Salsa

This hearty casserole is a great way to use up small amounts of rice. Or you can make it with one of the unseasoned blended-rice mixes now in the supermarkets. If you don't have tomatillos, use 2 green tomatoes. You can prepare the salsa ahead and keep it in the refrigerator for a few days.

Rice Mixture

550	ml vegetable stock (page 93)
4	tablespoons wild rice
4	tablespoons basmati rice
4	tablespoons jasmine or white rice
160	ml canned hominy, rinsed and drained
125	g chopped celery
90	g chopped carrots
1	teaspoon low-sodium soy sauce

Green Salsa

6	tomatillos
90	g finely chopped red onions
2	serrano chilli peppers, finely chopped (wear rubber gloves when handling)
2	tablespoons chopped fresh coriander
1	clove garlic, minced
½	teaspoon white-wine vinegar
¼	teaspoon sugar
	Salt (optional)

Vegetables

125	g broccoli florets
155	g cauliflower florets
2	large plum tomatoes, thinly sliced

1 *To make the rice mixture:* Bring the stock to a boil in a medium non-stick saucepan over medium-high heat. Add the wild rice. Reduce the heat to medium, cover and simmer for 25 minutes. Stir in the basmati rice and jasmine or white rice; cover and simmer for 15 to 20 minutes, or until the wild rice is tender.

2 Add the hominy, celery, carrots and soy sauce. Stir to combine.

3 Coat a 30 x 20 cm baking dish with non-stick spray. Spread the rice mixture evenly in the dish.

4 *To make the green salsa:* While the rice is cooking, remove and discard the papery skins from the tomatillos. Bring a medium saucepan of water to a boil over high heat. Add the tomatillos. Reduce the heat to medium. Simmer for 20 minutes, or until the tomatillo skins split. Drain and peel off the skins. Cut the flesh into quarters.

5 Place the tomatillos in a blender or food processor; process until puréed. Add the onions, peppers, coriander, garlic, vinegar and sugar. Pulse several times to combine. Season to taste with the salt (if using). Spoon over the grain mixture.

6 *To make the vegetables:* Preheat the oven to 180°C, Gas 4.

7 Bring 750 ml water to a boil in a large non-stick frying pan over medium-high heat. Add the broccoli and cauliflower. Reduce the heat to medium, cover and cook for 8 minutes, or until just tender. Drain and spread over the salsa. Top with the tomatoes. Bake for 20 minutes, or until heated through.

Makes **6** servings.

nutrition at a glance
per serving
0.9 g. total fat
0.1 g. saturated fat
144 calories
0 mg. cholesterol
258 mg. sodium
4.5 g. protein
28.9 g. carbohydrates
3.3 g. dietary fibre

Stuffed Potatoes

Steaming hot and heaped with an irresistible creamy vegetable filling, these baked potatoes are very satisfying. Our taste testers loved them. One of these potatoes is almost a meal in itself, sided with a Tossed Antipasto Salad (page 97).

4	large baking potatoes
185	g small broccoli florets
2	large tomatoes, diced
4	spring onions, thinly sliced
2	tablespoons water
375	ml fat-free soured cream
4	teaspoons fat-free Parmesan topping
4	tablespoons chopped fresh parsley

1 Preheat the oven to 180°C, Gas 4.

2 Wash and gently scrub the potatoes, but don't dry. Place at least 10 cm apart on the oven rack and bake for 1 hour, or until tender. Remove from the oven.

3 Coat a large non-stick frying pan with non-stick spray. Add the broccoli, tomatoes, spring onions and water. Cook over medium-high heat, stirring occasionally, for 4 to 6 minutes, or until the broccoli is bright green and crisp-tender. Remove from the heat and stir in the soured cream.

4 Cut a 2.5 cm-deep cross in each potato. Squeeze the ends to open the cut and push up the potato flesh slightly. Spoon the filling over the potatoes. Sprinkle with the Parmesan and parsley.

Makes **4** servings.

Many old rural homes still have dry cellars, where potatoes and other winter vegetables can be stored all through the cold months, as they were in the past century. In the days when seasonal eating was a reality for most people, long-keeping potatoes provided vitamin C, potassium, iron, and fibre.

nutrition at a glance	
per serving	
0.9 g.	total fat
0.2 g.	saturated fat
539	calories
0 mg.	cholesterol
155 mg.	sodium
17.3 g.	protein
117.3 g.	carbohydrates
11.7 g.	dietary fibre

Vegetable Side Dishes

You may have noticed that there are more recipes in

this chapter than in any other chapter in this

cookbook. The reason is clear: Vegetables are essen-

tial for a healthy low-fat eating plan.

Vegetables, along with fruits, are practically

perfect foods. With a few exceptions, most are close

to fat-free in their natural state. Vegetables provide a

density of nutrients – high quantities of vitamins such

as A, C and sometimes B, plus various minerals.

Vegetables also contain powerful substances called antioxidants, which may destroy the free radicals that can lead to cancer, heart disease and premature aging. All vegetables contain fibre, and many are terrific sources of the complex carbohydrates that give you a nice full feeling.

Cultivating the Vegetable Habit

Vegetables add excitement to cooking and eating: vivid colours, textures from crisp to creamy, a field of flavours from sweet to sharp. Vegetable variety is exceptional.

Get into the habit of trying at least one new vegetable a week. By year's end, you'll have 52 stalwart friends that will support your good health efforts.

Cooking with Flavour, Not Fat

Most vegetables are low in fat, so you don't want to undo all of nature's good work by pouring on the fat during cooking.

The secret to sautéing leeks, onions, mushrooms, peppers, courgettes, crookneck squash or celery without oil is to start the cooking in a covered non-stick frying pan that's coated with non-stick spray.

The water-filled vegetables will "sweat" their sweet juices, which caramelise on the bottom of the pan and create that wonderful browned flavour that we associate with fat-added cooking.

After the caramelisation starts, uncover and continue cooking. Stir occasionally, adding just a teaspoon or two of water to prevent sticking and to loosen those tasty browned bits.

For steamed or microwaved vegetables, try these flavour enhancers.

✳ Asparagus, broccoli, broccoflower, cauliflower: Steam or microwave with citrus juice mixed with an equal amount of vegetable stock or water. Add herbs, spices, ginger, onions or garlic.

✳ Carrots, sweet potatoes, winter squash: Steam or microwave in apricot juice or orange juice. Add a pinch of cinnamon, nutmeg or Cajun spice blend.

✳ Greens, kale, spinach or Swiss chard: Steam or microwave in vinegar or lemon juice combined with an equal amount of vegetable stock or water.

Peas and Leeks with Coriander

quick and **easy**

Fresh coriander and dark sesame oil add a bit of Asian intrigue to a simple dish of leeks and peas.

2	leeks, white and some green stem, sliced
1	tablespoon water
315	g fresh or frozen peas
1	tablespoon chopped fresh coriander
	Dark sesame oil in a spray bottle

1   Coat a large frying pan with non-stick spray. Add the leeks. Cover and cook over medium-high heat, stirring occasionally, for 3 to 4 minutes, or until the leeks start to release liquid. Uncover and reduce the heat to medium. Cook, stirring occasionally, for 2 to 3 minutes, or until golden. Add a few drops of the water if the mixture starts to stick.

2   Add the peas. Cover and cook over low heat for 3 to 5 minutes, or until tender. Sprinkle with the coriander and spray lightly with the oil. Toss to coat.

Makes **4** servings.

nutrition at a glance
per serving
0.6 g.	total fat
0.1 g.	saturated fat
99	calories
0 mg.	cholesterol
15 mg.	sodium
4.6 g.	protein
19.6 g.	carbohydrates
5.3 g.	dietary fibre

Sugar Snap Peas with Mint

quick and easy

This delicate fresh glaze is an easy and simple embellishment for crispy steamed sugar snaps.

500 g sugar snap peas
  1 tablespoon freshly squeezed lemon juice
  1 tablespoon honey
  1 tablespoon finely chopped fresh mint

1 Bring 250 ml water to a boil in a large saucepan over high heat. Add the peas; cover and cook for 2 to 3 minutes, or until the peas are bright green and crisp-tender. Drain and return to the saucepan. Add the lemon juice, honey and mint. Stir to coat the peas.

Makes **4** servings.

nutrition at a glance
per serving
0.3 g. total fat
0 g. saturated fat
66 calories
0 mg. cholesterol
8 mg. sodium
3.9 g. protein
12.9 g. carbohydrates
3.4 g. dietary fibre

Tomatoes with Herbed Crumbs

quick and easy

In the American south, some cooks stew tomatoes for at least 2 hours over very low heat until they are almost syrupy. In many areas, day-old bread cubes are added just before serving. My version is quicker and retains the fresh appeal of vine-ripened tomatoes. These are excellent served over fat-free mashed potatoes.

4	medium tomatoes, cut into quarters
250	ml tomato juice
2	stalks celery, finely chopped
2	teaspoons red-wine vinegar
1½	teaspoons sugar
½	teaspoon dried oregano
	Ground black pepper
	Salt (optional)
4	tablespoons fresh breadcrumbs (from 40-calorie-per-slice bread)
2	tablespoons chopped fresh parsley
2	tablespoons fat-free Parmesan topping

1 In a large non-stick saucepan, combine the tomatoes, tomato juice, celery, vinegar, sugar and oregano. Bring to a boil over medium-high heat. Reduce the heat to medium and simmer for 15 to 18 minutes, or until the tomatoes are very soft. If thicker tomatoes are desired, boil for 2 to 3 minutes longer. Season to taste with the pepper and salt (if using).

2 In a small bowl, combine the breadcrumbs, parsley and Parmesan. Sprinkle over the tomatoes just before serving.

Makes **4** servings.

nutrition at a glance
per serving
0.7 g.	total fat
0.1 g.	saturated fat
74	calories
0 mg.	cholesterol
332 mg.	sodium
3.8 g.	protein
15.8 g.	carbohydrates
2.6 g.	dietary fibre

Beetroot with their Greens

quick and easy

Orange brings out the natural sweetness of fresh beetroot. Make this dish when you have beetroot with fresh-looking tops.

5	red beetroot with greens attached
250	ml freshly squeezed orange juice
2	tablespoons grated orange rind
1	clove garlic, minced
	Salt (optional)

1 Cut the leafy greens from the beetroot stems. Stack the leaves, roll into a cylinder, and cut into thin slices. Place the leaves in a large non-stick pan.

2 Trim the bulbs from the remaining stems; discard the stems. Scrub the beetroot well and trim the stem and root ends. Peel the beetroot, if desired. Thinly slice the beetroot and set aside.

3 Add the orange juice and orange rind to the pan. Cover and bring to a boil over medium-high heat. Cook for 3 to 5 minutes, or until the leaves are wilted. Remove the greens with a slotted spoon or tongs (so the liquid remains in the pan). Set the greens aside.

4 Add the beetroot and garlic to the pan. Cover and cook over medium heat for 10 minutes, or until the beetroot are crisp-tender. Season to taste with the salt (if using).

5 If necessary, microwave the greens on high power for 1 minute to reheat. Arrange the greens on a serving platter. Top with the beetroot. Spoon some of the cooking liquid over the beetroot and greens.

Makes **4** servings.

Lynn's Kitchen Tip

If you're a home gardener or if you shop at a farmers market, look for young and tender beetroot greens. They're great to add to a tossed salad.

nutrition at a glance
per serving

0.3 g.	total fat
0 g.	saturated fat
74	calories
0 mg.	cholesterol
210 mg.	sodium
3.1 g.	protein
16.7 g.	carbohydrates
4.3 g.	dietary fibre

Beetroot with Pineapple Sauce

This beetroot dish is so versatile, it can be served hot or cold, as a side dish to any meat main dish, or as a salad on a bed of greens. Scrub the beetroot well, but don't peel them before roasting.

4	medium beetroot
1	teaspoon cornflour
1	tablespoon red-wine vinegar
125	ml crushed pineapple
4	tablespoons pineapple juice
1	teaspoon grated fresh ginger
½	teaspoon sugar
¼	teaspoon grated orange rind

1 Preheat the oven to 190°C, Gas 5.

2 Individually wrap the beetroot in foil. Place on a baking tray and bake for 45 minutes, or until tender when pierced with a sharp knife. Set aside until cool enough to handle.

3 Peel off the beetroot skins. Trim off the stem and root ends; discard. Cut each beetroot into 8 wedges; set aside.

4 Place the cornflour in a medium saucepan. Add the vinegar and stir to dissolve the cornflour. Add the pineapple, pineapple juice, ginger, sugar and orange rind. Bring to a boil over medium heat. Cook, stirring constantly, for 1 minute, or until the mixture thickens. Add the beetroot and stir to coat with the sauce. Cook for 1 minute. Serve hot or cold.

Makes **4** servings.

nutrition at a glance

per serving

0.1 g.	total fat
0 g.	saturated fat
55	calories
0 mg.	cholesterol
39 mg.	sodium
1 g.	protein
13.3 g.	carbohydrates
1.1 g.	dietary fibre

Sweet-and-Spicy Carrots

quick and easy

Spicy and slightly sweet, Jamaican jerk seasoning brings carrots alive. Our tasters raved about them.

500	g carrots, sliced
250	ml water
2	tablespoons brown sugar
1	teaspoon hot-pepper sauce
1	teaspoon freshly squeezed lemon juice
1	teaspoon ground cumin
2	cloves garlic, minced
½	teaspoon chilli powder
	Ground black pepper
	Salt (optional)

1 In a medium non-stick saucepan, combine the carrots and water. Bring to a boil over medium-high heat. Cook, stirring occasionally, for 10 minutes, or until the carrots are tender but still firm. Drain the carrots well and transfer to a bowl.

2 Dry the saucepan and coat with non-stick spray. Add the brown sugar, hot-pepper sauce, lemon juice, cumin, garlic and chilli powder. Cook, stirring, for 2 to 3 minutes, or until the sugar bubbles and the spices are fragrant. Add the carrots. Toss or stir to coat the carrots with the sauce. Season to taste with the black pepper and salt (if using).

Makes **4** servings.

Lynn's Kitchen Tip

Store carrots, celery, asparagus and radishes unwashed in resealable plastic bags in the refrigerator. If they get limp, rehydrate them by sprinkling a little water into the bag. Reseal and refrigerate for several hours. Pour out any excess water within 12 hours and then use the vegetables as soon as possible.

nutrition at a glance

per serving

0.4 g.	total fat
0.1 g.	saturated fat
78	calories
0 mg.	cholesterol
76 mg.	sodium
1.4 g.	protein
18.7 g.	carbohydrates
2.8 g.	dietary fibre

Carrots in Soured Cream

quick and easy

These rich-tasting carrots are delicious with barbecued pork tenderloin, turbot or turkey breast.

500	g baby carrots
1	small onion or shallot, chopped
2	tablespoons water
1	tablespoon frozen apple juice concentrate
1	teaspoon Dijon mustard
80	ml fat-free soured cream or fat-free natural yogurt
1	tablespoon chopped fresh parsley

1   Place the carrots in a steamer basket. Steam over boiling water in a covered saucepan for 10 minutes, or until crisp-tender.

2   In a large non-stick frying pan, combine the onions or shallots, water and apple juice concentrate. Cover and bring to a boil over medium-high heat. Reduce the heat to medium and cook for 2 to 3 minutes. Add the carrots and mustard. Toss over medium-high heat for 1 to 2 minutes, if necessary, to evaporate excess liquid.

3   Remove from the heat. Add the soured cream or yogurt and toss to coat. Sprinkle with the parsley.

Makes **4** servings.

nutrition at a glance

per serving

0.8 g.	total fat
0.1 g.	saturated fat
82	calories
0 mg.	cholesterol
87 mg.	sodium
2.5 g.	protein
16.9 g.	carbohydrates
3.9 g.	dietary fibre

Bottled condiments, herbs, spices and fat-free dairy products offer a wealth of effortless enhancements for simply cooked vegetables. For times when you want to up the flavour ante from a spritz of butter-flavoured spray and a squeeze of lemon juice, cash in with these easy seasonings.

Asparagus, Broccoli and Cauliflower

✳ Drizzle with lemon juice or balsamic vinegar. Top with a swirl of fat-free Cheddar topping from a squeeze bottle or a sprinkling of fat-free Parmesan topping.

✳ Sprinkle with toasted herbed breadcrumbs and ground black pepper.

✳ Drizzle with a spoonful of honey mustard.

French Beans

✳ Sprinkle with diced raw sweet red peppers or diced jarred roasted peppers and a few drops of hot-pepper sauce.

✳ Toss with soy sauce or Worcestershire sauce and a smidgen of minced garlic or garlic salt.

✳ Toss with mirin (sweet rice wine), a pinch of brown sugar and crushed chillies.

✳ Toss with chopped fresh savoury, chopped spring onions, diced tomatoes, and lemon juice or lime juice.

Beetroot

✳ Toss with lime juice and chopped fresh coriander.

✳ Mix cider vinegar, sugar and a small amount of cornflour. Toss with the beetroot in a saucepan over low heat to thicken.

✳ Toss with lemon juice, brown sugar, a pinch of ground ginger and a pinch of dry mustard.

✳ Mix orange juice and grated orange rind with a small amount of cornflour. Toss with the beetroot in a saucepan over low heat to thicken.

✳ Drizzle with cider vinegar and add a dollop of fat-free soured cream, yogurt or yogurt cheese. Toss to coat. Sprinkle with chopped fresh dill.

Leafy Greens

✳ Drizzle with cider vinegar, balsamic vinegar or lemon juice and diced fat-free ham.

✳ Toss with a spoonful of salsa and fat-free soured cream.

Carrots

✳ Toss with finely chopped fresh mint and honey.

✳ Drizzle with soy sauce and a sprinkle of ground ginger or chopped pickled ginger.

✳ Sprinkle lightly with brown sugar and a dollop of fat-free yogurt, yogurt cheese or soured cream. Toss to combine.

✳ Toss with toasted breadcrumbs and a pinch of ground cumin.

Green or Sweet Red Peppers

✳ Sprinkle with capers.

✳ Drizzle red-wine vinegar and a sprinkling of fresh basil or dried oregano over roasted peppers.

✳ Sprinkle fat-free Parmesan topping over baked, grilled or roasted pepper strips.

Baked Citrus Carrots

Either chopped flat-leaf parsley or coriander is a tasty addition to these sunny carrots.

500	g carrots, cut into 7.3 cm-long sticks
2	tablespoons chopped fresh chives or spring onions
2	tablespoons freshly squeezed lemon juice
2	tablespoons freshly squeezed orange juice
½	teaspoon grated orange rind
2	tablespoons fresh breadcrumbs (from 40-calorie-per-slice bread), optional

1 Preheat the oven to 180°C, Gas 5.

2 In an 20 x 20 cm baking dish, combine the carrots, chives or spring onions, lemon juice, orange juice and orange rind. Cover with foil and bake for 45 minutes, or until tender.

3 Remove the foil. Sprinkle with the breadcrumbs (if using). Coat with non-stick spray. Grill 10 cm from the heat for 1 to 2 minutes, or until the crumbs are golden.

Makes **4** servings.

nutrition at a glance
per serving
0.2 g.	total fat
0 g.	saturated fat
53	calories
0 mg.	cholesterol
69 mg.	sodium
1.3 g.	protein
12.5 g.	carbohydrates
2.7 g.	dietary fibre

Bayou French Beans

quick and easy

Our testers loved these spicy, bright French beans studded with nubbins of sautéed garlic. I leave the beans whole, but you can cut them in smaller pieces if you like.

1	medium onion, finely chopped
4	cloves garlic, minced
1	teaspoon Cajun spice blend
500	g French beans
2	tablespoons water
	Dash of liquid smoke

1   Coat a large non-stick frying pan with non-stick spray. Add the onions, garlic and Cajun spice blend. Cover and cook over medium-high heat, stirring often, for 3 to 4 minutes, or until the onions are golden.

2   Add the beans, water and liquid smoke. Cover and cook for 6 to 7 minutes, or until the beans are crisp-tender.

Makes **4** servings.

nutrition at a glance

per serving

0.4 g.	total fat
0.1 g.	saturated fat
55	calories
0 mg.	cholesterol
49 mg.	sodium
2.6 g.	protein
12.3 g.	carbohydrates
3.9 g.	dietary fibre

French Beans and Mushrooms

quick and easy

This is a simple dish with gentle flavours. It is just right with comfort foods such as baked or mashed potatoes topped with fat-free gravy. A modest serving of fish, turkey or chicken breast will complete the homey meal.

1 Coat a large non-stick saucepan with non-stick spray. Add the onions and 2 tablespoons of the water. Cook over medium heat, stirring, for 4 minutes, or until the onions are translucent. Add the mushrooms. Cook for 4 minutes, or until the mushrooms are cooked through.

2 Add the stock and bring to a boil. Simmer for 10 minutes to reduce the stock. Add the beans; cover and cook for 5 minutes, or until the beans are crisp-tender.

3 Place the cornflour in a cup. Add the remaining 2 tablespoons water and stir to dissolve the cornflour. Add to the saucepan. Cook, stirring constantly, for 2 to 3 minutes, or until thickened. Season to taste with the pepper and salt (if using).

Makes **4** servings.

nutrition at a glance
per serving

0.6 g.	total fat
0.1 g.	saturated fat
78	calories
0 mg.	cholesterol
15 mg.	sodium
3.4 g.	protein
17.6 g.	carbohydrates
5 g.	dietary fibre

Creamed Pearl Onions

quick and easy

Creamed-onion lovers, take heart. This is the flavourful fat-free recipe that you've been waiting for. If pearl onions are not available, this recipe is also delicious with coarsely chopped onions, shallots or leeks.

500	g pearl onions or 1 package (500 g) frozen pearl onions
250	ml water
2	tablespoons dry sherry or 1 teaspoon sherry extract
3	tablespoons plain flour
500	ml fat-free liquid creamer or evaporated skim milk
¼	teaspoon ground black pepper
	Pinch of ground nutmeg
	Pinch of salt (optional)
1	tablespoon chopped fresh parsley
	Paprika

1   In a medium non-stick saucepan, combine the onions, water and sherry or sherry extract. Cover and bring to a boil over medium-high heat. Reduce the heat to medium and cook for 10 minutes, or until the onions are tender. Drain. If using fresh onions, peel them. Set aside.

2   Wipe the saucepan dry. Add the flour. Gradually whisk in the creamer or evaporated milk to make a smooth mixture. Add the pepper, nutmeg and salt (if using). Cook over medium-high heat, whisking constantly, for 3 minutes, or until the mixture thickens.

3   Add the onions and cook for 1 minute to reheat them. Sprinkle with the parsley and paprika just before serving.

Makes **4** servings.

Photograph on page 243

Lynn's Fat-Free Flavour

If you like to cook with wine occasionally, here are a few tips. Never use cooking wine, which contains unnecessary added salt. Select a wine that you enjoy drinking with dinner and use a little bit in your cooking. You may not know it, but you are the ultimate wine expert. If it tastes good to you, it is the right choice.

nutrition at a glance
per serving

0.3 g.	total fat
0 g.	saturated fat
161	calories
0 mg.	cholesterol
266 mg.	sodium
2.2 g.	protein
32.5 g.	carbohydrates
2 g.	dietary fibre

Dilled Squash with Mushrooms

Baking accents the natural sweetness of this delicate summer squash. Fresh dill is essential for the flavour of this dish.

500	g butternut squash, cut into thin diagonal slices
125	g closed cap mushrooms, sliced
1	large onion, sliced
1	orange or yellow pepper, sliced
4	tablespoons chopped fresh dill
2	tablespoons chopped fresh chives
1	large clove garlic, minced
¼	teaspoon ground black pepper
	Pinch of salt (optional)
45	g fat-free Parmesan topping

1   Preheat the oven to 180°C, Gas 4. Coat a 30 x 20 cm baking dish with non-stick spray.

2   In a large bowl, combine the squash, mushrooms, onions, sliced peppers, dill, chives, garlic, black pepper and salt (if using). Toss to mix. Spread evenly in the prepared dish. Sprinkle with the Parmesan.

3   Cover with foil. Bake for 25 to 30 minutes, or until the squash is tender.

Makes **6** servings.

nutrition at a glance
per serving

0.4 g.	total fat
0.1 g.	saturated fat
61	calories
0 mg.	cholesterol
132 mg.	sodium
5.4 g.	protein
10.8 g.	carbohydrates
1.8 g.	dietary fibre

Sweet-and-Sharp Spaghetti Squash

quick and easy

Here's a simple, savoury way to prepare spaghetti squash. If you like a slightly less tangy mustard flavour, use a combination of fat-free mayonnaise and Dijon mustard.

1	spaghetti squash
90	g diced plum tomatoes
45	g currants or raisins
2	teaspoons Dijon mustard
2	teaspoons dry sherry or ½ teaspoon sherry extract
1	tablespoon water
1	teaspoon white-wine vinegar
1	teaspoon chopped fresh thyme
½	teaspoon sugar

1 Microwave the squash on high power for 2 minutes to make cutting easier. Cut the squash in half lengthwise. Wrap each half in greaseproof paper. Microwave each half on high power for 5 to 5½ minutes. Let stand for 3 minutes. Scoop out and discard the seeds and attached stringy membranes.

2 With a fork, pull out the strands of squash and place in a large non-stick frying pan. Add the tomatoes, currants or raisins, mustard, sherry or sherry extract, water, vinegar, thyme and sugar. Toss to combine.

3 Cook over medium heat, tossing frequently, for 3 to 4 minutes, or until hot.

Makes **4** servings.

Lynn's Fat-Free Flavour

Although the pulp of spaghetti squash resembles the pasta for which it's named, it has a mild flavour that can easily be overpowered by tomato-based sauces. It is best simply spritzed with butter-flavoured spray and a sprinkling of salt and ground black pepper. For a dressier treatment, toss with a simple white sauce (page 294) flavoured with dill.

nutrition at a glance

per serving

0.9 g.	total fat
0.1 g.	saturated fat
98	calories
0 mg.	cholesterol
103 mg.	sodium
2 g.	protein
21.9 g.	carbohydrates
3.9 g.	dietary fibre

Summer Succotash

quick and easy

**Fresh flavours shine through in this traditional American dish.
Diced courgettes can also be added.**

180	ml skimmed chicken stock (page 94)
1	large onion, chopped
1	green pepper, chopped
1	medium potato, diced
1	large clove garlic, minced
315	g fresh broad beans or 1 package (315 g) frozen baby broad beans, thawed
90	g fresh sweetcorn kernels or thawed frozen sweetcorn
1	small tomato, diced
2	tablespoons chopped fresh dill
2	tablespoons chopped fresh parsley
	Ground black pepper
	Salt (optional)

1   Coat a large non-stick saucepan with non-stick spray. Add the stock, onions, peppers, potatoes and garlic. Cook over medium-high heat, stirring occasionally, for 10 minutes.

2   Reduce the heat to medium. Add the beans; cover and cook for 5 minutes. Add the sweetcorn; cover and cook for 5 minutes. Add the tomatoes; cook, stirring, for 5 minutes. Stir in the dill and parsley. Season to taste with the pepper and salt (if using).

Makes **6** servings.

nutrition at a glance

per serving

0.8 g.	total fat
0.1 g.	saturated fat
107	calories
0 mg.	cholesterol
23 mg.	sodium
5 g.	protein
21.5 g.	carbohydrates
4.2 g.	dietary fibre

Oriental Vegetable Stir-Fry

quick and easy

The secret to good stir-fries is to cut all your vegetables before you begin cooking. For this recipe, feel free to vary the vegetables. Try bok choy, cabbage, French beans, asparagus or thinly sliced sweet potatoes. To heat things up, add crushed chillies. Garnish with chopped spring onions or bean sprouts.

1	tablespoon cornflour
125	ml vegetable stock (page 93)
	Dark sesame oil in a spray bottle
2	large carrots, cut into thin diagonal slices
2–3	cloves garlic, minced
2	teaspoons grated fresh ginger
2	teaspoons low-sodium soy sauce
5	spring onions, cut into 2.5 cm diagonal slices
1	can (185 g) sliced water chestnuts or bamboo shoots, drained
2	teaspoons dry sherry or ½ teaspoon sherry extract
185	g mangetout
½	teaspoon sugar
½	teaspoon sesame seeds or crushed chillies (optional)

1   Place the cornflour in a cup. Add half of the stock and stir to dissolve the cornflour. Set aside.

2   Coat a large non-stick frying pan or wok with a spritz of the oil. Add the carrots, garlic, ginger, 1 teaspoon of the soy sauce and 2 tablespoons of the remaining stock. Cook over medium-high heat, stirring, for 2 minutes.

3   Add the spring onions, water chestnuts or bamboo shoots, sherry or sherry extract and the remaining 2 tablespoons stock. Cook, stirring and tossing, for 2 minutes.

4   Add the mangetout, sugar, the remaining 1 teaspoon soy sauce and the cornflour mixture. Cook, tossing, for 1 minute, or until thickened. Spoon onto 4 dinner plates. Sprinkle with the sesame seeds or crushed chillies (if using).

Makes **4** servings.

nutrition at a glance

per serving
0.7 g.	total fat
0.1 g.	saturated fat
72	calories
0 mg.	cholesterol
128 mg.	sodium
2.4 g.	protein
14.7 g.	carbohydrates
3.6 g.	dietary fibre

10 Terrific Toppers for Baked Potatoes

A large potato, baked in its skin, is a good source of potassium and fibre, yet it contains only a trace amount of fat. For an easy satisfying meal, cut open a baked spud and spoon on one of these tasty accompaniments.

✳ Fat-free soured cream or fat-free ricotta mixed with chopped fresh chives, parsley, tarragon, basil or dill, herbes de Provence, Cajun spice blend or ground black pepper

✳ Barbecue sauce, fat-free soured cream and finely chopped spring onions

✳ Julienned fat-free ham and grated fat-free Cheddar cheese. Grill briefly to melt the cheese.

✳ Curried Vegetable-Turkey Sauce (page 289)

✳ Fat-free Chicken Gravy (page 293) or fat-free commercial gravy with fat-free sautéed mushrooms

✳ Salsa (heated in the microwave, if desired), fat-free natural yogurt, and chopped fresh coriander

✳ Lightly steamed sweetcorn kernels, chopped onions, chopped carrots and chopped sweet red peppers mixed in Basic White Sauce (page 294)

✳ Steamed broccoli florets topped with fat-free marinara sauce or fat-free Cheddar topping from a squeeze bottle

✳ Fiesta Chilli (page 186) or canned fat-free chilli

✳ Sauerkraut (rinsed, drained and heated)

Scalloped Potatoes and Fennel

The buttery-rich flavour of yellow-fleshed potatoes is seductive. Look for these wonderful varieties, which include Maris Piper, Catriona and Estima. The gentle flavour of fresh fennel beautifully complements the potatoes.

3	large yellow-fleshed potatoes, very thinly sliced
1	medium leek, white and some green stem, thinly sliced
185	g thinly sliced fennel
4	tablespoons plain flour
	Ground black pepper
	Salt (optional)
300	ml vegetable stock (page 93)
4	tablespoons fat-free Parmesan topping
	Paprika

1 Coat a 25 cm glass pie plate with non-stick spray. Add half of the potatoes in an even layer. Top with half of the leeks and half of the fennel. Sprinkle with 2 tablespoons of the flour and a dusting of pepper and salt (if using). Repeat to use the remaining vegetables, flour, pepper and salt.

2 Pour the stock into the pie plate. Cover tightly with cling film; slit the film twice with a sharp knife. Microwave on high power for a total of 12 to 15 minutes; rotate the pie plate after 6 minutes.

3 Carefully remove the cling film and discard. Sprinkle the top of the mixture with the Parmesan and paprika.

4 Preheat the oven to 220°C, Gas 7.

5 Bake for 30 to 35 minutes, or until the top is browned. Remove and let stand for 5 minutes before cutting into wedges.

Makes **8** servings.

Photograph on page 244

nutrition at a glance

per serving

0.2 g.	total fat
0 g.	saturated fat
115	calories
0 mg.	cholesterol
70 mg.	sodium
4.1 g.	protein
25.1 g.	carbohydrates
2.9 g.	dietary fibre

Potato-Carrot Mash

quick and easy

Dietitian Chris Louden told me of this recipe, which is pure comfort food. Sprinkle with chopped parsley and a whisper of ground nutmeg for a garnish.

4	medium baking potatoes, peeled and diced
500	g diced carrots
1	teaspoon salt (optional)
250	ml fat-free liquid creamer
	Ground black pepper

1 In a medium saucepan, combine the potatoes, carrots and enough cold water to cover them. Add the salt (if using). Bring to a boil over medium-high heat. Reduce the heat to medium and cook at a brisk simmer for 25 minutes, or until the carrots are tender.

2 Drain the potatoes and carrots and return to the saucepan. Mash with a potato masher, leaving some small lumps of carrots visible.

3 In a small saucepan over medium heat, warm the creamer. Add to the vegetables and stir to combine. Season to taste with the pepper.

Makes **4** servings.

nutrition at a glance

per serving

0.9 g.	total fat
0.2 g.	saturated fat
160	calories
0 mg.	cholesterol
134 mg.	sodium
1.9 g.	protein
35.8 g.	carbohydrates
5.6 g.	dietary fibre

Western Fries

Use the best chilli powder for these potatoes because the seasoning is important. I often add wedges of scrubbed unpeeled sweet potatoes and yuca, a root vegetable available in African and Spanish food shops and some large supermarkets.

3	very large baking potatoes
¼	teaspoon sugar
	Salt (optional)
2–3	teaspoons chilli powder
1	teaspoon Cajun spice blend (optional)

1 Preheat the oven to 200°C, Gas 6. Cover a large baking tray with foil.

2 Slice the potatoes lengthwise into eighths. Pat dry with paper towels. Place on the baking tray. Coat all sides of the potatoes with non-stick spray. Sprinkle evenly with the sugar and a little salt (if using). Sprinkle with the chilli powder and Cajun spice blend (if using). Use your fingers to coat the potatoes evenly.

3 Place the potatoes in the oven. Lower the heat to 180°C, Gas 4 and bake for 30 to 40 minutes, or until the potatoes are crisp on the outside and tender when pierced with a sharp knife.

Makes **4** servings.

Photograph on page 247

Photograph on page 247

Lynn's Kitchen Tip

Slicing potatoes into wedges is safe and easy when you keep your potato steady and your knife pointed toward the cutting board. Here's how: Place the potato, flattest side down, on a cutting board. With your non-cutting hand, hold the potato steady with your fingertips tucked toward the palm of your hand. Cut the potato in half lengthwise. Position both halves, cut side down; cut each in half lengthwise. You now have quarters. Position each quarter, skin side down, and cut in half to make 2 wedges. You will have 8 long wedges from each potato.

nutrition at a glance

per serving
- 0.5 g. total fat
- 0.1 g. saturated fat
- 208 calories
- 0 mg. cholesterol
- 34 mg. sodium
- 4.5 g. protein
- 47.7 g. carbohydrates
- 5 g. dietary fibre

Sweet-and-Sour Red Cabbage

quick and easy

This dish keeps well and is especially good after the sauce has permeated the cabbage. In cold weather, it's nice to have some on hand in the refrigerator to reheat as a topper for baked or boiled potatoes.

½	medium head red cabbage, thinly sliced
2	tart apples, chopped or shredded
1	small onion, chopped
4	tablespoons brown sugar
2	tablespoons cider vinegar
2	tablespoons freshly squeezed lemon juice
½	teaspoon grated lemon rind (optional)
	Pinch of salt (optional)
1	tablespoon cornflour
2	tablespoons water

1 In a large non-stick saucepan, combine the cabbage, apples, onions, brown sugar, vinegar, lemon juice, lemon rind (if using) and salt (if using). Cover and cook over low heat, stirring occasionally, for 15 minutes, or until the cabbage is tender.

2 Place the cornflour in a cup. Add the water and stir to dissolve the cornflour. Stir into the saucepan.

3 Increase the heat to medium. Cook, stirring constantly, for 2 minutes, or until thickened.

Makes **6** servings.

nutrition at a glance
per serving

0.3 g.	total fat
0.1 g.	saturated fat
88	calories
0 mg.	cholesterol
10 mg.	sodium
1 g.	protein
22.3 g.	carbohydrates
3 g.	dietary fibre

Creamed Kale

Creamed spinach has been an American favourite for decades. I've updated it with super-nutritious curly-leafed kale. (Of course, you can also make this dish with spinach, if you prefer.) Serve it as a side dish, a stuffing for baked potatoes or tomatoes or as a bed for poached fish. It can even be chilled and puréed for a dip.

2	small cloves garlic, minced
2	tablespoons plain flour
375	ml skimmed milk
6	tablespoons fat-free soured cream
2	tablespoons low-fat soured cream
4	tablespoons fat-free Parmesan topping
	Dash of ground nutmeg
	Salt (optional)
250	ml water
625	g kale, stems removed, coarsely chopped
	Ground black pepper

1 Place the garlic in a large non-stick frying pan. Coat with non-stick spray. Sauté over medium heat, stirring occasionally, for 1 to 2 minutes, or until the garlic is golden. Add the flour. Slowly whisk in the milk to form a smooth mixture.

2 Cook over medium heat, stirring constantly, for 4 minutes, or until thickened. Stir in the fat-free soured cream, low-fat soured cream, Parmesan and nutmeg. Season to taste with the salt (if using). Turn off the heat.

3 Meanwhile, place the water in a large non-stick pan. Bring to a boil over high heat. Add the kale. Cover and cook over medium-high heat for 7 to 9 minutes, or until the kale is crisp-tender. Drain and add to the cream sauce. Stir to combine. Cook over low heat for 1 to 2 minutes to reheat the sauce. Season to taste with the pepper.

Makes **4** servings.

nutrition at a glance

per serving

0.9 g.	total fat
0.4 g.	saturated fat
100	calories
3 mg.	cholesterol
136 mg.	sodium
7.4 g.	protein
16.2 g.	carbohydrates
2.1 g.	dietary fibre

Greek-Style Cauliflower

quick and easy

Tender cauliflower takes to this zesty tomato sauce sparked with cinnamon, a signature spice in Greek cuisine. Garnish with some crumbled low-fat feta cheese if you like.

½	large onion, chopped
2	cloves garlic, minced
1	teaspoon dried oregano
½	teaspoon crushed fennel seeds
¼	teaspoon ground cinnamon
1	medium head cauliflower, broken into florets
125	ml tomato sauce
1	tablespoon freshly squeezed lemon juice
	Ground black pepper
	Salt (optional)
¼	teaspoon crushed chillies (optional)

1 Coat a large non-stick frying pan with non-stick spray. Add the onions, garlic, oregano, fennel seeds and cinnamon. Cover and cook over medium-high heat for 3 to 4 minutes, or until the onions are golden. If necessary, add 1 to 2 teaspoons water to prevent sticking.

2 Add the cauliflower, tomato sauce and lemon juice. Season with the black pepper and salt (if using). Bring the mixture to a boil. Cover and reduce the heat to medium. Cook for 8 minutes, or until the cauliflower is tender. Sprinkle with the crushed chillies (if using).

Makes **4** servings.

nutrition at a glance
per serving
- 0.6 g. total fat
- 0.2 g. saturated fat
- 39 calories
- 1 mg. cholesterol
- 212 mg. sodium
- 2.2 g. protein
- 7.7 g. carbohydrates
- 2 g. dietary fibre

Cauliflower Purée with Garlic

quick and easy

If you keep puréed Roasted Garlic (page 304) on hand in the refrigerator or freezer, you can make this earthy cauliflower dish in minutes. For a variation, pour the purée into a baking dish, dust with fat-free Parmesan topping, and grill until the topping is golden.

375 ml vegetable stock (page 93)
1 medium head cauliflower, broken into florets
90 g chopped onions
2 tablespoons puréed Roasted Garlic (page 304)
  Ground black pepper
  Salt (optional)
1 tablespoon thinly sliced fresh basil

1 In a large non-stick saucepan over medium-high heat, bring the stock to a boil. Add the cauliflower and onions. Reduce the heat to medium, cover and simmer for 20 minutes, or until the vegetables are very tender. Drain in a colander (if desired, save the stock for soup or other uses).

2 Place the vegetables in a blender or food processor. Add the garlic. Season with the pepper and salt (if using). Purée until smooth. Stir in the basil. If desired, return to the saucepan to reheat gently for 2 to 3 minutes.

Makes **4** servings.

nutrition at a glance
per serving
0.8 g. total fat
0.1 g. saturated fat
59 calories
0 mg. cholesterol
27 mg. sodium
3.7 g. protein
11.6 g. carbohydrates
3.2 g. dietary fibre

Hungarian Broccoli and Mushrooms

quick and easy

The broccoli is cooked al dente, making the colour a glorious bright green. If you prefer it more tender, simply cook it a little longer.

500	g broccoli
250	g closed cap mushrooms, sliced
60	g finely chopped shallots
1½	tablespoons plain flour
1	teaspoon paprika
375	ml vegetable stock (page 93)
	Ground black pepper
	Ground cayenne pepper
	Salt (optional)

1 Cut the florets from the broccoli stems. Peel the stems, then cut into 6 cm - thick rounds.

2 In a large non-stick saucepan over high heat, bring 250 ml water to a boil. Add the broccoli stems; cover and cook for 2 minutes. Add the florets. Cover and cook for 3 to 4 minutes, or until crisp-tender. Drain and set aside.

3 Dry the saucepan. Coat it with non-stick spray. Add the mushrooms and shallots. Cover and cook over medium-high heat for 3 to 4 minutes, or until the mushrooms release some liquid. Uncover and reduce the heat to medium. Cook, stirring, for 2 to 3 minutes, or until the mushrooms are lightly browned. Remove the mixture from the pan. Set aside.

4 Off heat, place the flour and paprika in the saucepan. Gradually whisk in 60 ml of the stock to form a smooth paste. Whisk in the remaining stock. Cook over medium-high heat, whisking constantly, for 3 to 4 minutes, or until thick.

5 Add the mushroom mixture and the reserved broccoli; cook for 2 minutes, or until heated through. Season to taste with the black pepper, cayenne pepper and salt (if using).

Makes **4** servings.

nutrition at a glance

per serving

0.7 g.	total fat
0.1 g.	saturated fat
70	calories
0 mg.	cholesterol
41 mg.	sodium
5.2 g.	protein
14 g.	carbohydrates
5 g.	dietary fibre

Sicilian Broccoli

quick **quick and easy**

Sweet raisins play beautifully off the sharp, earthy flavour of broccoli. This is an attractive dish to serve, and it's simple to make. It even tastes great the next day as a salad.

500	g broccoli
2	plum tomatoes, chopped
4	cloves garlic, minced
2	tablespoons raisins
2	tablespoons thinly sliced fresh basil
	Salt (optional)
2	tablespoons chopped toasted pine nuts (optional)

1 Cut the florets from the broccoli stems. Peel the stems, then cut into 6 mm-thick rounds.

2 Bring 250 ml water to a boil in a large non-stick saucepan over high heat. Add the broccoli stems; cover and cook for 2 minutes. Add the florets. Cover and cook for 3 to 4 minutes, or until crisp-tender. Drain and set aside.

3 In the same saucepan, combine the tomatoes, garlic and raisins. Cook over medium heat, stirring frequently, for 4 to 5 minutes, or until the tomatoes soften. Add the basil and the broccoli. Cook, stirring, for 1 to 2 minutes, or until the broccoli is heated through. Season to taste with the salt (if using). Sprinkle with the pine nuts (if using).

Makes **4** servings.

Photograph on page 248

Lynn's Kitchen Tip

Cooking broccoli can be problematic, because the tender florets often overcook before the stem is tender. But both parts can cook in almost the same time with this method: Cut off the florets where they join the stem; separate them into equal-size florets. Slice the stem into 6 mm-thick rounds. Cook the stem pieces by blanching, stir-frying, or steaming for 2 minutes. Add the florets and continue cooking for 3 to 4 minutes, or until the stems are crisp-tender.

---

nutrition at a glance

per serving

0.5 g.	total fat
0.1 g.	saturated fat
55	calories
0 mg.	cholesterol
32 mg.	sodium
3.8 g.	protein
11.5 g.	carbohydrates
3.8 g.	dietary fibre

Mediterranean Vegetables

quick and easy

This lemony Mediterranean mélange is particularly good with grilled fish. Serve it topped with fat-free natural yogurt.

1	onion, chopped
2	large cloves garlic, minced
1	teaspoon ground cumin
1	teaspoon dried oregano
1	small plum tomato, diced
90	g cooked chickpeas
250	g spinach leaves, thinly sliced
30	g diced jarred roasted red peppers or pimientos
2	tablespoons freshly squeezed lemon juice
	Salt (optional)
	Crushed chillies (optional)

1 In a large non-stick saucepan, combine the onions, garlic, cumin and oregano. Cover and cook over medium-low heat, stirring occasionally, for 5 minutes, or until the onions are golden. If necessary, add 1 to 2 teaspoons water to prevent sticking.

2 Stir in the tomatoes and chickpeas. Cook for 2 to 3 minutes, or until the tomatoes soften.

3 Add the spinach, roasted peppers or pimientos and lemon juice. Cook over medium-high heat, stirring constantly, for 1 minute, or until the spinach wilts and excess moisture evaporates. Season to taste with the salt (if using) and crushed chillies (if using.)

Makes **4** servings.

nutrition at a glance

per serving

0.9 g.	total fat
0.1 g.	saturated fat
68	calories
0 mg.	cholesterol
92 mg.	sodium
4 g.	protein
12.8 g.	carbohydrates
2.9 g.	dietary fibre

Orange-Kissed Turnip Custards

It's fun to give the lowly turnip the Cinderella treatment with these elegant individual baked custards. They make a special side dish for celebration or Christmas dinner.

1	can (185 g) mandarin oranges
375	ml vegetable stock (page 93)
1	teaspoon low-sodium soy sauce
1	teaspoon brown sugar
¼	teaspoon minced fresh ginger
250	g sliced turnips
180	ml fat-free egg substitute
125	ml evaporated skim milk
	Ground black pepper

1 Coat four 180-ml ovenproof custard cups with non-stick spray.

2 Drain the oranges, reserving 125 ml of the juice. Place the juice in a medium non-stick saucepan. Set the oranges aside.

3 To the saucepan with the juice, add the stock, soy sauce, brown sugar and ginger. Bring to a boil over medium-high heat. Add the turnips. Cover, reduce the heat to medium and simmer for 15 minutes, or until tender. Drain well.

4 Preheat the oven to 180°C, Gas 4.

5 Place the turnip mixture in a blender or food processor. Purée until smooth. Add the egg substitute and milk. Process just to combine. Season to taste with the pepper.

6 Spoon into the prepared custard cups, tapping each one lightly. Smooth the tops and place in an 20 x 20 cm baking dish. Add hot water so that it comes halfway up the sides of the custard cups. Bake for 20 minutes, or until a knife inserted in the centre comes out clean.

7 Carefully remove the baking dish from the oven. Gently remove the cups from the water. Garnish with the reserved oranges.

Makes **4** servings.

Photograph on page 245

nutrition at a glance

per serving

0.1 g.	total fat
0.1 g.	saturated fat
85	calories
1 mg.	cholesterol
220 mg.	sodium
8 g.	protein
14 g.	carbohydrates
1.6 g.	dietary fibre

Sweet Potato Pudding

This luscious Louisiana pudding is hard to resist. I like to make it with dark-fleshed garnet sweet potatoes whenever I find them in the market. You can omit the ginger, but it does give the pudding a special flavour boost.

2	medium sweet potatoes
250	ml fat-free liquid creamer
4	tablespoons fat-free egg substitute
2	tablespoons brown sugar
1	tablespoon minced crystallised ginger (optional)
1	teaspoon grated lemon rind
1	teaspoon ground cinnamon
¼	teaspoon ground nutmeg
¼	teaspoon ground black pepper
	Pinch of ground allspice
	Pinch of salt (optional)
2	egg whites

1 Preheat the oven to 180°C, Gas 4. Coat a 1-litre baking dish with non-stick spray.

2 Pierce the sweet potatoes several times with a fork. Microwave on high power, rotating once, for 7 to 10 minutes, or until soft. (The sweet potatoes can also be baked directly on the oven rack at 200°C, Gas 6 for 1 hour, or until soft.) Set aside to cool slightly.

3 Peel the sweet potatoes and press through a ricer or fine sieve into a medium bowl. Add the creamer, egg substitute, brown sugar, ginger (if using), lemon rind, cinnamon, nutmeg, pepper, allspice and salt (if using). Stir to combine.

4 Place the egg whites in a medium bowl. Beat with an electric mixer until stiff peaks form. Fold into the sweet potato mixture.

5 Pour into the prepared baking dish. Cover with foil and bake for 45 minutes. Remove the foil and bake for 15 minutes, or until a knife inserted in the centre comes out clean. Serve hot or cold.

Makes **4** servings.

Lynn's Fat-Free Flavour

Crystallised ginger is fresh ginger that has been poached in sugar syrup and coated in coarse sugar. The process tames ginger's heat, making it a wonderful addition to both savoury and sweet dishes. It's expensive in supermarkets but can often be purchased much cheaper in bulk-food stores. Store tightly sealed in a cool, dry place. It keeps well for months.

---

nutrition at a glance

per serving

0.1 g.	total fat
0 g.	saturated fat
143	calories
0 mg.	cholesterol
61 mg.	sodium
4.3 g.	protein
29.6 g.	carbohydrates
2.1 g.	dietary fibre

Twice-Baked Sweet Potatoes

These sweet potatoes are rich and filling. Because the sweet potato skin is delicate, be sure to leave 6 mm layer of flesh next to the skin when scooping out the flesh. Garnish with a dusting of nutmeg.

3	medium sweet potatoes
60	g drained canned apricots, peaches or pears
½	teaspoon grated orange rind
⅛	teaspoon ground cinnamon
2	tablespoons brown sugar
	Salt (optional)
12	miniature marshmallows (optional)

1   Preheat the oven to 200°C, Gas 6.

2   Pierce the sweet potatoes several times with a fork. Place on a baking tray and bake for 1 hour, or until tender. Allow to cool for several minutes.

3   Cut each sweet potato in half lengthwise. Carefully scoop out most of the flesh from 4 of the halves, leaving 6 mm shell. Place the shells on the baking tray and set aside. Scoop the flesh completely from the remaining 2 halves; discard the skins.

4   Place the flesh in a medium bowl. Add the apricots, peaches or pears. Mash the mixture. Add the orange rind, cinnamon and 1 tablespoon of the brown sugar. Season to taste with the salt (if using). Stir or mash to combine.

5   Spoon the filling into the reserved shells, mounding it above the tops of the shells. Sprinkle with the remaining 1 tablespoon brown sugar. Dot with the marshmallows (if using).

6   Bake for 2 to 3 minutes, or until the filling is hot.

Makes **4** servings.

nutrition at a glance

per serving

0.1 g.	total fat
0 g.	saturated fat
128	calories
0 mg.	cholesterol
12 mg.	sodium
1.6 g.	protein
31.2 g.	carbohydrates
2.7 g.	dietary fibre

Brussels Sprouts with Apples

quick and easy

I like my Brussels sprouts bright and a bit crunchy. In this recipe, sweet apple juice balances the bite of the miniature cabbages. The sprouts are quartered to both speed cooking and enable them to absorb more apple flavour. The toasted walnuts are a wonderful complement and will add only about 1 gramme of fat per serving.

125	ml apple juice
½	teaspoon dried rosemary, crushed
500	g Brussels sprouts, cut into quarters
2	small tart apples, cut into quarters and sliced
1	teaspoon cornflour
1	tablespoon water
	Ground black pepper
	Salt (optional)
1	tablespoon finely chopped toasted walnuts (optional)

1   In a large non-stick frying pan, combine the apple juice and rosemary. Bring to a boil over medium-high heat. Add the Brussels sprouts. Cover, reduce the heat to medium and cook for 6 minutes. Add the apples.

2   Place the cornflour in a cup. Add the water and stir to dissolve the cornflour. Add to the frying pan. Cook, stirring gently but constantly, for 3 minutes, or until a glaze forms. Season to taste with the pepper and salt (if using). Stir in the walnuts (if using).

Makes **4** servings.

nutrition at a glance

per serving

0.9 g.	total fat
0.2 g.	saturated fat
97	calories
0 mg.	cholesterol
27 mg.	sodium
3.3 g.	protein
23 g.	carbohydrates
6.8 g.	dietary fibre

Oven-Glazed Swedes

Roasting really brings out the natural sweetness in swedes as well as other root vegetables. Try this technique with turnips, carrots or sweet potatoes.

4	swedes, ends trimmed
1	medium onion, coarsely chopped
¼	teaspoon ground black pepper
	Pinch of salt (optional)
1½	tablespoons brown sugar
1	small clove garlic, minced

1   Preheat the oven to 190°C, Gas 5.

2   Microwave the swedes on high power for 4 minutes, turning the swedes once, to make peeling easier. Allow to stand until cool enough to handle. Peel and cut into 2.5 cm cubes.

3   Coat a non-stick baking tray with non-stick spray. Place the swedes and onions on the tray. Mist with non-stick spray. Sprinkle with the pepper and salt (if using). Toss to coat. Spread in an even layer.

4   Bake for 35 minutes, stirring twice during baking time. Sprinkle evenly with the brown sugar and garlic. Bake for 10 minutes, or until the vegetables are tender and golden.

Makes **4** servings.

nutrition at a glance
per serving
0.3 g.	total fat
0.1 g.	saturated fat
72	calories
0 mg.	cholesterol
24 mg.	sodium
1.7 g.	protein
16.9 g.	carbohydrates
2.2 g.	dietary fibre

Roast Vegetables for Fabulous Flavour

Roasting brings out the sweet side of many vegetables. Good candidates include celery, fennel, leeks, onions, carrots, potatoes, courgettes, tomatoes, peppers, winter squash, cauliflower, broccoli, aubergine, broccoflower, turnips, kohlrabi, beetroot and sweet potatoes.

Some combinations are naturals. One of my favourites is onions, potatoes and carrots coated lightly with non-stick spray and a sprinkling of crushed fennel seeds or ground cumin.

To roast vegetables, cut them in like-size pieces (no smaller than 2.5 cm cubes) and place in a foil-lined baking dish. Lightly coat with non-stick spray. Season with ground spices, finely chopped herbs, minced garlic or salt. Toss and bake at 190°C, Gas 5, stirring occasionally, for 45 minutes to 1 hour, or until the vegetables are tender and browned. If the vegetables start to brown too quickly, cover them loosely with foil and continue baking until tender.

Roasted vegetables are tasty as side dishes or as a main course accompanied by a grain pilaf. You can also purée them in a blender or food processor to use as a base for sauces and soups.

Acorn Squash with Cranberries

quick and easy

A mulled cider mix makes a super seasoning for sweet acorn squash. This presentation is particularly attractive for an American Thanksgiving feast. Choose dark green acorn squash with a touch of orange or use one of the new golden acorn squash. You can also substitute small halved butternut squash.

2	acorn squash
125-180	ml apple juice, heated
45	g dried cranberries
2	tablespoons brown sugar
½	teaspoon ground cinnamon
	Dash of ground allspice

1   Pierce each squash several times with a fork. Place side by side in a microwave. Microwave on high power for 10 minutes. Turn the squashes over and microwave for 8 to 10 minutes, or until a sharp knife can pierce the flesh. Let stand for 5 minutes.

2   Cut each squash in half lengthwise. Scoop out and discard the seeds. Place the squash, cut side up, on a baking tray. Fill the cavities with the juice and the cranberries.

3   In a small bowl, mix the brown sugar, cinnamon and allspice. Sprinkle evenly over the squash. Grill 10 cm from the heat for 1 to 2 minutes, or until the sugar melts.

Makes **4** servings.

Photograph on page 246

nutrition at a glance

per serving

0.3 g.	total fat
0.1 g.	saturated fat
160	calories
0 mg.	cholesterol
10 mg.	sodium
1.8 g.	protein
41 g.	carbohydrates
7.7 g.	dietary fibre

Parsnips with Pearl Onions

quick and easy

Pearl onions, tomatoes, olives and thyme liven up mild parsnips.

250	ml vegetable stock (page 93)
375	g parsnips, cut into 1 cm pieces
125	g frozen pearl onions, thawed
2	plum tomatoes, diced
½	teaspoon dried thyme
1	teaspoon chopped stoned green olives or tiny capers
	Ground black pepper
	Salt (optional)

1 In a large non-stick frying pan over high heat, bring the stock to a boil. Add the parsnips; cover and cook for 4 to 5 minutes. Add the onions; cover and cook for 4 to 5 minutes.

2 Reduce the heat to medium-high. Add the tomatoes and thyme. Cook, stirring, until most of the liquid is absorbed. Add the olives or capers. Season to taste with the pepper and salt (if using).

Makes **4** servings.

nutrition at a glance
per serving

0.5 g.	total fat
0.1 g.	saturated fat
96	calories
0 mg.	cholesterol
35 mg.	sodium
1.9 g.	protein
22.7 g.	carbohydrates
4.5 g.	dietary fibre

Vegetable Stew with Beef (page 172)

Beef and Mushroom Fajitas (page 171)

Peking Turkey and Vegetables (page 166)

Turkey-Broccoli Divan (page 167)

Creamed Pearl Onions (page 215)

Scalloped Potatoes and Fennel (page 220)

Orange-Kissed Turnip Custards (page 231)

Acorn Squash with Cranberries (page 237)

Western Fries (page 223)

Sicilian Broccoli (page 229)

Herbed Bulgur Pilaf (page 282)

Mediterranean Beans (page 262)

Tubetti with Tomato and Ham (page 269)

Orzo with Asparagus (page 271)

Broccoli Alfredo Sauce (page 287) with fettuccine

Nectarine Salsa (page 303) on chicken

Beans, Pasta, Rice and Grains

Going with the grains is great advice for anyone
concerned with healthful eating. The Department of
Health's Food Guide Pyramid of healthy eating guidelines rests solidly on a base of grains – and with
good reason.

Grains, rice and pasta provide complex carbohydrates, which are an important source of energy in
any healthful eating plan. They also contain fibre,
vitamins and minerals. The Food Guide Pyramid

suggests 6 to 11 servings of these foods each day.

Explore Grains

If your grain vocabulary extends no further than wholewheat bread and oatmeal, it's time to get acquainted with the wonderful universe of grain products right on your supermarket shelves. Rice, cornmeal, bulgur, quinoa, millet, wild rice and barley are all waiting for you.

For a chart on cooking the grains featured in this chapter, see "Grains: A Cook's Guide" on page 281. Most of them can be cooked in double batches and the extras frozen to microwave for instant side dishes.

When you're really in a hurry, turn to couscous – tiny grains of precooked semolina – which rehydrates in hot water or stock in about 5 minutes. wholewheat couscous is sold in health food shops.

Benefit from Beans

Dry legumes mesh so well with grains because they, too, are integral to healthy low-fat eating. Dry beans, lentils and peas are excellent sources of fibre, vitamins and minerals. Among the many choices are navy, kidney, pinto, cannellini, lima and black beans; chickpeas, green and yellow split peas; and lentils in shades of green, red and brown.

Like red meat, beans are loaded with protein. But unlike red meat, beans are light on fat, particularly saturated fat. Compare 280 g cooked black beans with 90 g grilled beef sirloin. The beans contain 23 grammes of protein, 1 gramme of total fat and 0.4 gramme of saturated fat. By contrast, the beef contains 25 grammes of protein but also 10 grammes of total fat and 4 grammes of saturated fat.

For convenience, you can cook dry beans in a big batch, then freeze them in recipe-ready portions (see page 259). Cook beans in plain water or skimmed stock with no seasonings. That way, you'll be able to adapt them to the seasonings in any recipe.

For real speed, start with canned beans. They're as nutritious as dry beans cooked from scratch, but they cost a bit more. They also contain more sodium, so be sure to rinse them with cold water and drain before adding to a recipe.

The more you eat beans, grains and other high-fibre foods, the better your body will feel.

Curried Lentils with Fruit

These mildly spiced lentils, tossed with tart apples and sweet dried fruit, are a nice change from typical heavy lentil dishes. If you prefer a less sweet dish, reduce the dried fruit to 2 tablespoons.

500	ml vegetable stock (page 93)
185	g dry green lentils
2	stalks celery with leafy tops, diced
½	teaspoon curry powder
1	tart apple, diced
4	tablespoons dried currants or diced dried apricots
2	teaspoons grated fresh ginger
	Salt (optional)

1 In a medium non-stick saucepan, combine the stock, lentils, celery and curry powder. Bring to a boil over medium-high heat. Reduce the heat to medium-low, cover, and cook for 30 minutes, or until the lentils are soft but not mushy.

2 Add the apples, currants or apricots and ginger. Cover and cook for 5 minutes. Season to taste with the salt (if using).

Makes **4** servings.

nutrition at a glance

per serving
0.7 g.	total fat
0.1 g.	saturated fat
201	calories
0 mg.	cholesterol
28 mg.	sodium
12.2 g.	protein
39.2 g.	carbohydrates
7.5 g.	dietary fibre

Boston Baked Beans

This classic sweet-and-smoky American bean dish is perfect for a picnic or any other informal gathering. You may use canned beans or cook dry navy beans from scratch (start with about 470 g).

940	g cooked navy beans
1	medium onion, coarsely chopped
1	stalk celery with leafy tops, coarsely chopped
125	ml dark molasses
125	g dark brown sugar
2	teaspoons dry mustard
1	teaspoon liquid smoke
1	bay leaf
	Salt (optional)

1 Preheat the oven to 180°C, Gas 4.

2 In a 2-litre baking dish, combine the beans, onions, celery, molasses, brown sugar, mustard, liquid smoke and bay leaf. Cover and bake for 1½ hours. Season to taste with the salt (if using.) Remove and discard the bay leaf before serving.

Makes **8** servings.

nutrition at a glance

per serving
0.9 g.	total fat
0.2 g.	saturated fat
278	calories
0 mg.	cholesterol
19 mg.	sodium
10.3 g.	protein
59.1 g.	carbohydrates
10.4 g.	dietary fibre

Cooking dry beans isn't difficult. It's an easy kitchen project that takes little actual work on a stay-at-home day. Cook up 500 g or 1 kg of beans at a time as the basis for many fabulous fat-free dishes. Simply freeze the cooked beans in recipe-ready portions, so you have them ready for quick meals.

Cooking times for dry beans vary depending on the variety, the size, and the age of the beans. Generally, soaked dry beans take from 1½ to 3 hours to cook. For best results, follow the cooking directions on the package.

Lentils and dry split peas cook more quickly than other beans. And they do not need soaking before cooking. Dry beans, however, benefit from soaking. Soaking softens the tough skin and starts the rehydration process. Additionally, it helps decrease the flatulence-producing compounds in the beans. You can cook beans without soaking them first, but they'll take longer.

Before cooking beans, pick out and discard any stones, broken beans or other debris. Wash the beans well with cold water. Place in a large bowl and cover generously with cold water. Let stand for at least 3 hours – or overnight. (Alternatively, for a quicker method, place the beans in a large pan and cover generously with cold water. Bring to a boil over high heat. Remove from the heat, cover and allow to stand for 1 hour.) Discard the soaking water and rinse the beans. Cook according to the package directions or recipe instructions.

Mexican Beans

quick and easy

If you want to cook your own beans, be sure to make extra for other uses. Start with 500 g dry beans; soak and cook as usual. Refrigerate or freeze the extras for other side dishes, soups, or salads.

1	large red onion, coarsely chopped
2	cloves garlic, minced
1	teaspoon chilli powder
1	teaspoon ground cumin
560	g canned navy beans, rinsed and drained
125	ml water or skimmed chicken stock (page 94)
1	plum tomato, finely diced
125	g chopped spring onions
1	tablespoon chopped fresh coriander
	Hot-pepper sauce (optional)

1   Coat a large non-stick saucepan with non-stick spray. Add the onions; mist with non-stick spray. Cover and cook over medium-high heat for 2 minutes, or until the onions start to release moisture. Uncover and cook, stirring occasionally, for 2 to 3 minutes, or until browned. If necessary, add 1 to 2 teaspoons water to prevent sticking.

2   Add the garlic, chilli powder and cumin. Cook, stirring, for 2 minutes.

3   Add the beans and water or stock. Stir to mix well. Cover and simmer for 10 minutes. Add the tomatoes, spring onions and coriander. Stir to combine. Season with the hot-pepper sauce (if using).

Makes **6** servings.

nutrition at a glance

per serving

0.7 g.	total fat
0.1 g.	saturated fat
130	calories
0 mg.	cholesterol
9 mg.	sodium
8.3 g.	protein
23.8 g.	carbohydrates
8.3 g.	dietary fibre

Puerto Rican Black Beans

This traditional Caribbean bean dish is usually served with rice, a sprinkling of chopped raw onions, hot-pepper sauce and a squirt of fresh lime juice.

185	g dry black beans
1	Spanish onion, chopped
1	carrot, grated
1	stalk celery with leafy top, finely chopped
1	tomato, chopped
3	cloves garlic, minced
1	teaspoon ground cumin
½	teaspoon dried basil
¼	teaspoon dried thyme
¼–½	teaspoon finely chopped jalapeño peppers (wear rubber gloves when handling)
1	bay leaf
750	ml water
	Salt (optional)

1   Place the beans in a large non-stick pan and cover generously with cold water. Bring to a boil over medium-high heat. Remove from the heat, cover and allow to stand for 1 hour. Drain; discard the soaking water and rinse the beans. Return to the pan.

2   Add the onions, carrots, celery, tomatoes, garlic, cumin, basil, thyme, peppers, bay leaf and water. Bring to a boil over medium-high heat.

3   Reduce the heat to medium-low, cover and simmer for 1½ to 2 hours, or until the beans are tender. Remove and discard the bay leaf.

4   Transfer half of the mixture to a blender and purée. Return the mixture to the pan. (The beans can also be partially puréed in the pan with a hand blender.) Season to taste with the salt (if using).

Makes **4** servings.

nutrition at a glance

per serving

0.9 g.	total fat
0.2 g.	saturated fat
190	calories
0 mg.	cholesterol
29 mg.	sodium
11.6 g.	protein
35.2 g.	carbohydrates
11.7 g.	dietary fibre

Mediterranean Beans

quick and easy

These robust legumes are a great match for a big cos lettuce salad, a small serving of grilled swordfish and crusty bread.

1	medium onion, coarsely chopped
1½	tablespoons finely diced fat-free smoked ham
1	carrot, sliced
1	stalk celery, sliced
2	cloves garlic, minced
1	can (470 g) cannellini, rinsed and drained
125	ml skimmed chicken stock (page 94)
2	tablespoons thinly sliced fresh basil
1	teaspoon dried oregano
10	cherry tomatoes, cut into quarters
4	tablespoons Marsala wine (optional)
	Ground black pepper
	Salt (optional)

1 Coat a large non-stick saucepan with non-stick spray. Add the onions and ham; mist with non-stick spray. Cover and cook over medium-high heat for 2 to 3 minutes, or until the onions start to release moisture. Uncover and cook, stirring occasionally, for 2 to 3 minutes, or until the onions are browned. If necessary, add 1 to 2 teaspoons water to prevent sticking.

2 Add the carrots, celery and garlic. Cook, stirring occasionally, for 7 minutes. Add the beans, stock, basil and oregano. Bring to a boil. Reduce the heat to medium-low and cook, stirring occasionally, for 8 to 10 minutes, or until the liquid is almost evaporated.

3 Add the tomatoes and wine (if using). Bring to a boil over medium heat. Cook for 2 minutes. Season to taste with the pepper and salt (if using).

Makes **4** servings.

Photograph on page 250

nutrition at a glance
per serving

0.6 g.	total fat
0 g.	saturated fat
96	calories
1 mg.	cholesterol
229 mg.	sodium
4.7 g.	protein
18.5 g.	carbohydrates
4.5 g.	dietary fibre

French White Beans

quick and easy

**Use cannellini or navy beans for this easy side dish that's dotted
with sweet roasted peppers. Leftovers are excellent served at
room temperature, sprinkled with lemon juice or balsamic
vinegar.**

1	large leek, white and some green stem, thinly sliced
155	g thinly sliced fennel
125	ml water
1	can (470 g) white beans, rinsed and drained
155	g fresh or thawed frozen peas
315	g diced jarred roasted sweet red peppers
½	teaspoon vinegar
¼	teaspoon chopped fresh thyme
	Ground black pepper

1 In a large non-stick skillet,
combine the leeks, fennel and water. Cover and cook
over medium heat for 5 minutes, or until the fennel is
crisp-tender. Drain and return the vegetables to the
frying pan.

2 Add the beans, peas, red
peppers, vinegar and thyme. Cook for 4 to 5 minutes,
or until hot. Season to taste with the black pepper.

Makes **4** servings.

**Lynn's
Fat-Free
Flavour**

When red and
yellow peppers are
abundant and cheap
in the late summer,
it's smart to roast a
number of them on
the barbecue over
hot charcoal.
Blacken them on all
sides, then place in
a large plastic bag
to steam for 10
minutes. When cool
enough to handle,
peel off the black-
ened skin and
discard. Discard the
stems and seeds.
Dice or cut into
strips. Roasted
peppers can be
refrigerated for a
week or frozen for
several months.

nutrition at a glance

per serving

0.5 g.	total fat
0.1 g.	saturated fat
175	calories
0 mg.	cholesterol
238 mg.	sodium
10.6 g.	protein
33.8 g.	carbohydrates
8.5 g.	dietary fibre

Tex-Mex Pinto Beans

quick and easy

Fresh sweetcorn makes this simple dish really special. It's great with spicy turkey fillets, a large green salad and apple pie.

125	ml water
1	medium onion, diced
1	stalk celery, diced
	Kernels from 1 ear sweetcorn
1	can (470 g) pinto beans, rinsed and drained
2	cloves garlic, minced
1	teaspoon dried oregano
½	teaspoon ground cumin
	Hot-pepper sauce
1	tablespoon chopped fresh coriander (optional)

1   In a large non-stick frying pan, bring the water to a boil over medium-high heat. Add the onions and celery. Cover and cook for 5 minutes. Add the sweetcorn and cook for 2 minutes. Drain and return the vegetables to the frying pan.

2   Add the beans, garlic, oregano and cumin. Cook over medium heat, stirring occasionally, for 5 minutes, or until the beans are hot. Season to taste with the hot-pepper sauce. Sprinkle with the coriander (if using).

Makes **4** servings.

nutrition at a glance

per serving

0.8 g.	total fat
0.1 g.	saturated fat
143	calories
0 mg.	cholesterol
197 mg.	sodium
7.6 g.	protein
28.2 g.	carbohydrates
7.8 g.	dietary fibre

Confetti Black Beans

quick and easy

Garnish individual portions of this festive side dish with a dollop of fat-free soured cream, chopped lettuce and coriander leaves.

185	g chopped onions
2	large cloves garlic, minced
125	ml water
1	sweet red pepper, diced
2	plum tomatoes, chopped
90	g sweetcorn kernels
1	bay leaf
185	g cooked black beans
2	tablespoons chopped fresh coriander
1	tablespoon fresh lime juice
⅛	teaspoon cayenne pepper
	Ground black pepper
	Salt (optional)

1 Coat a large non-stick saucepan with non-stick spray and place over medium heat. Add the onions and garlic; stir. Cover and cook for 2 minutes, or until the onions start to release moisture. Uncover and cook, stirring, for 2 to 3 minutes, or until golden. Add the water, diced red peppers, tomatoes, sweetcorn and bay leaf. Cook for 2 minutes. Add the beans.

2 Reduce the heat and simmer for 15 minutes, or until the liquid is almost gone. Add the coriander, lime juice and cayenne pepper. Season to taste with the black pepper and salt (if using). Cook for 1 minute. Remove and discard the bay leaf.

Makes **4** servings.

nutrition at a glance

per serving

0.7 g.	total fat
0.1 g.	saturated fat
105	calories
0 mg.	cholesterol
8 mg.	sodium
5.4 g.	protein
21.2 g.	carbohydrates
5.5 g.	dietary fibre

Pasta e Fagioli

quick and easy

This simply prepared dish will please both bean and pasta lovers. And it will especially please the youngsters. During one tasting session, the two-year-old daughter of one of our testers ate her mother's entire portion. If you don't have pinto beans, substitute pink or red ones.

1	onion, chopped
1	clove garlic, minced
500	ml water
185	g canned pinto beans, rinsed and drained
1	tablespoon tomato paste
½	teaspoon honey
185	g low-fat miniature shell pasta or tube pasta (0.5 g. fat per 60-g serving)
1	tablespoon thinly sliced fresh basil
2	tablespoons chopped fresh parsley
	Ground black pepper
	Salt (optional)
4	tablespoons fat-free Parmesan topping

1   Coat a large non-stick saucepan with non-stick spray. Add the onions. Cover and cook over medium heat for 5 minutes, or until the onions start to release moisture. Add the garlic. Cook, stirring frequently, for 3 to 4 minutes, or until the onions are golden. If necessary, add 1 to 2 teaspoons water to prevent sticking.

2   Add the water, beans, tomato paste and honey; stir to combine. Add the pasta and stir. Cover and simmer for 10 to 15 minutes, or until the pasta is tender. Stir in the basil and parsley. Season to taste with the pepper and salt (if using). Serve sprinkled with the Parmesan.

Makes **4** servings.

nutrition at a glance

per serving

0.9 g.	total fat
0.2 g.	saturated fat
238	calories
0 mg.	cholesterol
235 mg.	sodium
11.8 g.	protein
46 g.	carbohydrates
5.6 g.	dietary fibre

Autumn Couscous with Mint

quick and easy

Other types of winter squash or even sweet potatoes can be substituted for the butternut squash in this dish.

1	small McIntosh apple, chopped
1	tablespoon freshly squeezed lemon juice
500	g butternut squash, peeled, seeded and cut in 2.5 cm cubes
½	teaspoon ground cinnamon
375	ml water
185	g couscous
2	tablespoons chopped fresh mint
1	tablespoon grated lemon rind
½	teaspoon salt (optional)

1 Place the apples in a small bowl. Sprinkle with the lemon juice and toss to coat. Set aside.

2 Place the squash in a steamer basket. Sprinkle with the cinnamon and toss to coat. Place the basket in a large saucepan. Add 2.5 cm of water to the pan, cover, and bring to a boil over medium-high heat. Reduce the heat to medium and steam for 7 to 9 minutes, or until the squash is tender.

3 Meanwhile, in a medium non-stick saucepan over medium-high heat, bring the 375 ml water to a boil. Stir in the couscous. Cover, remove from the heat and set aside for 5 minutes.

4 Transfer the couscous to a large bowl; fluff with a fork. Lightly stir in the squash, mint, lemon rind and salt (if using). Sprinkle with the apples.

Makes **4** servings.

Lynn's Kitchen Tip

Couscous – tiny precooked dried granules of semolina – has caught on in popularity because it's as satisfying as pasta and even quicker to make. The type that's sold in most supermarkets needs only to be soaked in a hot liquid for 5 minutes.

nutrition at a glance

per serving

0.6 g.	total fat
0.1 g.	saturated fat
243	calories
0 mg.	cholesterol
19 mg.	sodium
7.5 g.	protein
53.3 g.	carbohydrates
6.9 g.	dietary fibre

Couscous with Sweetcorn and Cumin

quick and **easy**

This side dish is wonderful in late summer, when fresh sweetcorn is at its prime.

185	g fresh sweetcorn or thawed frozen sweetcorn
375	ml water
185	g couscous
½	jalapeño pepper, seeded and finely chopped (wear rubber gloves when handling)
125	g chopped sweet red or green peppers
1	clove garlic, minced
½	teaspoon ground cumin
½	teaspoon salt (optional)
2	tablespoons chopped fresh coriander

1 Place the sweetcorn in a small saucepan; add enough cold water to cover. Cook over medium heat for 3 to 4 minutes, or until tender. Drain and set aside.

2 In a medium non-stick saucepan, bring the 375 ml water to a boil over medium-high heat. Stir in the couscous. Cover, remove from the heat and set aside for 5 minutes.

3 Coat a large non-stick frying pan with non-stick spray. Warm over medium heat for 1 minute. Add the jalapeño peppers and red or green peppers; cook for 3 minutes, or until softened. Add the garlic, cumin and salt (if using). Cook, stirring, for 1 minute. Stir in the sweetcorn.

4 Transfer the couscous to a large bowl; fluff with a fork. Stir in the sweetcorn mixture and coriander.

Makes **4** servings.

Lynn's Kitchen Tip

To accurately measure liquid ingredients, use glass or plastic measuring jugs with a pour spout and measurements marked on the side of the jug. A set of good measuring spoons is also a handy tool to keep in the kitchen.

nutrition at a glance

per serving
0.9 g.	total fat
0.1 g.	saturated fat
227	calories
0 mg.	cholesterol
16 mg.	sodium
7.5 g.	protein
47.4 g.	carbohydrates
3.7 g.	dietary fibre

Tubetti with Tomato and Ham

quick and easy

Any small dry pasta such as macaroni, shells or pennetti may be substituted for the tubetti, which are short lengths of tubes. I like to garnish this dish with plenty of chopped parsley.

1½	tablespoons diced fat-free ham or prosciutto trimmed of all visible fat
1	medium onion, chopped
3	cloves garlic, minced
125	g diced tomatoes
	Ground black pepper
	Salt (optional)
185	g low-fat tubetti pasta (0.5 g. fat per 60-g serving)
4	tablespoons fat-free Parmesan topping

1 In a large non-stick frying pan over medium-high heat, cook the ham or prosciutto, stirring occasionally, for 5 minutes, or until browned. Remove from the pan and set aside.

2 Off the heat, coat the frying pan with non-stick spray. Add the onions. Cover and cook over medium-high heat, stirring occasionally, for 5 to 6 minutes, or until golden. If necessary, add 1 to 2 teaspoons water to prevent sticking.

3 Add the garlic and cook for 2 to 3 minutes. Add the tomatoes and the reserved ham or prosciutto. Stir to combine. Season to taste with the pepper and salt (if using). Keep warm over low heat.

4 Meanwhile, bring a large pan of water to a boil over high heat. Add the pasta and cook according to the package directions. Reserve 4 tablespoons of the cooking water, then drain the pasta.

5 Return the pasta to the pan. Add the onion mixture and 1 to 2 tablespoons of the cooking water. Toss to combine. Add a bit more cooking water, if needed, to moisten. Sprinkle with the Parmesan.

Makes **4** servings.

Photograph on page 251

Lynn's Fat-Free Flavour

To boost the flavour of fat-free cheeses and still keep the fat content very low, mix 1 part standard cheese to 4 parts of the fat-free version.

---

nutrition at a glance

per serving

0.9 g.	total fat
0.1 g.	saturated fat
218	calories
1 mg.	cholesterol
144 mg.	sodium
10.1 g.	protein
42.3 g.	carbohydrates
2.3 g.	dietary fibre

Macaroni Cheese

quick and easy

Macaroni cheese is a classic and, unfortunately, usually almost all fat. But this fabulous fat-free adaptation has an added boost of calcium and protein from cottage cheese. For extra colour, add 4 tablespoons pimientos or green peppers and sprinkle on some paprika for garnish.

250	g macaroni (0.5 g. fat per 60-g serving)
375	g fat-free cottage cheese
125	ml buttermilk
1	tablespoon plain flour
1	teaspoon prepared mustard
	Salt (optional)
90	g fat-free Cheddar cheese, finely chopped

1 Bring a large pan of water to a boil over high heat. Add the macaroni and cook according to the package directions. Drain and return to the pan. Set aside.

2 Meanwhile, in a blender or food processor, combine the cottage cheese, buttermilk, flour and mustard. Process for 1 minute, or until very smooth. Season to taste with the salt (if using).

3 Pour the cottage-cheese mixture into a medium non-stick saucepan. Bring to a boil over medium-low heat, stirring constantly. Boil, stirring constantly, for 5 minutes. Remove from the heat. Add the Cheddar and stir until melted. Let stand for 5 minutes to thicken.

4 Pour over the macaroni; toss to combine. Pour into a shallow 1.5-litre baking dish. Grill 10 cm from the heat for 2 to 3 minutes, or until golden brown.

Makes **4** servings.

nutrition at a glance

per serving

0.6 g.	total fat
0 g.	saturated fat
317	calories
10 mg.	cholesterol
436 mg.	sodium
24.9 g.	protein
49.7 g.	carbohydrates
2.1 g.	dietary fibre

Orzo with Asparagus

quick and **easy**

For a creamed version of this dish, whisk together 250 ml fat-free liquid creamer and 1 tablespoon flour. Cook over medium heat, stirring, until thickened. Add a pinch of ground nutmeg. Omit the cooking water from the final step of the recipe and toss the orzo mixture with the cream sauce.

185	g low-fat orzo pasta (0.5 g. fat per 60-g serving)
250	g thinly sliced asparagus
1	medium onion, finely chopped
2	cloves garlic, minced
125	g drained canned mushroom pieces
1	plum tomato, diced
4	tablespoons chopped fresh parsley
2	tablespoons diced sweet red peppers
8	fresh basil leaves, thinly sliced
	Ground black pepper
	Salt (optional)

1 Bring a large pan of water to a boil over high heat. Add the orzo and cook according to the package directions; add the asparagus during the last 2 minutes of cooking time. Reserve 125 ml of the cooking water, then drain. Return the orzo and asparagus to the pan. Set aside.

2 Meanwhile, coat a large non-stick frying pan with non-stick spray. Add the onions. Cover and cook over medium heat, stirring occasionally, for 5 minutes, or until golden. Add the garlic. Cook for 2 minutes.

3 Add the mushrooms, tomatoes, parsley, red peppers, and basil. Cover and cook for 1 to 2 minutes. Add the orzo and asparagus. Season to taste with the black pepper and salt (if using).

4 Add about 60 ml of the reserved cooking water; toss to combine. Add a bit more cooking water, if needed, to moisten.

Makes **4** servings.

Photograph on page 252

Lynn's Kitchen Tip

Tinned mushrooms in the can often be a real lifesaver. Chopped, sliced and whole button mushrooms make quick and convenient fat-free additions to pasta, bean, grain, vegetable and rice dishes.

nutrition at a glance

per serving

0.9 g.	total fat
0.1 g.	saturated fat
188	calories
0 mg.	cholesterol
95 mg.	sodium
7.3 g.	protein
38.2 g.	carbohydrates
3 g.	dietary fibre

Rice and Orzo Pilaf

Look for packages of quick-cooking brown rice in your supermarket that say "cooks in 30 minutes." I prefer the taste and texture of this rice over the instant brown rice that cooks in 10 minutes.

90	g low-fat orzo pasta (0.5 g. fat per 60-g serving)
185	g chopped onions
½	teaspoon dried marjoram
¼	teaspoon dried rosemary, crumbled
	Pinch of ground turmeric
800	ml skimmed chicken stock (page 94)
¼	teaspoon ground black pepper
	Pinch of salt (optional)
105	g quick-cooking brown rice (ready in 30 minutes)
90	g long-grain white rice

1 Coat a large non-stick frying pan with non-stick spray. Add the orzo and mist with the non-stick spray. Cook over medium heat, stirring, for 2 to 3 minutes, or until browned. Add the onions and cook, stirring, for 2 to 3 minutes. Cover and cook for 1 minute.

2 Add the marjoram, rosemary and turmeric. Cook, stirring constantly, for 1 to 2 minutes. Add the stock, pepper and salt (if using).

3 Cover and bring to a boil over medium-high heat. Stir in the brown rice. Reduce the heat to medium-low, cover and simmer for 15 minutes. Add the white rice. Cover and simmer for 20 minutes, or until the rice is tender and the liquid is absorbed. Fluff with a fork.

Makes **6** servings.

Lynn's Kitchen Tip

Traditionally, pilafs were made by first sautéing the grain in oil or butter to toast and gently heat the kernels, so they could absorb the water or stock that is added later. You can achieve the same effect with virtually no fat by lightly coating the grains with non-stick spray before toasting.

nutrition at a glance

per serving

0.9 g.	total fat
0.1 g.	saturated fat
188	calories
0 mg.	cholesterol
13 mg.	sodium
4.9 g.	protein
39.8 g.	carbohydrates
2.5 g.	dietary fibre

Saffron Rice

quick and easy

Moist and creamy saffron rice is a treat fit for guests. You can always use a little more saffron if you like its distinctive flavour. Garnish with chopped fresh parsley or chives.

500	ml skimmed chicken stock (page 94) or vegetable stock (page 93)
¼	teaspoon crushed saffron threads
375	g chopped leeks
2	cloves garlic, minced
4	tablespoons white wine (optional)
185	g long-grain white rice
	Pinch of salt (optional)

1 In a microwaveable measuring jug or medium bowl, combine the stock and saffron. Microwave on high power for 2 minutes, or until hot. Remove and set aside for 5 minutes.

2 Coat a medium non-stick saucepan with non-stick spray. Warm over medium heat. Add the leeks and garlic. Cover and cook, stirring occasionally, for 3 minutes, or until golden. Add the wine (if using) and bring to a boil. Stir in the rice.

3 Stir in the saffron stock and salt (if using). Bring to a boil over medium-high heat. Reduce the heat to medium-low, cover and cook for 20 minutes, or until the rice is tender and the liquid is absorbed. Fluff with a fork.

Makes **4** servings.

nutrition at a glance

per serving

0.6 g.	total fat
0.1 g.	saturated fat
228	calories
0 mg.	cholesterol
19 mg.	sodium
4.8 g.	protein
47.8 g.	carbohydrates
2.2 g.	dietary fibre

Spanish Green Rice

quick and easy

This savoury green rice is terrific with a hot bean soup and a salad. Serve with lemon or lime wedges and hot sauce.

500	ml water or vegetable stock (page 93)
140	g long-grain white rice
	Pinch of salt (optional)
90	g chopped fresh coriander
60	g finely chopped spring onions
4	tablespoons chopped fresh parsley
½	teaspoon finely diced jalapeño peppers (wear rubber gloves when handling)

1 In a medium non-stick saucepan, combine the water or stock, rice and salt (if using). Bring to a boil over medium-high heat. Reduce the heat to medium-low, cover and cook for 20 minutes, or until the rice is tender and the liquid is absorbed.

2 Fluff the rice with a fork. Add the coriander, spring onions, parsley and peppers (if using). Stir with a fork.

Makes **4** servings.

nutrition at a glance
per serving

0.4 g.	total fat
0.1 g.	saturated fat
146	calories
0 mg.	cholesterol
10 mg.	sodium
3.3 g.	protein
31.4 g.	carbohydrates
1.1 g.	dietary fibre

North Woods Wild Rice

If you can't find fresh ripe Bing or yellow Queen Anne cherries, substitute tinned or frozen ones. Or use halved seedless tangerine or canned mandarin orange wedges.

1	package (0.35 ounce) dried mushrooms
500	ml boiling water
1	tablespoon molasses
1	bay leaf
185	g wild rice
4	tablespoons sweet cherries, stoned and cut into quarters
	Ground black pepper
	Salt (optional)

1 Place the mushrooms in a medium bowl. Add the water and set aside to soak for 10 minutes. Strain through a fine sieve lined with a paper coffee filter or paper towel; reserve the liquid. Chop the mushrooms, discarding any tough stems.

2 Add enough water to the mushroom liquid to equal 625 ml. Transfer to a large non-stick saucepan. Add the molasses and bay leaf. Bring to a boil over medium-high heat.

3 Add the rice and stir. Reduce the heat to low. Cover and cook for 50 to 55 minutes, or until the rice is tender and most of the liquid is absorbed. Fluff with a fork.

4 Add the cherries. Season to taste with the pepper and salt (if using). Stir to combine. Cook for an additional 1 to 2 minutes, or until the cherries are heated through. Remove and discard the bay leaf.

Makes **4** servings.

nutrition at a glance

per serving

0.8 g.	total fat
0.1 g.	saturated fat
204	calories
0 mg.	cholesterol
7 mg.	sodium
7 g.	protein
44.5 g.	carbohydrates
2.9 g.	dietary fibre

Rice and Vegetable Ring

quick and easy

A rice mould is pretty to serve and easy to make. Prepare it in a non-stick ring mould, a gelatine mould or a Bundt pan. For variety, replace the broccoli with asparagus cut into 1 cm pieces.

375	g long-grain white rice
1.12	ml skimmed chicken stock (page 94) or vegetable stock (page 93)
	Pinch of salt (optional)
185	g broccoli florets
1	medium onion, finely chopped
90	g finely chopped carrots
	Ground black pepper

1 In a large non-stick saucepan, combine the rice, stock and salt (if using). Bring to a boil over medium-high heat. Reduce the heat to medium-low, cover and cook for 10 minutes. Add the broccoli, onions and carrots. Cover and cook for 10 minutes, or until the rice is tender and the liquid is absorbed. Season to taste with the pepper.

2 Coat a 2-litre ring mould with non-stick spray. Spoon the rice and vegetables into the mould, packing it firmly. Cover with foil and let stand for 5 minutes. Invert onto a platter and unmould.

Makes **8** servings.

nutrition at a glance

per serving

0.6 g.	total fat
0.1 g.	saturated fat
211	calories
0 mg.	cholesterol
24 mg.	sodium
5 g.	protein
45.8 g.	carbohydrates
2.3 g.	dietary fibre

Lemon-Dill Rice

quick and easy

Rice, lemon and dill are a refreshingly satisfying mix. Cook a double batch so that you have leftovers for rice salad: Toss the cold rice with cooked vegetables, seafood and your favourite fat-free dressing.

375 ml skimmed chicken stock (page 94)
185 g jasmine, basmati or long-grain white rice
1 tablespoon grated lemon rind
¼ teaspoon ground black pepper
Pinch of salt (optional)
1 tablespoon chopped fresh dill or 1 teaspoon dried
1 tablespoon freshly squeezed lemon juice

1 In a small non-stick saucepan over medium heat, bring the stock to a boil. Stir in the rice, lemon rind, pepper and salt (if using). Return to a boil. Stir. Reduce the heat to low, cover and simmer for 20 minutes, or until the rice is tender and the liquid is absorbed.

2 Fluff the rice with a fork. Add the dill and lemon juice. Mix lightly with a fork.

Makes **4** servings.

nutrition at a glance

per serving

0.4 g.	total fat
0.1 g.	saturated fat
193	calories
0 mg.	cholesterol
110 mg.	sodium
4.6 g.	protein
41.2 g.	carbohydrates
1 g.	dietary fibre

Cajun Red Beans and Rice

quick and easy

Beans and rice are a traditional favourite in many parts of the world. I like to use dark red kidney beans because they have more texture than some other varieties. If you like garnishes, sprinkle coriander leaves on top for colour.

185	g finely chopped onions
185	g finely chopped green peppers
1	large clove garlic, minced
1	can (470 g) dark red kidney beans, rinsed and drained
1	can (440 g) low-sodium chicken broth, skimmed
185	g long-grain white rice
60	g fat-free smoked ham or turkey breast, finely chopped
1	bay leaf
½	teaspoon dried thyme
	Salt (optional)

1 In a large non-stick saucepan, combine the onions, peppers and garlic. Cook over medium heat, stirring often, for 3 minutes. Add the beans, broth, rice, ham or turkey, bay leaf and thyme. Season to taste with the salt (if using).

2 Bring the mixture to a boil over medium-high heat. Reduce the heat to low, cover and simmer for 20 minutes, or until the rice is tender and the liquid is absorbed. Fluff the mixture with a fork. Remove and discard the bay leaf.

Makes **4** servings.

nutrition at a glance

per serving

0.6 g.	total fat
0.1 g.	saturated fat
212	calories
3 mg.	cholesterol
314 mg.	sodium
9 g.	protein
41.9 g.	carbohydrates
5.2 g.	dietary fibre

Barley with Mushrooms

Earthy barley acquires even deeper, richer flavour when simmered with hearty dried mushrooms. Brighten this cold-weather side dish with a sprinkling of chopped parsley.

1	package (0.35 ounce) dried mushrooms
500	ml hot water
375	g sliced fresh closed cap or chestnut mushrooms
140	g diced carrots
1	medium onion, chopped
2	stalks celery, chopped
2	cloves garlic, minced
100	g barley
½	teaspoon dried thyme
¼	teaspoon dried rosemary, crumbled
	Pinch of salt (optional)
	Ground black pepper

1 Place the dried mushrooms in a small bowl. Add 250 ml of the water and set aside to soak for 10 minutes. Strain through a fine sieve lined with a paper coffee filter or paper towel; reserve the liquid. Chop the mushrooms, discarding any tough stems; set aside.

2 Meanwhile, coat a large non-stick saucepan with non-stick spray. Add the closed cap or chestnut mushrooms, carrots, onions, celery and garlic. Cover and cook over medium heat, stirring occasionally, for 6 minutes, or until the onions start to brown.

3 Add the barley, thyme, rosemary, and salt (if using). Stir in the remaining 250 ml water, the reserved mushroom liquid and the soaked mushrooms. Bring to a boil over medium-high heat.

4 Reduce the heat to medium, cover and cook for 30 minutes, or until the barley is tender and the liquid is absorbed. Fluff with a fork. Season to taste with the pepper.

Makes **4** servings.

nutrition at a glance

per serving

0.9 g.	total fat
0.2 g.	saturated fat
126	calories
0 mg.	cholesterol
36 mg.	sodium
4.6 g.	protein
26.7 g.	carbohydrates
6.7 g.	dietary fibre

Oriental Millet with Carrots

Tiny round yellow millet grains look pretty cooked in this pilaf-like side dish with carrots, spring onions and coriander. Serve it with lemon wedges and pass around the crushed chillies for those who like things spicy.

375	ml water or skimmed chicken stock (page 94)
1	onion, coarsely chopped
10	baby carrots, diced
60	g millet
2	pieces (10 cm each) fresh lemongrass (optional)
3	cloves garlic, minced
	Pinch of salt (optional)
3	spring onions, chopped
2	tablespoons chopped fresh coriander
2	teaspoons low-sodium soy sauce
	Ground black pepper

1   In a large non-stick saucepan, combine the water or stock, onions, carrots, millet, lemongrass (if using), garlic and salt (if using). Cover and bring to a boil over medium-high heat. Reduce the heat to medium, cover and cook for 35 to 40 minutes, or until the millet is tender and the liquid is absorbed.

2   Stir in the spring onions, coriander and soy sauce. Season to taste with the pepper. Remove and discard the lemongrass (if using).

Makes **6** servings.

nutrition at a glance	
per serving	
0.9 g.	total fat
0.2 g.	saturated fat
117	calories
0 mg.	cholesterol
79 mg.	sodium
3.6 g.	protein
23.6 g.	carbohydrates
2 g.	dietary fibre

Grains: A Cook's Guide

Cook grains in water, stock or vegetable juice in a covered heavy-bottomed pan. Season if you like with herbs, spices, other aromatics or salt.

Follow the same basic method for all the following grains. Bring the grain and liquid to a boil, then reduce the heat to low so the mixture simmers. Cover and cook for the allotted time. Remove from the heat and set aside, covered, to steam for 5 minutes. Fluff with a fork before serving.

Remember that the amount of liquid and the time listed are approximate. The age of the grain, the weather, and the heat intensity of your stove top can all affect the amount of liquid that the grain absorbs and the time needed to absorb it.

Grain (185 g)	Liquid (ml)	Cooking Time (min.)
Barley	750	35
Brown rice, quick-cooking	500	30
Brown rice, standard	500	45
Bulgur, medium or coarse	500	20–25
Millet	625	30
Quinoa	500	15
White rice	500	15
Wild rice	750	45–50

Herbed Bulgur Pilaf

Bulgur is made from wheat berries that have been steamed, dried and crushed. It's available in fine, medium and coarse grinds in health food stores and some supermarkets. I prefer a fine-grind bulgur for this recipe because it cooks quickly.

90	g chopped spring onions
60	g grated carrots
185	g bulgur
½	teaspoon herbes de Provence
500	ml water
4	tablespoons chopped fresh parsley
	Pinch of salt (optional)
	Ground black pepper
	Fat-free Parmesan topping (optional)

1 Coat a medium non-stick saucepan with non-stick spray. Add the spring onions and carrots. Mist with non-stick spray. Cover and cook over medium heat, stirring occasionally, for 4 to 5 minutes, or until the vegetables release moisture.

2 Uncover and cook, stirring, for 3 to 4 minutes, or until the spring onions are golden. Add the bulgur and herbes de Provence. Cook, stirring, for 2 to 3 minutes, or until the bulgur is lightly toasted.

3 Add the water, parsley and salt (if using). Bring to a boil over medium-high heat. Reduce the heat to medium-low, cover and cook for 18 to 20 minutes, or until the bulgur is tender and the liquid is absorbed.

4 Fluff with a fork. Season to taste with the pepper. Serve sprinkled with the Parmesan (if using).

Makes **4** servings.

Photograph on page 249

Photograph on page 249

Lynn's Kitchen Tip

It's easy to change the personality of a grain pilaf just by substituting a different dried herb, spice or seasoning mix for the one called for in the original recipe. Try equal parts dried oregano and basil for Italian or equal parts dried oregano and ground cumin for Mexican.

nutrition at a glance
per serving

0.6 g.	total fat
0.1 g.	saturated fat
131	calories
0 mg.	cholesterol
18 mg.	sodium
4.8 g.	protein
29.2 g.	carbohydrates
7.3 g.	dietary fibre

Grilled Polenta with Mushrooms

quick and easy

This robust side dish is also good served as an appetizer for a formal Autumn dinner.

4	slices (1 cm thick) prepared fat-free polenta in a tube
125	g chestnut or shiitake mushrooms, sliced
2	cloves garlic, minced
80	ml dry white wine or water
2	tablespoons chopped fresh chives or parsley
1	teaspoon fat-free Parmesan topping

1   Coat a barbecue grill rack or heavy cast iron grill pan with non-stick spray. Prepare a barbecue or warm the frying pan over high heat.

2   Add the polenta to the rack or frying pan. Cook for 4 to 5 minutes on each side.

3   Meanwhile, coat a large non-stick frying pan with non-stick spray. Warm over medium heat for 1 minute. Add the mushrooms and cook for 2 to 3 minutes. Add the garlic and cook for 1 minute. Add the wine or water and bring to a boil. Reduce the heat to low. Cook for 2 to 3 minutes, or until the mushrooms are tender. Stir in the chives or parsley and Parmesan. Spoon over the polenta.

Makes **4** servings.

nutrition at a glance

per serving

0.2 g.	total fat
0.1 g.	saturated fat
83	calories
0 mg.	cholesterol
232 mg.	sodium
2.3 g.	protein
15.3 g.	carbohydrates
2.2 g.	dietary fibre

Orange Quinoa with Raisins

quick and easy

The fluffy texture and delicate flavour of quinoa belie its nutritional power. It is one of the finest sources of vegetable protein.

5	spring onions
1	large clove garlic, minced
½	teaspoon ground cumin
¼	teaspoon ground cinnamon
250	ml skimmed chicken stock (page 94)
90	g quinoa, rinsed and drained
90	g sultanas
	Pinch of salt (optional)
1	teaspoon grated orange rind

1 Cut the green stems from the spring onions; chop finely and set aside. Chop the white parts and set aside.

2 Coat a small non-stick saucepan with non-stick spray. Add the white parts of the spring onions, garlic, cumin and cinnamon. Mist with non-stick spray. Cook over medium heat, stirring, for 1 minute.

3 Stir in the stock, quinoa, sultanas and salt (if using). Bring to a boil over medium-high heat. Reduce the heat to low, cover and cook for 15 minutes, or until the quinoa is tender and the liquid is absorbed.

4 Fluff with a fork. Stir in the orange rind and reserved spring onion greens.

Makes **4** servings.

nutrition at a glance
per serving

0.9 g.	total fat
0.1 g.	saturated fat
102	calories
0 mg.	cholesterol
55 mg.	sodium
2.9 g.	protein
22 g.	carbohydrates
1.6 g.	dietary fibre

Sauces, Gravies and Condiments

Judging from the contents of my refrigerator,

sauces, gravies and condiments are the most important foods in my kitchen. I have more of these flavour enhancers – especially condiments – than any other single item.

I also have a freezer stocked with recipe-ready portions of sauces and gravies, which I can thaw in the microwave to top cooked pasta, a baked potato, steamed courgettes or pancakes.

Perfect sauces – such as Broccoli Alfredo Sauce and Mushroom and Bacon Sauce – dress up pasta, mashed potatoes or rice. Dill Sauce on grilled halibut entices even fish phobics. Caramelised Onion Compote or Nectarine Salsa – served with grilled turkey breast – makes a most favourable flavour impression.

Sauce Support

Sauces play an extremely important supporting role in fat-free cooking. With their range of textures and tastes, they keep us from feeling deprived.

Most of my fat-free sauces don't take much time, and many can be made ahead and even frozen. When I'm in the mood, I'll have a sauce-making day and prepare several sauces to freeze in serving portions in plastic bags. So I always have the perfect fat-free sauce when I need it.

With my master Basic White Sauce, which is a simple three-ingredient wonder (five, if you count the salt and pepper), you can make Cheese Sauce, Dill Sauce, Garlic Sauce, Lemon Sauce, Mushroom Sauce and Onion Sauce.

Serve It Right

How much sauce makes a serving?
* My sauces for pasta and rice are 125 ml, which is a good quantity for 60 g cooked pasta or rice. (That amount of starch contains less than 1 gramme of fat per serving.)
* The sauces for poultry and seafood, with the exception of the Spicy Peanut Sauce, are 60 ml. Because the peanut sauce is both naturally higher in fat and more filling, 3 tablespoons is a good serving size.
* The sweet sauces – for cakes, frozen desserts, pancakes, French toast or cooked cereals – are 60 ml each.
* Condiments tend to have more assertive flavours, so a little bit of each of them will go a long way. Servings of all my condiments – except for the Roasted Garlic – are 2 tablespoons.

I consider both the Roasted Garlic and the Yogurt Cheese to be indispensable condiments. Use Roasted Garlic as a spread, or add it to dips, puréed cooked vegetables, sauces or grain pilafs. Yogurt cheese, which is made by draining natural fat-free yogurt to release much of the liquid, is a cream-cheese substitute that adds richness and true dairy flavour to dips, spreads, desserts, sauces and many other dishes.

Broccoli Alfredo Sauce

quick and easy

If you're serving the sauce with pasta, the broccoli can be added to the pasta pan instead of being cooked separately.

4	tablespoons plain flour
500	ml skimmed milk
375	ml fat-free liquid creamer
250	g fat-free cream cheese
30	g low-fat Provolone cheese, grated
	Pinch of ground nutmeg
1	medium onion, diced
2	tablespoons dry sherry or 1 teaspoon sherry extract
	Pinch of ground red pepper
315	g broccoli florets
	Ground black pepper
4	tablespoons fat-free Parmesan topping

1 Place the flour in a medium non-stick saucepan. Gradually whisk in the milk until smooth. Add the creamer and cream cheese. Cook over medium heat, stirring constantly and breaking the cream cheese into small pieces, for 5 to 7 minutes, or until the mixture thickens.

2 Add the Provolone and nutmeg. Cook, stirring, for 2 minutes, or until the Provolone melts. Reduce the heat to low. Cover and cook, stirring occasionally, for 5 minutes.

3 Meanwhile, coat a large non-stick frying pan with non-stick spray. Add the onions and cook, stirring, for 4 to 5 minutes, or until the onions soften. Add the sherry or sherry extract and the red pepper. Cook over medium heat until the sherry evaporates. Add the onions to the saucepan with the Provolone mixture.

4 Bring a medium pan of water to a boil. Add the broccoli; cook for 3 to 4 minutes, or until crisp-tender. Drain and add to the sauce. Season to taste with the black pepper. Stir in the Parmesan.

Makes about **1.5** litres.

Photograph on page 253

Photograph on page 253

Lynn's Kitchen Tip

To freeze the Alfredo sauce, it's best to prepare it without the broccoli, which will lose some of its bright colour in the freezer. At serving time, add the broccoli to the pasta pan a few minutes before the pasta is done cooking. Gently reheat the Alfredo sauce over low heat. Drain the broccoli with the pasta and toss both with the Alfredo sauce to reheat it.

nutrition at a glance

per 125 ml

0.9 g.	total fat
0.4 g.	saturated fat
108	calories
5 mg.	cholesterol
265 mg.	sodium
9.8 g.	protein
13.6 g.	carbohydrates
0.9 g.	dietary fibre

Marinara Sauce

quick and easy

This sauce is endlessly versatile. It's good with lasagna or simply spooned over cooked pasta. Sprinkle with a combination of grated fat-free mozzarella, low-fat mozzarella and fat-free Parmesan topping before serving.

1	large onion, coarsely chopped
3	cloves garlic, minced
1	can (500 g) tomatoes, chopped (with juice)
500	ml tomato juice
2	plum tomatoes, coarsely chopped
4	tablespoons chopped fresh parsley
1	teaspoon dried oregano
⅛	teaspoon crushed chillies (optional)
½	teaspoon sugar (optional)
3	tablespoons thinly sliced fresh basil
	Ground black pepper
	Salt (optional)

1 Coat a large non-stick frying pan with non-stick spray. Add the onions and garlic. Mist with non-stick spray. Cook over medium-low heat, stirring, for 5 minutes, or until the onions soften.

2 Add the canned tomatoes (with juice), tomato juice, plum tomatoes, parsley, oregano, crushed chillies (if using) and sugar (if using). Cover and simmer over low heat, stirring occasionally, for 15 minutes, or until the tomatoes are softened. With the back of a large spoon, break some of the tomatoes to thicken the sauce.

3 Stir in the basil. Season to taste with the pepper and salt (if using).

Makes about **1** litre.

nutrition at a glance

per 125 ml

0.3 g.	total fat
0 g.	saturated fat
35	calories
0 mg.	cholesterol
316 mg.	sodium
1.5 g.	protein
8 g.	carbohydrates
1.3 g.	dietary fibre

Curried Vegetable-Turkey Sauce

quick and easy

Serve each portion of this creamy sauce over 315 g cooked basmati rice, which will add less than 1 gramme of fat.

625	ml water or skimmed chicken stock (page 94)
125	g boneless, skinless turkey breast, trimmed of all visible fat and cut into bite-size pieces
4	tablespoons chopped onions
1	teaspoon minced fresh ginger
2	tablespoons plain flour
250	ml skimmed milk
185	g chopped carrots
1	tablespoon curry powder
90	g broccoli florets
1	teaspoon freshly squeezed lemon juice
1½	teaspoons sugar
1	teaspoon cornflour
1	tablespoon water
	Salt (optional)
90	g chopped spring onions

1 In a large non-stick frying pan over medium-high heat, bring 250 ml of the water or stock to a boil. Reduce the heat to medium. Add the turkey and simmer for 2 minutes, or until no longer pink. With a slotted spoon, remove the turkey and set aside.

2 Add the onions and ginger to the frying pan. Cook for 1 minute. Sift the flour through a fine sieve into the frying pan; cook, stirring constantly, for 1 minute. Slowly add the milk and the remaining 375 ml water or stock. Cook, stirring constantly, for 1 to 2 minutes, or until the mixture starts to thicken.

3 Add the carrots and curry powder; cook for 5 minutes. Add the broccoli; cook for 3 minutes. Add the lemon juice, sugar, and reserved turkey.

4 Place the cornflour and water in a cup. Stir to dissolve. Add to the sauce. Cook, stirring constantly, for 1 to 2 minutes. Season to taste with the salt (if using). Stir in the spring onions.

Makes about **1** litre.

nutrition at a glance

per 125 ml

0.4 g.	total fat
0.1 g.	saturated fat
53	calories
10 mg.	cholesterol
34 mg.	sodium
5.4 g.	protein
7.4 g.	carbohydrates
1.2 g.	dietary fibre

Mushroom and Bacon Sauce

quick and easy

Big, thick mushroom slices make this pasta sauce taste and look decadent. I use the large stuffer-size button mushrooms, but you can substitute the more earthy portobellos. Capers make a piquant garnish.

Add fresh basil to a dish just before serving to preserve its distinctive aroma and colour.

1	large onion, chopped
5	cloves garlic, minced
375	g large mushrooms, cut into 1 cm-thick slices
2	stalks celery, sliced
125	ml water or skimmed chicken stock (page 94)
1½	teaspoons dried oregano
	Pinch of dried thyme
3	medium tomatoes, coarsely chopped
60	g lean smoked ham, cut into matchsticks
60	g chopped fresh parsley
4	tablespoons thinly sliced fresh basil
1	tablespoon red-wine vinegar or cider vinegar
	Ground black pepper
	Salt (optional)

1 Coat a large non-stick frying pan with non-stick spray. Add the onions and garlic. Cook over medium heat, stirring occasionally, for 5 minutes, or until lightly browned.

2 Add the mushrooms, celery, water or stock, oregano and thyme. Cook, stirring occasionally, for 20 minutes, or until the sauce is thick and the vegetables are tender.

3 Add the tomatoes, bacon, parsley, basil and vinegar. Cook, stirring, for 3 to 4 minutes, or until the tomatoes are hot. Season to taste with the pepper and salt (if using).

Makes about **1** litre.

nutrition at a glance

per 125 ml

0.9 g.	total fat
0.2 g.	saturated fat
46	calories
4 mg.	cholesterol
117 mg.	sodium
3.2 g.	protein
7.5 g.	carbohydrates
1.9 g.	dietary fibre

Roasted Pepper Sauce

Here's a pepper-packed sauce for rice, noodles, baked potatoes, sliced braised mushrooms or turkey cutlets.

1	yellow pepper
1	sweet red pepper
2	tablespoons finely chopped onions
1	small clove garlic, minced
2	tablespoons finely diced tomatoes
1	tablespoon finely chopped celery leaves
1	teaspoon finely chopped fresh parsley
1	can (440 g) low-sodium chicken broth, skimmed
1½	tablespoons cornflour
	Ground black pepper
	Salt (optional)

1 Cut the yellow pepper and red pepper in half; discard the stems, membranes and seeds. Place the peppers, cut side down, on a foil-lined grill pan. Grill 10 cm from the heat for 10 to 12 minutes, or until blackened. Remove from the oven and wrap the foil tightly around the peppers. Set aside for 10 minutes. Peel and discard the skin.

2 Finely dice the red peppers. Coarsely dice the yellow peppers; set both aside.

3 Coat a medium non-stick saucepan with non-stick spray. Add the onions and garlic. Cook over medium-low heat for 2 to 3 minutes, or until the onions start to soften. Add the tomatoes, celery and parsley. Cook, stirring, for 5 minutes. Add the red peppers and 375 ml of the broth to the saucepan. Pour the mixture into a blender or food processor. Purée. Return the mixture to the saucepan. Cook over medium heat, stirring, until the mixture comes to a boil.

4 Place the cornflour in a cup. Add the remaining broth and stir to dissolve the cornflour. Add to the pan. Cook, stirring constantly, for 3 minutes, or until thickened. Add the yellow peppers. Cook for 1 minute. Season to taste with the black pepper and salt (if using).

Makes about **625** ml.

nutrition at a glance

per 125 ml
- 0.1 g. total fat
- 0 g. saturated fat
- 39 calories
- 0 mg. cholesterol
- 71 mg. sodium
- 3.5 g. protein
- 6.3 g. carbohydrates
- 1.3 g. dietary fibre

All-American Barbecue Sauce

quick and easy

Use this thick, dark, basic barbecue sauce for basting skinless poultry, lean pork and beef, seafood, mushrooms, potato wedges or other vegetables. The sauce will keep, refrigerated, for 2 weeks. If sodium is a concern, you can use low-sodium tomato purée and tomato juice, which will reduce the amount of sodium by about two-thirds.

2	large onions, coarsely chopped
1	tablespoon liquid smoke
500	ml tomato purée
375	ml tomato juice
125	ml molasses
3	tablespoons Dijon mustard
75	g brown sugar
2	tablespoons cider vinegar
1½	tablespoons chilli powder
1	teaspoon ground black pepper
½	teaspoon hot-pepper sauce

1   Coat a large non-stick frying pan with non-stick spray. Add the onions and ½ tablespoon of the liquid smoke. Cook over medium heat, stirring occasionally, for 6 minutes, or until the onions soften. Add the tomato purée, tomato juice, molasses, mustard, brown sugar, vinegar, chilli powder, black pepper, hot-pepper sauce and the remaining ½ tablespoon liquid smoke. Stir to combine well.

2   Reduce the heat to medium-low. Cook, stirring occasionally, for 20 minutes, or until the sauce is thickened.

Makes about **1** litre.

Lynn's Kitchen Tip

Take a tip from the professional barbecue cooks and baste meat, poultry or vegetables with barbecue sauce shortly after cooking is completed. You can cook for 1 to 2 minutes more just to heat the sauce. If brushed on too early, the sugar in the sauce will burn.

nutrition at a glance

per 125 ml

0.5 g.	total fat
0 g.	saturated fat
75	calories
0 mg.	cholesterol
292 mg.	sodium
1.2 g.	protein
18.3 g.	carbohydrates
1.4 g.	dietary fibre

Chicken Gravy

quick and easy

You won't find a richer-tasting poultry gravy than this. It can be made with turkey breast instead of chicken. For a smooth version, purée the finished gravy in a blender or food processor.

4	tablespoons finely chopped onions
4	tablespoons finely chopped mushrooms
4	tablespoons finely chopped celery
4	tablespoons finely chopped carrots
1	small clove garlic, minced
30	g skinless, boneless chicken breast, trimmed of all visible fat and finely diced
60	g plain flour
2	cans (440 g each) low-sodium chicken broth, skimmed
	Pinch of dried thyme
	Pinch of dried rosemary, crumbled
	Pinch of dried sage
	Ground black pepper
	Salt (optional)

1   Coat a large non-stick saucepan with non-stick spray. Add the onions, mushrooms, celery, carrots and garlic. Cook over medium heat, stirring constantly, for 5 minutes.

2   Add the chicken. Cook, stirring, for 1 to 2 minutes, or until the chicken is no longer pink. Remove the chicken and vegetables; set aside.

3   Add the flour to the pan. Cook over medium heat, stirring, for 5 minutes, or until light tan in colour. Remove from the heat and gradually whisk in the broth until smooth. Add the thyme, rosemary and sage.

4   Cook over medium heat, whisking constantly, for 2 to 3 minutes, or until thick.

5   Add the reserved chicken and vegetables. Reduce the heat to low; simmer for 5 minutes, or until the vegetables are hot. Season to taste with the pepper and salt (if using).

Makes about **1** litre.

Lynn's Kitchen Tip
A "pinch" of an herb is about ¹⁄₁₆ teaspoon. If the herb is dried, I rub it between my thumb and forefinger to release more flavour.

nutrition at a glance
per 125 ml

0.1 g.	total fat
0 g.	saturated fat
21	calories
1 mg.	cholesterol
43 mg.	sodium
2.4 g.	protein
2.5 g.	carbohydrates
0.2 g.	dietary fibre

Basic White Sauce with Variations

quick and easy

This versatile "mother sauce" can be used by itself or as a base for many flavoured sauces (I've given some variations below to get you started). It stores beautifully in the freezer in recipe-ready portions.

3	tablespoons plain flour
250	ml skimmed milk
250	ml fat-free liquid creamer
	Pinch of ground black pepper or nutmeg
	Salt (optional)

1 Place the flour in a medium non-stick saucepan. Gradually whisk in the milk until smooth. Add the creamer. Cook over medium heat, whisking constantly, for 4 to 5 minutes, or until the sauce thickens. Add the pepper or nutmeg. Season to taste with the salt (if using).

Makes **500** ml.

Cheese Sauce: To the finished basic sauce, add 60 g grated fat-free Cheddar cheese; whisk over medium-low heat until melted.

Dill Sauce: To the finished basic sauce, add 2 to 3 tablespoons chopped fresh dill.

Garlic Sauce: To the finished basic sauce, add 4 tablespoons puréed Roasted Garlic (page 304).

Lemon Sauce: To the finished basic sauce, add 4 tablespoons lemon juice and ½ teaspoon grated lemon rind.

Mushroom Sauce: To the finished basic sauce, add 250 g mushrooms (thinly sliced and sautéed) and 1 small onion (sliced and sautéed).

Onion Sauce: To the finished basic sauce, add 90 g sautéed chopped onions, 90 g grated fat-free mozzarella cheese, and 2 tablespoons fat-free Parmesan topping.

nutrition at a glance	
per 60 ml	
0 g.	total fat
0 g.	saturated fat
41	calories
1 mg.	cholesterol
16 mg.	sodium
1.3 g.	protein
7.7 g.	carbohydrates
0 g.	dietary fibre

Spicy Peanut Sauce

quick and easy

This piquant easy-to-make sauce can be served as a hot or cold topper for grilled turkey, chicken, prawns, fish fillets or vegetables. Sprinkle the sauce with chopped fresh coriander just before serving for added colour and flavour.

90	g finely chopped onions
3	tablespoons low-fat peanut butter
1	tablespoon grated fresh ginger
1	teaspoon ground coriander
3	cloves garlic, minced
2	teaspoons brown sugar
2	teaspoons low-sodium soy sauce
½	teaspoon crushed chillies
1	teaspoon finely chopped jalapeño or serrano peppers (wear rubber gloves when handling)
	Dash of ground cloves
625	ml skimmed chicken stock (page 94)
2	tablespoons cornflour
2–3	tablespoons freshly squeezed lemon juice or lime juice

1   In a medium non-stick saucepan, combine the onions, peanut butter, ginger, coriander, garlic, brown sugar, soy sauce, crushed chillies, jalapeño or serrano peppers and cloves. Add the stock. Bring to a simmer over medium heat. Reduce the heat to low and cook for 15 minutes, or until the onions are tender.

2   Transfer the mixture to a blender or food processor. Purée until smooth. Return to the saucepan.

3   Place the cornflour in a cup. Add the lemon juice or lime juice and stir to dissolve the cornflour. Add to the saucepan. Cook over medium-low heat, stirring constantly, for 2 to 3 minutes, or until thickened.

Makes about **625** ml.

Lynn's Lore

In Indonesia and Thailand, spicy peanut sauce usually accompanies satay – skewered and grilled cubes of marinated poultry or meat.

nutrition at a glance

per 3 tablespoons
0.9 g.	total fat
0.2 g.	saturated fat
31	calories
1 mg.	cholesterol
51 mg.	sodium
1.4 g.	protein
3.9 g.	carbohydrates
0.2 g.	dietary fibre

Mexican Sauce

This version of Mexican mole sauce is deeply flavoured, slightly sweet and pleasantly spicy. Pour it over boneless, skinless chicken breasts before baking. Or spoon it over pan-seared turkey cutlets or cooked rice, beans or even baked potatoes.

1	dried chipotle pepper (wear rubber gloves when handling)
1	onion, finely chopped
1	large clove garlic, minced
1	teaspoon cocoa powder
250	ml skimmed chicken stock (page 94)
1	can (250 g) tomato sauce
2	teaspoons chilli powder
1	teaspoon ground cumin
½	teaspoon sugar
¼	teaspoon ground allspice
¼	teaspoon ground cinnamon
2	teaspoons freshly squeezed lime juice

1 Place the pepper in a small bowl and add hot water to cover. Set aside for 30 minutes, or until softened. Drain.

2 Split the pepper and discard the seeds, membranes and stem. Chop the pepper finely and set aside.

3 Coat a large non-stick saucepan with non-stick spray. Add the onions, garlic and cocoa. Mist with non-stick spray. Cook over medium heat, stirring, for 8 minutes, or until the onions are softened.

4 Add the reserved peppers. Cook, stirring, for 2 minutes. Add the stock, tomato sauce, chilli powder, cumin, sugar, allspice and cinnamon. Stir well to combine. Reduce the heat to low. Cook for 15 minutes, or until thickened. Add the lime juice and stir well.

Makes about **500** ml.

Lynn's Lore

According to Mexican cooking authority Diana Kennedy, the word *mole* comes from the Nahuatl word *molli*, meaning "concoction". Traditional mole poblano is a complex blend of dried peppers, spices, seeds and a touch of unsweetened chocolate.

nutrition at a glance

per 4 tablespoons

0.3 g.	total fat
0.1 g.	saturated fat
22	calories
0 mg.	cholesterol
181 mg.	sodium
0.8 g.	protein
5 g.	carbohydrates
1.1 g.	dietary fibre

Citrus-Honey Sauce

quick and easy

This smooth sweet-tart sauce is a delight with angel food cake, fat-free pudding, fat-free vanilla ice cream or fresh ripe berries. For a special treat, make it with limes.

1	tablespoon cornflour
80	ml freshly squeezed lemon juice
125	ml water
4	tablespoons sugar
2	tablespoons honey
½	teaspoon grated lemon rind
½	teaspoon grated orange rind

1　Place the cornflour in a medium non-stick saucepan. Add the lemon juice and stir to dissolve the cornflour. Add the water, sugar, honey, lemon rind and orange rind. Whisk until smooth.

2　Cook over medium heat, whisking constantly, for 4 to 5 minutes, or until thickened.

Makes about **250** ml.

nutrition at a glance

per 4 tablespoons

0 g.	total fat
0 g.	saturated fat
94	calories
0 mg.	cholesterol
2 mg.	sodium
0.1 g.	protein
24.8 g.	carbohydrates
0.2 g.	dietary fibre

Blueberry Sauce

quick and easy

Serve this berry good sauce warm with hot cereal, pancakes or waffles. Or chill it to top fat-free ice cream, fat-free vanilla yogurt, fat-free pudding, angel food cake or lemon sorbet.

1	tablespoon cornflour
250	ml water
100	g sugar
2	tablespoons freshly squeezed lemon juice
2	teaspoons grated lemon rind
500	g blueberries
1	teaspoon vanilla

1   Place the cornflour in a cup. Add 4 tablespoons of the water and stir to dissolve the cornflour. Set aside.

2   In a medium non-stick saucepan, combine the sugar, lemon juice, lemon rind and the remaining 180 ml water. Bring to a boil over medium heat. Reduce the heat to medium-low. Add the blueberries and stir gently. Add the cornflour mixture. Cook, stirring gently, for 30 seconds, or until thickened. Remove from the heat. Stir in the vanilla.

Makes about **500** ml.

nutrition at a glance

per 4 tablespoons

0.1 g.	total fat
0 g.	saturated fat
74	calories
0 mg.	cholesterol
3 mg.	sodium
0.3 g.	protein
18.9 g.	carbohydrates
1 g.	dietary fibre

Tomato Relish

quick and easy

The ingredients for this sweet-sharp relish can be chopped and mixed in a wink in a food processor. It's a terrific accompaniment to Black Bean and Rice Cakes (page 181) or nearly any bean recipe. For best results, refrigerate the salsa for several hours to develop the flavour.

2   plum tomatoes, coarsely chopped
2   small spring onions, finely chopped
1   small carrot, finely chopped or grated
1   tablespoon freshly squeezed lemon juice
2   teaspoons crystallised ginger, minced
2   teaspoons thinly sliced fresh basil
1   clove garlic, minced
    Salt (optional)
    Hot-pepper sauce (optional)

1   In a medium bowl, combine the tomatoes, spring onions, carrots, lemon juice, ginger, basil and garlic. Season to taste with the salt (if using) and hot-pepper sauce (if using). Mix well.

Makes about **250** ml.

Photograph on page 320

nutrition at a glance

per 2 tablespoons

0.1 g.	total fat
0 g.	saturated fat
13	calories
0 mg.	cholesterol
6 mg.	sodium
0.4 g.	protein
3 g.	carbohydrates
0.6 g.	dietary fibre

Rémoulade Sauce

quick and easy

This adaptation of the classic savoury New Orleans condiment is superb on chilled cooked turkey, chicken, fish or shellfish. It's also a fine spread for sandwiches. Make it with a fat-free mayonnaise that's not heavily sweetened.

250	g fat-free mayonnaise
2	tablespoons chopped fresh parsley
1	tablespoon chopped gherkins
2	teaspoons Dijon mustard
½	teaspoon cider vinegar
½	teaspoon low-sodium Worcestershire sauce
½	teaspoon dried tarragon
1	teaspoon capers, rinsed and drained

1 In a medium bowl, combine the mayonnaise, parsley, gherkins, mustard, vinegar, Worcestershire sauce and tarragon. Chop the capers and add to the bowl. Mix well.

Makes about **250** ml.

nutrition at a glance
per 2 tablespoons

0.1 g.	total fat
0 g.	saturated fat
21	calories
0 mg.	cholesterol
248 mg.	sodium
0.2 g.	protein
3.9 g.	carbohydrates
0 g.	dietary fibre

Caramelised Onion Compote

quick and easy

The flavour of this sweet-and-sour condiment will really develop if it is refrigerated for a few days after cooking. Serve with cooked poultry, beef, beans or grilled vegetables.

2	large onions, chopped
4	tablespoons finely chopped yellow peppers
½	teaspoon minced garlic
2	tablespoons chopped raisins
2	tablespoons sugar
2	teaspoons brewed coffee
180	ml white wine or non-alcoholic white wine
1	teaspoon dried thyme
½	teaspoon dried rosemary, crumbled
	Ground black pepper
	Salt (optional)

1 Coat a large non-stick saucepan with non-stick spray. Add the onions, peppers and garlic. Mist with non-stick spray. Cover and cook over medium heat, stirring occasionally, for 4 to 5 minutes, or until the onions start to release moisture. Uncover and reduce the heat to medium-low. Cook, stirring occasionally, for 5 to 6 minutes, or until golden. If necessary, add 1 to 2 teaspoons water to prevent sticking.

2 Add the raisins, sugar and coffee. Cook over low heat for 2 minutes, or until the sugar dissolves. Add the wine. Cook over medium heat, stirring occasionally, for 5 minutes, or until the liquid has nearly evaporated.

3 Add the thyme and rosemary. Cook over low heat for 5 minutes. Season to taste with the pepper and salt (if using).

Makes about **500** ml.

nutrition at a glance

per 2 tablespoons

0.1 g.	total fat
0 g.	saturated fat
20	calories
0 mg.	cholesterol
1 mg.	sodium
0.3 g.	protein
3.6 g.	carbohydrates
0.3 g.	dietary fibre

Pinto Bean Salsa with Chipotle

A quicker version of this salsa – different but still delicious – can be made by combining all the ingredients raw.

1	small dried chipotle pepper (wear rubber gloves when handling)
3	medium tomatoes
2	cloves garlic, unpeeled
½	jalapeño pepper (wear rubber gloves when handling)
1	teaspoon dried oregano
¼	teaspoon cumin seeds, crushed
185	g cooked pinto beans
1	small onion, chopped
2	tablespoons finely chopped green peppers
2	tablespoons freshly squeezed lime juice
1	tablespoon chopped fresh parsley
	Salt (optional)

1 Place the chipotle pepper in a small bowl and add hot water to cover. Set aside for 30 minutes, or until softened. Drain.

2 Split the pepper and discard the seeds, membranes and stem. Chop the pepper finely and place in a medium bowl.

3 In a large non-stick frying pan, combine the tomatoes, garlic and jalapeño pepper. Cook over medium-high heat, turning occasionally, for 10 minutes, or until the tomato skins are blackened on all sides. Remove and set aside cool.

4 Add the oregano and cumin to the frying pan. Cook over medium heat, tossing constantly, for 2 to 3 minutes, or until fragrant. Transfer to the bowl with the chipotle peppers.

5 Core and peel the tomatoes; discard the cores and skin. Chop the tomatoes coarsely. Add to the bowl.

6 Peel the garlic. Finely chop the garlic and the jalapeño pepper. Add to the bowl. Add the beans, onions, green peppers, lime juice and parsley. Mix well. Season to taste with the salt (if using).

Makes about **625** ml.

nutrition at a glance

per 2 tablespoons

0.1 g.	total fat
0 g.	saturated fat
19	calories
0 mg.	cholesterol
22 mg.	sodium
0.9 g.	protein
3.7 g.	carbohydrates
1 g.	dietary fibre

Nectarine Salsa

quick and easy

Refreshing fruit salsas add terrific tastes to summer meals.
Serve with fish, meat, poultry, pork or bean dishes. Peaches can
easily substitute for the nectarines. Just be sure that the fruit you
use is ripe and sweet.

3	nectarines, diced
4	spring onions, chopped
4	tablespoons freshly squeezed lime juice
1	teaspoon finely chopped jalapeño peppers (wear rubber gloves when handling)
1	small clove garlic, minced
1	teaspoon chopped fresh mint
1–2	teaspoons sugar (optional)

1 In a medium bowl, combine the nectarines, spring onions, lime juice, peppers, garlic and mint. Mix well. If the fruit is not sweet enough, add 1 to 2 teaspoons sugar. Cover and refrigerate for 30 minutes. Drain off excess liquid before serving.

Makes about **625** ml.

Photograph on page 254

nutrition at a glance

per 2 tablespoons

0.1 g.	total fat
0 g.	saturated fat
12	calories
0 mg.	cholesterol
1 mg.	sodium
0.3 g.	protein
2.9 g.	carbohydrates
0.4 g.	dietary fibre

Roasted Garlic

Garlic that has been roasted has a mellow flavour and spreadable consistency. It can replace butter as a bread spread. Or it can be mixed with cooked rice or pasta or whisked into savoury sauces. Be sure to use 4 whole bulbs garlic, not individual cloves.

4   large bulbs garlic, unpeeled

1   Preheat the oven to 180°C, Gas 4. Cut the tops from the garlic bulbs to expose just the tips of the garlic cloves. Place the garlic bulbs in the centre of a large piece of foil. Mist with non-stick spray. Seal the foil tightly, leaving some air space around the garlic. Bake for 55 to 60 minutes, or until tender.

2   Open the foil and set aside to cool slightly. One clove at a time, squeeze the roasted garlic out of its skin. Discard the foil and skins. Purée the garlic in a blender or food processor, adding 1 teaspoon water, if necessary, to facilitate blending. Refrigerate for up to 1 week.

Makes about **125** ml.

Photograph on page 322

Photograph on page 322

nutrition at a glance

per 1 tablespoon

0.1 g.	total fat
0 g.	saturated fat
34	calories
0 mg.	cholesterol
4 mg.	sodium
1.4 g.	protein
7.5 g.	carbohydrates
0.5 g.	dietary fibre

Yogurt Cheese

Be sure to buy yogurt without added gelatine, which prevents the whey from separating from the curd to make cheese. To test your yogurt, remove a spoonful from the carton. If the space fills with liquid within a few minutes, you can make yogurt cheese from it.

500   ml fat-free natural yogurt

1   Line a fine mesh sieve with muslin or use a plastic mesh-lined yogurt cone. Spoon the yogurt into the sieve or cone. Set over a large glass measuring jug or other tall container. Refrigerate for at least 4 hours, or until well-drained.

2   Remove the yogurt from the sieve or cone. Store, tightly covered, in the refrigerator.

Makes about **250** ml.

nutrition at a glance

per 2 tablespoons

0.1 g.	total fat
0 g.	saturated fat
34	calories
1 mg.	cholesterol
47 mg.	sodium
3.5 g.	protein
4.7 g.	carbohydrates
0 g.	dietary fibre

Breakfast, Brunch and Lunch

Dinners are certainly important on a low-fat

eating plan, but there are only seven dinners in

a week.

Breakfasts, brunches and lunches provide many

more opportunities to eat healthfully.

Too often, these meals are treated as an

afterthought. With some forethought, however, break-

fasts, brunches and lunches can become important

occasions to incorporate nutrient- and fibre-packed

grains, vegetables and fruits into your eating plan.

Breakfast

Many of us are from a farm heritage and think that the ideal breakfast is big and rich. Traditional offerings are oozing with butter or other animal fats. Bacon, ham, sausage, potatoes, eggs, French toast, and fried bread are as much an anachronism as the horse and carriage.

An enlightened breakfast for modern lifestyles is whole-grain cereal, skimmed milk and fruit juice or fresh fruit. Toasted bagels or muffins are also good options. Serve with jam, preserves, honey or marmalade – all of which are fat-free. Or drizzle with fat-free butter from a squeeze bottle.

For those on the go, a bag of my Orange Granola makes a handy desk companion. Or a banana smoothie is quick to whip up to sip on the way to the office. (Cut a frozen banana into chunks – store peeled overripe bananas in the freezer for just such occasions. Purée in a blender or food processor with a scoop of fat-free vanilla frozen yogurt, skimmed milk to thin and a dash of cinnamon.)

Brunch

Weekends are more leisurely and can include brunch fare that tastes as luscious as it is nutritious.

Omelettes, scrambled eggs, quiches and French toast can all be made fat-free using egg substitutes. Fat-free egg substitutes, available refrigerated or frozen, are made mostly from egg whites. They are also pasteurised, which makes them safe to eat even when slightly undercooked.

My Spinach Quiche in Potato Crust, Salmon-Stuffed Mushrooms, Cranberry Biscotti and assorted filled omelettes will make any brunch special.

Lunch

Whether you're eating at home or at your office desk, lunch is the second-most important meal of the day. My lunch main dishes are based on vegetables, grains and lean proteins to fuel your body and keep your energy high throughout the busy afternoon.

My Spaghetti with Fresh Vegetables and Baked Potatoes Italiano are the kinds of carbohydrate-rich dishes that stick to your ribs. My Hearty Vegetable Sauté, Malaysian Curried Rice and Polenta with Roasted Ratatouille make great packed lunches to heat in an office microwave. You might want to make double batches so that you have leftovers on hand for lunch.

Orange Granola

Orange juice and fresh ginger give this granola a spirited new flavour. For the fruit, use a mixture of dates, figs, tart cherries, apricots and prunes – or whatever dried fruit you have on hand. Both old-fashioned rolled oats and the quick-cooking kind work fine in this recipe.

280   g finely chopped mixed dried fruit
  2   tablespoons orange juice
  1   teaspoon grated fresh ginger
125   ml maple syrup
185   g rolled oats

1   Preheat the oven to 165°C, Gas 3.

2   In a medium microwaveable bowl, combine the fruit, orange juice, ginger and half of the maple syrup. Microwave on high power for 1½ to 2 minutes, or until hot.

3   Coat a Swiss roll pan with non-stick spray. Place the oats in the pan. Drizzle with the remaining maple syrup; toss lightly to coat. Spread the oats in an even layer and bake for 20 minutes, stirring once.

4   Pour the fruit mixture over the oats; stir well to mix. Spread in an even layer. Bake for 20 minutes, stirring every 5 minutes, or until the mixture is crisp and golden.

5   Allow to cool, then store in an airtight container in a cool spot.

Makes **500** g.

nutrition at a glance
per 30 g

0.9 g.	total fat
0.1 g.	saturated fat
113	calories
0 mg.	cholesterol
2 mg.	sodium
2 g.	protein
26 g.	carbohydrates
1.9 g.	dietary fibre

Hot Porridge with Scalloped Apples

The scalloped apple topping makes this breakfast cereal even more special. Add dried cranberries, dried cherries or chopped dried apricots to the scalloped apples instead of the raisins if you like. Serve with fat-free liquid creamer or skimmed milk.

Scalloped Apples

2	large Granny Smith apples, thinly sliced
2	tablespoons freshly squeezed lemon juice
2	tablespoons sugar
¼	teaspoon ground cinnamon
	Pinch of ground allspice
4	tablespoons raisins (optional)

Porridge

500	ml skimmed milk
90	g superfine oatmeal
4	tablespoons water
1	tablespoon oat bran
¼	teaspoon salt (optional)

1 *To make the scalloped apples:* In a medium microwaveable bowl, combine the apples, lemon juice, sugar, cinnamon and allspice. Cover loosely with greaseproof paper. Microwave on high power, stirring occasionally, for 15 minutes, or until the apples are almost tender. Add the raisins (if using). Microwave on high power for 5 minutes more; set aside.

2 *To make the porridge:* In a medium microwaveable bowl, combine the milk, oatmeal, water, oat bran and salt (if using). Cover loosely with greaseproof paper. Microwave on medium power, stirring frequently, for 10 to 12 minutes, or until the cereal is thick and smooth. Serve topped with the apples.

Makes **6** servings.

nutrition at a glance

per serving

0.9 g.	total fat
0.2 g.	saturated fat
196	calories
1 mg.	cholesterol
157 mg.	sodium
6 g.	protein
42 g.	carbohydrates
2.4 g.	dietary fibre

Pancakes with Nectarines

quick and easy

You can substitute other fruits for the nectarines in these light and fluffy pancakes. Try cherries, raspberries, blueberries, peaches, plums, strawberries or bananas. If using bananas, be sure to toss the slices with a few teaspoons lemon juice to prevent discolouring.

125	g fat-free cottage cheese
4	tablespoons fat-free egg substitute
3	tablespoons sugar
75	g plain flour
½	teaspoon bicarbonate of soda
½	teaspoon baking powder
½	teaspoon ground cinnamon
4	egg whites
2	nectarines, chopped

1 Place the cottage cheese in a sieve. Set over a bowl and allow to drain for 10 minutes. Transfer to a blender or food processor. Blend, scraping the sides of the container occasionally, for 3 to 5 minutes, or until completely smooth. Add the egg substitute and sugar. Process briefly to mix. Set aside.

2 In a small bowl, combine the flour, bicarbonate of soda, baking powder and cinnamon. Mix well.

3 Place the egg whites in a large bowl. Beat with an electric mixer until stiff peaks form. Sift the flour mixture over the egg whites. Fold to combine. Add the cottage-cheese mixture. Fold to combine.

4 Coat a large non-stick frying pan with non-stick spray. Warm over low heat. Spoon the batter in 60 ml measures into the pan. Sprinkle 2 tablespoons of the nectarines over each pancake, pressing in lightly. Cook for 5 minutes, or until the bottoms are golden. Flip and cook for 4 minutes, or until golden. Remove to a platter. Cover to keep warm while cooking the remaining pancakes.

Makes **8** pancakes.

Photograph on page 325

Photograph on page 325

Lynn's Kitchen Tip

Plain thick pancakes freeze well for quick weekday breakfasts. Allow the cooked pancakes to cool, then stack with pieces of greaseproof paper between the pancakes. Place in a plastic freezer bag and seal tightly. Freeze. Remove just the number of pancakes that you need. Allow to stand at room temperature for 15 minutes, then heat in a toaster, toaster oven, or conventional oven.

nutrition at a glance

per pancake

0.2 g.	total fat
0 g.	saturated fat
84	calories
1 mg.	cholesterol
189 mg.	sodium
5.2 g.	protein
15.6 g.	carbohydrates
0.9 g.	dietary fibre

Baked Winter Fruits

This luscious baked fruit compote is delicious as a topping for fat-free natural yogurt or as a sweet in its own right – drizzle it with some evaporated skimmed milk.

1	baking apple
1	ripe but firm pear
125	ml apple juice
4	tablespoons raisins
4	tablespoons chopped dates
1½	tablespoons cherry jam
2	teaspoons freshly squeezed lemon juice
	Pinch of ground nutmeg
	Pinch of ground cinnamon

1 Preheat the oven to 190°C, Gas 5.

2 Cut the apple and pear into lengthwise quarters. Cut out the seeds and discard. Place in an 20 x 20 cm baking dish.

3 In a small bowl, combine the apple juice, raisins, dates, jam, lemon juice, nutmeg and cinnamon. Pour over the apples and pears. Stir to mix.

4 Cover with foil. Bake, basting occasionally with the sauce, for 35 to 40 minutes, or until the fruit is tender.

Makes **4** servings.

nutrition at a glance
per serving

0.5 g.	total fat
0.1 g.	saturated fat
141	calories
0 mg.	cholesterol
5 mg.	sodium
0.9 g.	protein
36.6 g.	carbohydrates
3.3 g.	dietary fibre

French Toast

quick and easy

This French toast is so easy to make that it's sure to become a weekend favourite. Let the bread slices sit out overnight to dry slightly so they keep their shape when dipped in the egg mixture. Serve with a dollop of fruit jam or a drizzle of warm maple syrup or honey. Using a large frying pan to cook the French toast will allow you to do them in 2 batches.

180	ml fat-free egg substitute
250	ml skimmed milk
¼	teaspoon vanilla
	Pinch of ground cinnamon
8	slices (40-calorie-per-slice) white bread
2	teaspoons icing sugar

1 In a large shallow bowl, combine the egg substitute, milk, vanilla and cinnamon. Whisk to combine.

2 Coat a large non-stick frying pan with non-stick spray. Warm over medium heat. Dip one bread slice at a time into the egg mixture, turning to coat both sides and to soak up as much of the mixture as possible. Add to the frying pan. Cook for 4 minutes, or until golden. Flip and cook for 4 minutes, or until golden. Remove and keep warm.

3 Wipe the frying pan with a paper towel to remove any browned bits. Off the heat, coat the frying pan with non-stick spray. Warm over medium heat. Dip and cook more bread slices. Repeat to cook all the bread slices.

4 Place the icing sugar in a small fine sieve. Sprinkle over the French toast just before serving.

Makes **8** slices.

nutrition at a glance

per slice

0.6 g.	total fat
0.1 g.	saturated fat
66	calories
1 mg.	cholesterol
144 mg.	sodium
5 g.	protein
11.4 g.	carbohydrates
1.9 g.	dietary fibre

Salmon-Stuffed Mushrooms

These savoury stuffed mushrooms make a lovely addition to the brunch table. Serve with scrambled fat-free egg substitute and toasted muffins.

8	large mushrooms (7.3 cm diameter)
125	g diced French bread
1	clove garlic, minced
⅛	teaspoon dried thyme
⅛	teaspoon dried crumbled rosemary
250	ml fat-free egg substitute
1	egg white
2	tablespoons fat-free mayonnaise
1	teaspoon finely chopped fresh dill
3	spring onions, chopped
4	tablespoons chopped smoked salmon
	Salt (optional)
3	tablespoons fat-free soured cream

1   Preheat the oven to 190°C, Gas 5.

2   Remove the stems from the mushrooms. Set aside the caps. Chop the stems and set aside.

3   Coat a large non-stick frying pan with non-stick spray. Warm over medium-high heat. Place the caps in the pan, round side down. Reduce the heat to medium, cover, and cook for 4 minutes. Turn the mushrooms. Cover and cook for 4 minutes, or until softened. Place the caps, round side down, in a 30 x 20 cm baking dish. Set aside.

4   Add the bread, garlic, thyme and rosemary to the frying pan. Mist with non-stick spray. Cook over medium heat, tossing frequently, for 4 minutes, or until golden. Add the mushroom stems. Cook, tossing, for 4 minutes, or until the stems soften.

5   In a small bowl, mix the egg substitute, egg white, mayonnaise, dill and half of the spring onions. Add to the frying pan. Cook, stirring, for 3 to 5 minutes, or until the eggs start to set. Add the salmon and mix to combine. Season to taste with the salt (if using).

6   Remove from the heat. Divide the filling among the mushroom caps. Bake for 8 to 10 minutes, or until the stuffing is hot.

7   Top each cap with a dollop of the soured cream and sprinkle with the remaining spring onions.

Makes **8** mushrooms.

nutrition at a glance	
per mushroom	
0.4 g.	total fat
0.1 g.	saturated fat
50	calories
1 mg.	cholesterol
146 mg.	sodium
5.5 g.	protein
5.9 g.	carbohydrates
0.7 g.	dietary fibre

Basic Omelette with Variations

Omelettes are one of the easiest and most versatile dishes for breakfast or brunch. They can be made without fat just by using fat-free egg substitute and egg whites. After you master the basic omelette, try any my fillings below or create your own. For best results if doubling the recipe, don't increase the size of the pan. Instead, cook the omelettes in two batches.

250 ml fat-free egg substitute
2 egg whites
Pinch of ground black pepper
Pinch of salt (optional)

1 In a medium bowl, combine the egg substitute, egg whites, pepper and salt (if using). Whisk until slightly frothy.

2 Coat a medium non-stick frying pan or omelette pan with non-stick spray. Warm over medium-high heat. Add the egg mixture. Cook over high heat for 3 to 4 minutes, occasionally lifting the edges of the egg mixture to let the uncooked eggs run underneath. When the eggs are almost set, use a spatula to loosen the edges.

3 With the spatula, fold the eggs in half to create a half-moon. Reduce the heat to low and cook for 2 minutes, or until the eggs are cooked through. Cut in half.

nutrition at a glance
per serving
0 g. total fat
0 g. saturated fat
79 calories
0 mg. cholesterol
255 mg. sodium
15.5 g. protein
3 g. carbohydrates
0 g. dietary fibre

Makes **2** servings.

Cheese Omelette: Add a pinch of nutmeg to the egg mixture instead of the pepper. Just before folding the omelette, sprinkle with 4 tablespoons grated fat-free Cheddar cheese or fat-free mozzarella cheese. Fold and cook for 2 minutes, or until the cheese melts. Sprinkle with finely chopped spring onions.

Greek Omelette: Coat a large non-stick frying pan with non-stick spray. Add 60 g torn spinach leaves, 1 spring onion (chopped), and ¼ teaspoon dried oregano. Cook over medium heat, stirring, for 2 to 3 minutes, or until the spinach wilts. Add 1 small tomato (chopped). Cook for 2 minutes. Set aside while preparing the omelette. Just before folding the omelette, spoon the mixture over the eggs. Sprinkle with 1 tablespoon crumbled low-fat feta cheese. Fold and cook for 2 minutes, or until the filling is hot. Sprinkle with chopped fresh dill.

Ham Omelette: Just before folding the omelette, sprinkle with 60 g diced fat-free ham. Fold and cook for 2 minutes, or until the filling is hot. Sprinkle with finely chopped fresh parsley.

Jam Omelette: Add ½ teaspoon sugar to the egg mixture instead of the pepper. Just before folding the omelette, spoon 3 tablespoons jam over the eggs. Fold and cook for 2 minutes, or until the filling is hot.

Mushroom Omelette: Coat a large non-stick frying pan with non-stick spray. Add 125 g mushrooms, sliced. Cover and cook over medium heat for 3 to 4 minutes, or until the mushrooms start to release moisture. Uncover and cook, stirring occasionally, for 2 to 3 minutes, or until softened. Set aside while preparing the omelette. Just before folding the omelette, spoon the mushrooms over the eggs. Fold and cook for 2 minutes, or until the filling is hot. Sprinkle with fat-free Parmesan topping.

Onion Omelette: Coat a large non-stick frying pan with non-stick spray. Add 90 g chopped onions. Cover and cook over medium heat for 3 to 4 minutes, or until the onions start to release moisture. Uncover and cook, adding 1 to 2 teaspoons water if needed to prevent sticking, for 2 to 3 minutes, or until golden. Set aside while preparing the omelette. Just before folding the omelette, sprinkle the onions over the eggs. Fold and cook for 2 minutes, or until the filling is hot. Sprinkle with finely chopped fresh parsley.

Spanish Omelette: Coat a large non-stick frying pan with non-stick spray. Add 1 small potato (diced), 1 small onion (diced), and 1 small clove garlic (minced). Mist with non-stick spray. Cook over medium-high heat, without stirring, for 3 to 4 minutes. Stir. Cook, stirring occasionally, for 8 to 10 minutes, or until the potatoes are tender. Set aside while preparing the omelette. Just before folding the omelette, spoon the potato mixture over the eggs. Fold and cook for 2 minutes, or until the filling is hot. Sprinkle with finely diced tomatoes.

Tex-Mex Omelette: Coat a large non-stick frying pan with non-stick spray. Add 45 g finely diced onions, 45 g finely diced green peppers, 45 g finely diced tomatoes, and 1 clove garlic (minced). Mist with the non-stick spray. Cook over medium heat, stirring occasionally, for 4 to 6 minutes, or until the peppers are softened. Season with ¼ teaspoon chilli powder, ¼ teaspoon ground cumin, and ¼ teaspoon dried oregano. Set aside while preparing the omelette. Just before folding the omelette, spoon the mixture over the eggs. Fold and cook for 2 minutes, or until the filling is hot. Sprinkle with chopped fresh coriander.

Photograph on page 324

Creamy Banana Bowl

quick and easy

I sometimes sprinkle these bananas with a bit of toasted coconut or brown sugar just before serving. A sprig of fresh mint makes a lovely garnish.

125	ml fat-free natural yogurt
1	tablespoon sugar
2	ripe but firm bananas, sliced
	Ground cinnamon or nutmeg

1   In a medium bowl, combine the yogurt and sugar. Stir to dissolve the sugar. Add the bananas. Stir to combine. Sprinkle with the cinnamon or nutmeg.

Makes **4** servings.

nutrition at a glance	
per serving	
0.3 g.	total fat
0.1 g.	saturated fat
82	calories
1 mg.	cholesterol
24 mg.	sodium
2.4 g.	protein
18.8 g.	carbohydrates
1.2 g.	dietary fibre

Spinach Quiche in Potato Crust

Using potato slices as a quiche crust eliminates the astronomically high amount of fat that comes with a traditional pastry crust. In fact, this recipe is so low in fat that I was able to use some real Parmesan cheese without raising the total fat above 1 gramme per serving.

Potato Crust

2	medium baking potatoes, thinly sliced
	Salt (optional)

Spinach Filling

1	large onion, sliced
1	package (315 g) frozen chopped spinach, thawed
500	ml fat-free egg substitute
375	ml fat-free liquid creamer
2	tablespoons plain flour
¼	teaspoon ground nutmeg
60	g grated fat-free Cheddar or mozzarella cheese
¼	teaspoon salt (optional)
2	tablespoons grated Parmesan cheese

1 *To make the potato crust:* Preheat the oven to 200°C, Gas 6.

2 Cover a large baking tray with foil and coat with non-stick spray. Arrange the potatoes, slightly overlapping, in rows. Mist with non-stick spray. Sprinkle lightly with the salt (if using). Bake for 10 minutes, or until golden. Remove the potatoes from the oven.

3 Reduce the oven temperature to 180°C, Gas 4.

4 Coat a 25 cm deep pie plate with non-stick spray. Arrange the potatoes in overlapping circles to cover the bottom. Overlap slices on the sides so that slices protrude above the edge of the plate. If you have extra potatoes, place them on the bottom. Set aside.

5 *To make the spinach filling:* Coat a large non-stick frying pan with non-stick spray. Add the onions. Cover and cook over medium heat, stirring occasionally, for 6 minutes, or until golden. If necessary, add 1 to 2 teaspoons water to prevent sticking.

6 Add the spinach and cook for 2 minutes, or until the spinach is hot.

7 In a large bowl, combine the egg substitute, creamer, flour and nutmeg. Whisk to combine. Add the Cheddar or mozzarella, onions, spinach and salt (if using). Mix to combine. Pour into the prepared pie plate. Sprinkle with the Parmesan.

8 Bake for 40 minutes, or until a knife inserted in the centre comes out clean.

Makes **8** servings.

Photograph on page 323

Photograph on page 323

> ## Lynn's Health Watch
>
> Incorporating fat-free, or even low-fat, cheeses into your cooking is one of the most important fat-reducing changes that you can make.

nutrition at a glance
per serving
0.6 g.	total fat
0.3 g.	saturated fat
128	calories
1.7 mg.	cholesterol
217 mg.	sodium
10.5 g.	protein
18.5 g.	carbohydrates
1.5 g.	dietary fibre

Quiche in Tomato Shells

On a chilly day, a piping hot quiche baked in a tomato shell makes a warm and inviting dish.

2	large firm tomatoes
250	ml fat-free egg substitute
2	tablespoons minced spring onions
2	tablespoons chopped fresh parsley
1	tablespoon capers, rinsed and drained
¼	teaspoon ground black pepper
	Pinch of salt (optional)
4	teaspoons fresh breadcrumbs (from 40-calorie-per-slice bread)
4	teaspoons fat-free Parmesan topping

1 Preheat the oven to 180°C, Gas 4.

2 Cut the tomatoes in half crosswise. Scoop out the pulp, leaving a 6 mm shell. Set the shells, upside down, on paper towels to drain.

3 Chop the pulp and place in a medium bowl. Add the egg substitute, spring onions, parsley, capers, pepper and salt (if using). Stir to combine.

4 Place 4 custard cups in an 20 x 20 cm baking dish. Place a tomato shell, cut side up, in each cup. Divide the egg mixture among the shells. Sprinkle with the breadcrumbs and Parmesan.

5 Bake for 40 minutes, or until a knife inserted in the filling comes out clean. If desired, grill for 2 minutes to brown the tops.

Makes **4** servings.

Lynn's Kitchen Tip

Try baking quiche in hollowed courgette halves, baby aubergine halves, or acorn squash halves. Make sure to partially cook the vegetable so that it will be thoroughly cooked when the quiche filling is done.

---

nutrition at a glance

per serving

0.4 g.	total fat
0 g.	saturated fat
61	calories
0 mg.	cholesterol
227 mg.	sodium
8 g.	protein
7.2 g.	carbohydrates
1.4 g.	dietary fibre

Thai Peanut Dressing (page 116) on mixed salad greens

Tomato Relish (page 299) and Black Bean and Rice Cakes (page 181)

Baked Potatoes Italiano (page 342)

Roasted Garlic (page 304)

Spinach Quiche in Potato Crust (page 316)

Tex-Mex Omelette (page 315)

Pancakes with Nectarines (page 309)

Stacked-High Apple Pie (page 359)

Pineapple-Caramel Cake (page 348)

Lemon Bars (page 369)

Key Lime Cheesecake (page 347)

Daffodil Cake with Lemon Sauce (page 354)

Almond Tapioca and Lime-Blackberry Parfaits (page 372)

Chocolate-Raspberry Cake (page 350)

Chocolate-Banana Pie (page 360)

Glazed Tropical Fruit Cake (page 356)

Cranberry Biscotti

For a fancy party or holiday treat, use a mixture of candied red and green cherries and coarsely chopped candied pineapple in place of the dried cranberries. These crunchy biscuits are the perfect close for any brunch. Offer hot coffee or tea for dunking.

3	egg whites
½	teaspoon cream of tartar
105	g sugar
½	teaspoon almond essence
155	g plain flour
60	g sliced almonds
185	g dried cranberries or tart cherries

1   Preheat the oven to 180°C, Gas 4.

2   Place the egg whites and cream of tartar in a large bowl. Beat with an electric mixer until soft peaks form. Continue beating, adding 1 tablespoon sugar at a time, until stiff peaks form. Add the almond essence and beat briefly. Sprinkle the flour over the egg-white mixture; fold to combine. Sprinkle the almonds and cranberries or cherries over the egg-white mixture; fold to combine.

3   Coat an 20 x 10 cm loaf tin with non-stick spray. Dust lightly with flour, shaking out the excess. Spread the dough evenly in the tin. Bake for 30 minutes, or until lightly browned. Remove from the oven and set aside to cool completely.

4   Reduce the oven temperature to 135°C, Gas 1.

5   Remove the biscotti loaf from the tin. Cut in half lengthwise into 2 strips. Cut each strip into 15 slices. Place the biscotti on a baking tray. Bake for 35 minutes, or until golden and dry. Cool to room temperature before serving.

Makes **30** biscotti.

nutrition at a glance

per biscotto

0.9 g.	total fat
0 g.	saturated fat
53	calories
0 mg.	cholesterol
6 mg.	sodium
1.1 g.	protein
10 g.	carbohydrates
0.6 g.	dietary fibre

Mediterranean Stuffed Tomatoes

quick and easy

Best with summer-ripe tomatoes, this versatile luncheon dish can be served warm or hot from the oven. If you like, you can substitute cooked bulgur or orzo pasta for the rice. Serve with dollops of fat-free natural yogurt or soured cream. Cuke and Zuke Raita (page 105) makes a fine accompaniment.

2	large firm tomatoes
45	g chopped onions
½	teaspoon dried oregano
⅛	teaspoon ground cinnamon
4	tablespoons skimmed chicken stock (page 94)
2	tablespoons chopped raisins
125	g cooked rice
1	teaspoon chopped fresh mint
	Salt (optional)

1   Preheat the oven to 180°C, Gas 4.

2   Cut the tomatoes in half crosswise. Scoop out the pulp, leaving a 6 mm shell. Set the shells, upside down, on paper towels to drain.

3   Chop the pulp and place in a medium bowl.

4   Coat a large non-stick frying pan with non-stick spray. Add the onions, oregano and cinnamon. Cover and cook over medium-low heat for 2 to 3 minutes. Add the chopped tomatoes, stock and raisins.

5   Bring to a boil over medium heat. Reduce the heat to low and simmer, stirring often, for 3 to 4 minutes, or until the tomatoes start to soften. Remove from the heat. Stir in the rice and mint. Season to taste with the salt (if using).

6   Coat an 20 x 20 cm baking dish with non-stick spray. Place the tomatoes in the dish. Divide the tomato mixture among the shells. Bake for 15 minutes, or until the stuffing is hot.

Makes **4** servings.

nutrition at a glance

per serving

0.4 g.	total fat
0.1 g.	saturated fat
72	calories
0 mg.	cholesterol
12 mg.	sodium
2 g.	protein
16 g.	carbohydrates
2 g.	dietary fibre

Spaghetti with Fresh Vegetables

quick and easy

I chop the vegetables while the pasta cooks, then toss them all, except the garlic, in a bowl so that the flavours blend for a few minutes. If you like, you can substitute finely chopped broccoli florets, fresh spinach or fresh or thawed frozen peas for the sugar snap peas. Garnish with fat-free Parmesan topping and chopped fresh parsley.

250	g low-fat spaghetti (0.5 g. fat per 60-g serving)
2	cloves garlic, minced
4	ripe plum tomatoes, diced
4	spring onions, finely chopped
1	stalk celery, finely chopped
90	g sugar snap peas sliced 6 mm thick
3	tablespoons capers, rinsed and drained
	Ground black pepper
	Salt (optional)
2	tablespoons thinly sliced fresh basil

1 Bring a large pan of water to a boil over high heat. Add the spaghetti and cook according to the package directions. Drain and let stand in the colander.

2 Coat the pan with non-stick spray. Add the garlic and cook over low heat, stirring, for 30 seconds. Add the tomatoes, spring onions, celery, peas and capers. Toss for 1 minute to heat. Season to taste with the pepper and salt (if using). Add the spaghetti and basil; toss.

Makes **4** servings.

Lynn's Kitchen Tip

Here's how to save on washing up when making a pasta dish, such as pasta primavera, that requires cooked broccoli, asparagus or other vegetables. Simply add the chopped vegetables to the pasta cooking water a few minutes before the pasta is done. Drain and add sauce according to the recipe.

nutrition at a glance

per serving

0.9 g.	total fat
0.1 g.	saturated fat
252	calories
0 mg.	cholesterol
255 mg.	sodium
10 g.	protein
51 g.	carbohydrates
5 g.	dietary fibre

Hearty Vegetable Sauté

quick and easy

This dish offers big flavour. Serve it with grilled fish or turkey – or with cooked rice or quinoa as a vegetarian luncheon dish.

1	onion, thinly sliced
½	orange or sweet red pepper, cut into thin strips
2	cloves garlic, minced
1	small courgette, sliced
185	g cap mushrooms, sliced
½	teaspoon dried oregano
¼	teaspoon dried thyme
75	g frozen peas, thawed
1	plum tomato, sliced
2	teaspoons white-wine Worcestershire sauce
2	tablespoons thinly sliced fresh basil
4	tablespoons fat-free Parmesan topping

1 Coat a large non-stick frying pan or wok with non-stick spray. Add the onions, peppers and garlic. Cover and cook over medium-high heat, stirring occasionally, for 3 to 4 minutes, or until the onions are golden. If necessary, add 1 to 2 teaspoons water to prevent sticking.

2 Add the courgette, mushrooms, oregano and thyme. Cover and cook for 3 to 4 minutes, or until the mushrooms give off liquid. Uncover and cook, stirring constantly, for 1 to 2 minutes, or until the liquid evaporates.

3 Add the peas, tomatoes and Worcestershire sauce. Cook, stirring, for 3 to 4 minutes, or until the tomatoes soften. Stir in the basil. Sprinkle with the Parmesan. Toss to combine.

Makes **4** servings.

nutrition at a glance

per serving

0.9 g.	total fat
0.4 g.	saturated fat
78	calories
1 mg.	cholesterol
152 mg.	sodium
6 g.	protein
14 g.	carbohydrates
3 g.	dietary fibre

Garlicky Spinach Potatoes

Mellow roasted garlic makes these spinach-stuffed potatoes really special. If you don't have any roasted garlic on hand, simply bake a head of garlic at the same time you do the potatoes. Garnish with thin strips of pimientos.

4	large baking potatoes
315	g spinach leaves, chopped
125	ml water
250	g fat-free ricotta cheese
125	ml fat-free liquid creamer or evaporated skimmed milk
2	tablespoons puréed Roasted Garlic (page 304)
¼	teaspoon ground black pepper
	Pinch of dried tarragon
	Salt (optional)

1 Preheat the oven to 180°C, Gas 4. Wash and gently scrub the potatoes, but don't dry. Place at least 10 cm apart on the oven rack and bake for 1 hour, or until tender. Remove from the oven. Do not turn off the oven.

2 Cut each potato in half lengthwise. Set aside for 10 minutes, or until cool enough to handle. Scoop the pulp from the potatoes, leaving 6 mm-thick shells. Place the pulp in a large bowl. Set the shells aside.

3 Place the spinach and water in a large non-stick saucepan. Cover and cook for 3 to 4 minutes, or until the spinach is wilted. Drain well and press with paper towels to squeeze out excess moisture. Set aside.

4 Mash the potato pulp until smooth. Add the ricotta, creamer or milk, garlic, pepper, tarragon and spinach. Season to taste with the salt (if using). Mix well. Spoon into the potato shells.

5 Place the potatoes in a single layer in a 33 x 23 cm baking dish. Cover loosely with foil. Bake for 10 minutes, or until the potatoes puff slightly. Remove the foil and bake for 3 to 5 minutes, or until lightly browned.

Makes **4** servings.

nutrition at a glance

per serving

0.5 g.	total fat
0.1 g.	saturated fat
303	calories
5 mg.	cholesterol
243 mg.	sodium
14 g.	protein
59.7 g.	carbohydrates
5.3 g.	dietary fibre

Malaysian Curried Rice

quick and easy

For a lovely luncheon main dish, top this aromatic rice with steamed prawns or scallops, chopped spring onions, grated carrots and sliced cucumbers. Add a pinch of cayenne pepper for a hint of heat. For a slightly sweeter version, add a few tablespoons chopped dried apricots, figs, raisins or dates.

750	ml water
280	g long-grain white rice
	Pinch of salt (optional)
1	medium onion, thinly sliced
2	teaspoons minced fresh ginger
2	cloves garlic, minced
1½	teaspoons plain flour
250	ml evaporated skimmed milk
80	ml peach or mango chutney
½	teaspoon coconut extract
½	teaspoon curry powder
½	teaspoon honey
1	tablespoon freshly squeezed lemon juice
1	tablespoon chopped fresh coriander

1   In a medium non-stick saucepan, combine the water, rice and salt (if using). Bring to a boil over medium-high heat. Reduce the heat to medium-low, cover and cook for 20 minutes, or until the rice is tender and the liquid is absorbed.

2   Meanwhile, coat a large non-stick frying pan with non-stick spray. Warm the frying pan over medium heat. Add the onions, ginger and garlic. Mist with non-stick spray. Cover and cook, stirring occasionally, for 2 to 3 minutes, or until the onions start to release moisture. Uncover and cook, stirring occasionally, for 3 to 4 minutes, or until golden. If necessary, add 1 to 2 teaspoons water to prevent sticking.

3   Place the flour in a small bowl. Gradually whisk in the milk until smooth. Add to the frying pan. Cook, whisking constantly, for 2 to 3 minutes, or until thickened. Add the chutney, coconut, curry powder and honey.

4   Remove from the heat. Add the lemon juice; whisk to combine.

5   Fluff the rice with a fork. Serve the sauce over the rice. Sprinkle with the coriander.

Makes **4** servings.

nutrition at a glance

per serving

0.6 g.	total fat
0.1 g.	saturated fat
211	calories
0 mg.	cholesterol
24 mg.	sodium
5 g.	protein
46 g.	carbohydrates
2 g.	dietary fibre

Baked Potatoes Italiano

I whipped up this easy oven dish one cold evening, and it's been a satisfying favourite ever since. The sauce cooks at the same time the potatoes are baking. Sprinkle with fat-free Parmesan topping just before serving.

4	large baking potatoes
2	medium tomatoes, diced
½	large onion, coarsely chopped
½	green pepper, cut into 1 cm chunks
90	g coarsely chopped fresh parsley
1	tablespoon finely chopped dry-pack sun-dried tomatoes
2	cloves garlic, minced
2	teaspoons dried oregano
3	tablespoons thinly sliced fresh basil
	Ground black pepper
	Salt (optional)

1 Preheat the oven to 180°C, Gas 4.

2 Wash and gently scrub the potatoes, but don't dry.

3 Coat a 30 x 20 cm baking dish with non-stick spray. Layer the fresh tomatoes, onions, green peppers, parsley, sun-dried tomatoes, garlic and oregano in the dish. Cover tightly with foil.

4 Place the dish in the oven. Poke each potato several times with a fork. Place the potatoes directly on the oven rack next to the dish. Bake for 1 hour, or until the vegetables are tender and the potatoes can be easily pierced with a sharp knife.

5 Stir the basil into the vegetable sauce. Season to taste with the black pepper and salt (if using).

6 Cut a 2.5 cm-deep cross in each potato. Squeeze the ends to open the cut and push up the flesh slightly. Top with the vegetable sauce.

Makes **4** servings.

Photograph on page 321

> ## Lynn's Fat-Free Flavour
> Romano are the finest choice for baking. With their low moisture and high starch content, the interior bakes into fluffy perfection.

nutrition at a glance

per serving

0.9 g.	total fat
0.2 g.	saturated fat
237	calories
0 mg.	cholesterol
34 mg.	sodium
5.8 g.	protein
53.6 g.	carbohydrates
6.3 g.	dietary fibre

Poached Vegetables with Lemon-Horseradish Sauce

A sprightly horseradish-lemon sauce brings a fresh note to this satisfying cold-weather favourite.

1	small head green cabbage, cored and cut into 8 wedges
2	large potatoes, each cut into 4 wedges
2	medium carrots, cut into 5 cm lengths
1	large onion, cut into 8 wedges
500	ml skimmed chicken stock (page 94)
½	teaspoon caraway seeds, crushed
¼	teaspoon ground black pepper
	Pinch of salt (optional)
2	tablespoons fat-free soured cream
1	tablespoon prepared horseradish
1	teaspoon grated lemon rind
4	tablespoons chopped fresh parsley

1   In a non-stick flameproof casserole, combine the cabbage, potatoes, carrots and onions. Add the stock, caraway seeds, pepper and salt (if using). Cover and simmer over medium heat for 35 minutes, or until the carrots are tender. With a slotted spoon, carefully remove the vegetables to a serving platter.

2   Pour off all but 125 ml of the stock from the saucepan. (Reserve for another use.) Over low heat, whisk in the soured cream, horse-radish and lemon rind. Cook, stirring, just until hot. Pour over the vegetables. Sprinkle with the parsley.

Makes **4** servings.

nutrition at a glance

per serving
0.9 g.	total fat
0.1 g.	saturated fat
176	calories
0 mg.	cholesterol
52 mg.	sodium
5 g.	protein
40 g.	carbohydrates
8 g.	dietary fibre

Polenta with Roasted Ratatouille

Polenta, the Italian version of cornmeal mush, is easy to make from scratch. But if you're pressed for time, you can serve this quick-roasted ratatouille over slices of cooked fat-free polenta from a tube, which is available in most supermarkets.

Roasted Ratatouille

1	small aubergine, cut into 2.5 cm pieces
1	large onion, coarsely chopped
1	medium courgette, cut into 2.5 cm pieces
1	small sweet red pepper, cut into 2.5 cm pieces
4	large cloves garlic, coarsely chopped
	Salt (optional)
500	g canned tomatoes, coarsely chopped (with juice)
4	tablespoons balsamic vinegar
2	teaspoons dried oregano

Polenta

750	ml skimmed milk
125	g yellow cornmeal
125	ml fat-free natural yogurt

1 *To make the roasted ratatouille:* Preheat the oven to 230°C, Gas 8.

2 Coat a non-stick roasting tin with non-stick spray. Add the aubergine, onions, courgette, peppers and garlic. Mist with non-stick spray. Season lightly with the salt (if using). Roast for 15 minutes.

3 Stir in the tomatoes (with juice), vinegar and oregano. Mist with non-stick spray. Roast for 15 minutes, or until the vegetables are tender.

4 *To make the polenta:* Meanwhile, in a medium non-stick saucepan over medium heat, bring the milk to a boil. Add the cornmeal in a slow, steady stream, stirring constantly. Reduce the heat to medium-low. Cook, stirring constantly, for 8 to 10 minutes, or until the cornmeal is soft. Stir in the yogurt.

5 To serve, spoon the ratatouille over the polenta.

Makes **6** servings.

nutrition at a glance

per serving

0.9 g.	total fat
0.2 g.	saturated fat
160	calories
0 mg.	cholesterol
156 mg.	sodium
5 g.	protein
34 g.	carbohydrates
5 g.	dietary fibre

Cakes, Pies and Other Sweets

Nutritionists tell us that a perfectly ripe piece of
fresh fruit is the healthy way to close a meal. We
know they're right, but in our hearts we long for
cheesecake.

So let it be cheesecake – as long as it's a wedge
of fabulous fat-free Key Lime Cheesecake. The
cheesecake and all the other desserts in this
chapter are crammed with satisfaction, yet none
contain more than 1 gramme of fat per (generous)

serving. Occasional indulgences like this won't upset your nutritional apple cart.

Feast on Chocolate-Banana Pie, Pineapple-Caramel Cake, Stacked-High Apple Pie, Pumpkin Pudding, Lemon Bars, Raisin and Spice Oatmeal Biscuits and more.

My desserts are based on intensely flavoured, naturally low fat ingredients – such as cocoa powder, citrus, ripe fruits and spices. These old-fashioned ingredients deliver honest flavour. To these I add a host of fat-free versions of dairy products – cream cheese, sweetened condensed milk, buttermilk, natural yogurt and soured cream. These products deliver excellent texture and flavour in baked and cooked desserts.

Occasionally, I call for prune purée, applesauce or golden syrup to replace fat. They trap moisture in baked goods in much the same way that fat does.

For other cakes, biscuits and pies, I rely on fat-free egg-white meringues to lightly carry sweetness and flavours. And many of the low-fat and fat-free biscuits now in supermarkets make delicious crumb pie shells without all the fat that's needed in pastry shell.

Don't you dare tell your family and friends that these desserts are fat-free. Because otherwise, they'll never know.

A Note about Ingredients

I created these recipes using large eggs and plain flour. Most of the recipes do not require sifting the flour before measuring. When it is necessary for a lighter result, for example, in the Daffodil Cake, I specify "sifted flour," which means that you should sift it first. If you have access to soft wheat flour, you can substitute it for the plain flour. It will produce a more tender crumb.

Be sure to use pure essences – vanilla, maple, almond and such – for the highest quality results.

For fruit desserts like Fresh Berry Angel Tart or Plum and Blueberry Tart, use the ripest berries available. Choose berries that are deeply coloured with no soft spots.

For Glazed Tropical Fruit Cake, Rice Pudding with Nectarines and Summer Fruits in Phyllo, select fruits with smooth skin and no blemishes or bruises. Ripe fruits yield slightly when gently pressed. To ripen hard plums, peaches, nectarines, papayas or mangoes, store them at room temperature in a brown paper bag with some bananas. They'll ripen in one or two days and can then be stored in the refrigerator until you're ready to use them.

Key Lime Cheesecake

If you can't find Key lime juice, substitute standard lime juice. Low-fat digestive biscuits can be substituted for the low-fat ginger snaps. You can make the cheesecake 1 or 2 days in advance, but top it with the sliced kiwifruit just before serving.

Ginger Snap Shell

30	low-fat ginger snaps
2	tablespoons sugar
1	egg white

Key Lime Cheesecake

2	tablespoons cold water
1	teaspoon powdered gelatine
2	packages (250 g each) fat-free cream cheese, at room temperature
1	can (440 g) fat-free sweetened condensed milk
125	ml Key lime juice
2	egg whites
2	tablespoons cornflour
1	teaspoon grated lime zest

Kiwifruit Topping

3	kiwifruit
1	tablespoon icing sugar

1 *To make the ginger snap shell:* Preheat the oven to 180°C, Gas 4. Coat a 23 cm springform tin with non-stick spray.

2 Break the ginger snaps and place in a food processor. Process until the ginger snaps are broken into fine crumbs. Add the sugar and egg white; process until evenly blended and slightly moist. Press into the bottom and 1 cm up the sides of the tin.

3 Bake for 10 minutes, or until the shell is lightly browned. Set aside. Do not turn off the oven.

4 *To make the Key lime cheesecake:* Place the water in a cup. Sprinkle with the gelatine and set aside for 5 minutes to soften.

(continued)

Lynn's Lore

Key lime pie is one of the most renowned regional American desserts. It is made from the juice of the Key lime, which is smaller and has more yellow skin than the green Persian lime we're all familiar with. It's also known as the West Indian lime or Mexican lime.

5 Rinse out the bowl of the food processor. Add the cream cheese, condensed milk, lime juice, egg whites, cornflour and lime zest. Process until smooth. Add the gelatine mixture and process until completely incorporated.

6 Pour into the warm shell. Bake for 55 minutes, or until a knife inserted in the centre comes out clean. Cool on a wire rack, then chill for at least 2 hours.

7 *To make the kiwifruit topping:* Peel and thinly slice the kiwifruit.

8 Remove the outer ring from the springform tin. Arrange the kiwifruit in a spiral pattern on top of the cheesecake. Dust with the icing sugar.

Makes **10** servings.

Photograph on page 329

Pineapple-Caramel Cake

You won't find a more luscious version of the classic pineapple upside-down cake. Dried tart cherries also work beautifully in this cake in place of the dried cranberries.

125	g soft brown sugar
4	tablespoons fat-free prepared caramel topping
6	canned pineapple slices (reserve the juice)
4	tablespoons dried cranberries
2	egg whites, at room temperature
¼	teaspoon salt
1	teaspoon vanilla
125	g sugar
100	g plain flour
¾	teaspoon baking powder

Lynn's Fun Food Fact
During the 1700s, fashionable Europeans cultivated pineapples in hothouses.

1   Preheat the oven to 180°C, Gas 4. Coat a 23 cm round cake tin with non-stick spray.

2   Spread the brown sugar evenly over the bottom of the tin and drizzle evenly with the caramel topping. Top with the pineapple in a decorative pattern. Sprinkle with the cranberries and 2 tablespoons of the reserved pineapple juice. Set aside.

3   Place the egg whites and salt in a large bowl. Beat with an electric mixer until soft peaks form. Beat in the vanilla. Gradually beat in the sugar until the whites are stiff but not dry.

4   In a small bowl, sift together the flour and baking powder. Sift half of the flour mixture over the egg whites. Gently fold in with a large rubber spatula.

5   Fold 4 tablespoons of the reserved pineapple juice into the egg-white mixture. Sift the remaining flour mixture over the egg-white mixture and fold in.

6   Spread the batter evenly over the pineapple mixture. Bake for 30 to 35 minutes, or until a wooden cocktail stick inserted in the centre comes out clean. Cool in the tin for 2 minutes; invert onto a serving plate. Cool for at least 1 hour before serving.

Makes **8** servings.

Photograph on page 327

nutrition at a glance
per serving

0.2 g.	total fat
0 g.	saturated fat
219	calories
0 mg.	cholesterol
168 mg.	sodium
2.5 g.	protein
53.2 g.	carbohydrates
1.1 g.	dietary fibre

Chocolate-Raspberry Cake

This dark layer cake with a tender crumb will satisfy devil's-food longings. For a variation, frost the cake with marshmallow whip or fat-free whipped topping instead of the raspberry fruit spread.

235	g plain flour
90	g cocoa powder
1½	teaspoons baking powder
½	teaspoon ground cinnamon
6	egg whites, at room temperature
½	teaspoon salt
2	teaspoons vanilla
375	g sugar
250	ml fat-free buttermilk
4	tablespoons raspberry all-fruit spread
	icing sugar
375	ml fat-free whipped topping (optional)

1   Preheat the oven to 180°C, Gas 4. Coat two 23 cm round cake tins with non-stick spray. Dust with flour, shaking out the excess.

2   In a medium bowl, sift together the flour, cocoa, baking powder and cinnamon. Set aside.

3   Place the egg whites and salt in a large bowl. Beat with an electric mixer until soft peaks form. Beat in the vanilla. Gradually beat in the sugar until the whites are stiff but not dry.

4   Sift about one-half of the cocoa mixture over the egg-white mixture; gently fold in with a large rubber spatula. Add 125 ml of the buttermilk and fold into the batter. Repeat with the remaining cocoa mixture and the remaining125 ml buttermilk.

5   Divide the batter between the prepared tins and spread evenly. Bake for 20 to 25 minutes, or until a wooden cocktail stick inserted in the centre comes out clean. Cool on a wire rack for 5 minutes. Turn the cakes out of the tins onto wire racks to cool completely.

6 Place 1 cake layer on a serving plate. Cover with the raspberry spread. Top with the second cake layer. Dust the top with icing sugar. Serve with dollops of the whipped topping (if using).

Makes **12** servings.

Photograph on page 332

Coffee Angel Food Cake

To prevent any specks of grease from inhibiting the foaming action of the egg whites, wash your mixing bowl, beaters and the tube tin with hot, soapy water, then rinse thoroughly and dry before starting the recipe. And remember to use an ungreased tube tin so that the egg-white proteins can climb up the sides for a high rise. To make a vanilla angel food cake, omit the coffee and increase the vanilla to 1½ teaspoons.

190	g sifted plain flour
2½	teaspoons instant coffee granules
440	g sugar
450	ml egg whites, at room temperature
1½	teaspoons cream of tartar
¼	teaspoon salt
1	teaspoon vanilla essence

1 Position an oven rack in the lower third of the oven. Preheat the oven to 190°C, Gas 5.

2 In a medium bowl, sift together the flour, coffee, and 185 g of the sugar; press the coffee granules through the mesh with a spoon if necessary. Sift 2 more times. Set aside.

3 Place the egg whites, cream of tartar and salt in a large bowl. Beat with an electric mixer until soft peaks form. Beat in the vanilla. Gradually beat in the remaining sugar until the egg whites are stiff but not dry.

(continued)

Lynn's Lore

Several years ago, I inherited an angel food tin from my maternal grandmother, Ocean Irwin. Inscribed in the metal are the words "Swans Down Cake Pan 1/3/23". Although it has become blackened with time and rusts if I don't dry it by hand, it makes the best angel food cake. It has two cleverly designed slides on each side that open to reveal a hidden 1 cm space at the bottom of the tin. The slides are kept closed to trap heat during baking but are opened to allow air to circulate around the cake for faster cooling.

4 Sift about one-third of the flour mixture over the egg-white mixture. Gently fold in with a large rubber spatula. Repeat with the remaining flour mixture, adding 4 tablespoons at a time.

5 Spoon the batter into an ungreased 25 cm tube tin. Run a knife gently through the batter in a swirling motion to remove air pockets.

6 Bake in the lower third of the oven for 40 to 50 minutes, or until a long wooden skewer inserted in the centre comes out clean.

7 Remove from the oven. If the tin has feet on the rim, turn it upside down to cool. If the tin doesn't have feet on the rim, position the tube over a narrow-necked bottle. Let cool for several hours, or until no longer warm.

8 Stand the cake upright. Run a long, thin knife between the cake and tin to loosen. Invert onto a platter. Cut with a serrated knife.

Makes **10** servings.

nutrition at a glance	
per serving	
0.2 g.	total fat
0 g.	saturated fat
217	calories
0 mg.	cholesterol
125 mg.	sodium
6.1 g.	protein
48 g.	carbohydrates
0 g.	dietary fibre

Citrus-Glazed Carrot Cake

This moist cake has all the spicy savour of traditional carrot cake, without all the excess fat. A sprightly citrus glaze is an excellent substitute for traditional cream-cheese icing.

Carrot Cake

325	g plain flour
2	teaspoons bicarbonate of soda
2	teaspoons ground cinnamon
1	teaspoon ground ginger
125	g sugar
350	g grated carrots
1	can (250 g) crushed pineapple (with juice)
125	ml puréed prunes
235	g soft brown sugar
4	tablespoons golden syrup
4	egg whites, at room temperature
1	teaspoon cream of tartar

Citrus Glaze

2	tablespoons fat-free soured cream
1½	teaspoons freshly squeezed lemon juice
1	teaspoon freshly squeezed orange juice
1	teaspoon grated lemon zest
¼	teaspoon grated orange zest
235	g sifted icing sugar

1 *To make the carrot cake:* Preheat the oven to 180°C, Gas 4. Coat a 3-litre Bundt tin with non-stick spray. Dust with flour, shaking out the excess.

2 In a medium bowl, combine the flour, bicarbonate of soda, cinnamon, ginger and half the white sugar. Mix well and set aside.

3 In a large bowl, combine the carrots, pineapple (with juice), prunes, brown sugar and golden syrup. Mix well. Add the flour mixture and blend well.

4 Place the egg whites and cream of tartar in a large bowl. Beat with an electric mixer until soft peaks form. Gradually beat in the remaining white sugar until the egg whites are stiff but not dry. Fold into the carrot mixture with a large rubber spatula. Pour into the Bund tin.

5 Bake for 50 minutes, or until a wooden cocktail stick inserted in the centre comes out clean. Cool on a wire rack for 10 minutes. Turn the cake out of the tin onto a wire rack to cool.

6 *To make the citrus glaze:* In a medium bowl, combine the soured cream, lemon juice, orange juice, lemon zest and orange zest. Whisk well to combine. Whisk in 155 g of the icing sugar. With a spoon, blend in the remaining icing sugar until smooth. Drizzle over the cake.

Makes **10** servings.

nutrition at a glance

per serving

0.4 g.	total fat
0.1 g.	saturated fat
320	calories
0 mg.	cholesterol
304 mg.	sodium
4.7 g.	protein
76 g.	carbohydrates
2.4 g.	dietary fibre

Daffodil Cake with Lemon Sauce

This light and elegant cake is delightful for a wedding shower or other special occasion. If you like, you can make the lemon sauce and the cake a day before serving. Reheat the sauce gently in a saucepan or microwave it in a glass measuring jug just until warm. For a special touch, decorate with crystallised violets and tiny fresh mint leaves.

Daffodil Cake

190	g + 2 tablespoons sifted plain cake flour
440	g + 2 tablespoons sugar
450	ml egg whites, at room temperature
1½	teaspoons cream of tartar
¼	teaspoon salt
1½	teaspoons vanilla
4	tablespoons fat-free egg substitute
1	tablespoon grated lemon zest

Warm Lemon Sauce

250	g sugar
1	tablespoon cornflour
125	ml water
3	tablespoons freshly squeezed lemon juice
1	tablespoon grated lemon zest

1 *To make the daffodil cake:* Position an oven rack in the lower third of the oven. Preheat the oven to 190°C, Gas 5.

2 Sift 190 g of the flour and 185 g of the sugar together 3 times. Set aside.

3 Place the egg whites, cream of tartar and salt in a large bowl. Beat with an electric mixer until soft peaks form. Beat in the vanilla. Gradually beat in 250 g of the remaining sugar until the egg whites are stiff but not dry.

4 Sift about one-third of the flour mixture over the egg-white mixture. Gently fold in with a large rubber spatula. Repeat with the remaining flour mixture, adding 4 tablespoons at a time.

5 Transfer one-third of the batter to a medium bowl. Set aside.

6 In another medium bowl, combine the egg substitute, the remaining 2 tablespoons flour and the remaining 2 tablespoons sugar. Beat with an electric mixer for 3 minutes, or until thickened. Stir in the lemon zest. Pour over the reserved batter in the medium bowl. Gently fold in with a large rubber spatula.

7 Spoon the white and yellow batters alternately into an ungreased 25 cm tube tin. Run a knife gently through the batter in a swirling motion to remove air pockets and to marble the batter slightly.

8 Bake in the lower third of the oven for 40 to 45 minutes, or until a long wooden skewer inserted in the centre comes out clean.

9 Remove from the oven. If the tin has feet on the rim, turn it upside down to cool. If the tin doesn't have feet on the rim, position the tube over a narrow-necked bottle. Let cool for several hours, or until no longer warm.

10 *To make the warm lemon sauce:* In a small non-stick saucepan, combine the sugar and cornflour. Stir in the water. Whisk over medium heat for 10 minutes, or until smooth and thickened. Add the lemon juice and lemon zest. Cook, whisking constantly, for 2 to 3 minutes, or until the mixture boils. Remove from the heat and set aside.

11 Stand the cake upright. Run a long, thin knife carefully around the edge, between the cake and tin, to loosen. Invert onto a platter. Cut with a serrated knife. Serve topped with the warm lemon sauce.

Makes **10** servings.

Photograph on page 330

nutrition at a glance

per serving

0.2 g.	total fat
0 g.	saturated fat
311	calories
0 mg.	cholesterol
135 mg.	sodium
6.7 g.	protein
71.5 g.	carbohydrates
1 g.	dietary fibre

Glazed Tropical Fruit Cake

This beautiful dessert is a sponge cake moistened with tropical fruit syrup and crowned with colourful fruits. You can use either bottled or reconstituted frozen mango, passion fruit or other tropical fruit juice for the glaze.

Sponge Cake

6	egg whites, at room temperature
2	eggs, at room temperature
1	teaspoon vanilla
¼	teaspoon salt
375	g sugar
235	g plain flour
1½	teaspoons baking powder

Tropical Fruit Glaze

180	ml tropical fruit juice
125	g sugar

Tropical Fruit Topping

90	g sliced papayas
90	g sliced mangoes
1	kiwifruit, sliced
1	banana, sliced
	icing sugar (optional)

1 *To make the sponge cake:* Preheat the oven to 180°C, Gas 4. Coat a 23 cm springform tin with non-stick spray. Dust with flour, shaking out the excess.

2 Place the egg whites, eggs, vanilla and salt in a large bowl. Beat with an electric mixer until light and fluffy. Gradually beat in the sugar. Beat for 5 minutes, or until thick.

3 In a medium bowl, sift together the flour and baking powder. Sift over the egg mixture. Gently fold in with a large rubber spatula. Pour the batter into the prepared tin.

4   Bake for 30 to 35 minutes, or until a wooden cocktail stick inserted in the centre comes out clean. Cool on a wire rack.

5   *To make the tropical fruit glaze:* In a small non-stick saucepan, combine the fruit juice and sugar. Whisk over medium heat and bring to a boil. Boil for 3 minutes, or until the sugar dissolves.

6   Using a wooden cocktail stick or skewer, poke holes about 2.5 cm apart all over the cake. Spoon all but 2 tablespoons of the syrup over the cake. Set aside to cool.

7   *To make the tropical fruit topping:* Remove the outer ring from the springform tin. Place the cake on a serving plate. Top with the papayas, mangoes, kiwifruit and bananas. Brush with the remaining 2 tablespoons syrup. Dust with the icing sugar (if using) just before serving.

Makes **12** servings.

Photograph on page 334

nutrition at a glance

per serving

0.8 g.	total fat
0.2 g.	saturated fat
177	calories
27 mg.	cholesterol
109 mg.	sodium
3.5 g.	protein
39.7 g.	carbohydrates
1 g.	dietary fibre

Ripe summer berries – blueberries, strawberries, boysenberries, blackberries and raspberries – make desserts that are as elegant as they are healthy. When the ice is on the berry vines, turn to loose-pack frozen berries to re-create summer memories. Whether you start with fresh or frozen, these quick desserts are the berry best.

Berry Berry. Intensify the berry bounty by stirring a handful of fresh berries into berry yogurt.

Blueberry Thrill. Top fresh blueberries with a sauce of puréed ripe mangoes or papayas seasoned to taste with freshly squeezed lime juice and sugar.

Citrus Twist. Any berries will benefit from a rich, tart sauce made from lemon yogurt mixed with a tablespoon of freshly squeezed lemon juice or lime juice. Use 1 tablespoon juice for each container (250 ml) of yogurt.

Lickety Split. Line old-fashioned glass banana boats with 2 banana halves each. Top with scoops of fat-free vanilla, chocolate and strawberry ice cream or frozen yogurt. Spoon on separate sauces: lightly mashed and sweetened strawberries, lightly mashed and sweetened raspberries and blueberries that have been briefly cooked with a bit of sugar, then cooled. Top with dollops of marshmallow fluff and a generous drizzle of fat-free chocolate sauce. Sprinkle with finely chopped walnuts and a long-stem maraschino cherry for a real retro touch.

Parfait Perfection. In parfait glasses, layer blueberries, raspberries or sliced strawberries with fat-free vanilla ice cream, frozen yogurt or citrus sorbet. Crown with fat-free whipped topping, a berry and a fresh mint sprig.

Short Cake – Tall Taste. For an instant fat-free strawberry shortcake, spoon sliced fresh strawberries over slices of angel food cake. Top with fat-free whipped cream or vanilla ice cream.

Strawberry Yields Forever. Choose the largest, reddest strawberries (on the stems, if possible) to serve with bowls of fat-free chocolate sauce, fat-free soured cream (sweetened with brown sugar), and fat-free whipped topping.

A Toast to Melba. Cover stoned ripe peach halves with fat-free vanilla ice cream and a sauce of puréed raspberries mixed with sugar, cinnamon and freshly squeezed lemon juice.

Stacked-High Apple Pie

If you thought you'd never see a delicious fat-free apple pie, you will be delighted with this. Our testers loved it so much that it disappeared immediately. The secret to the shell is using fat-free cinnamon-and-honey biscuits. Low-fat digestives or ginger snaps also work beautifully. Serve slightly warm from the oven – solo or accompanied by fat-free frozen yogurt, ice cream or whipped topping.

6	tart apples, cut into quarters and sliced
185	g sugar
3	tablespoons freshly squeezed lemon juice
3	tablespoons quick-cooking tapioca
¾	teaspoon ground cinnamon
⅛	teaspoon ground allspice
1	egg white
280	g fat-free cinnamon-and-honey biscuit crumbs

1 Preheat the oven to 180°C, Gas 4. Coat a 23 cm pie plate with non-stick spray.

2 In a large bowl, combine the apples, sugar, lemon juice, tapioca, cinnamon and allspice. Mix well. Cover and let stand, stirring occasionally, for 15 minutes.

3 Place the egg white in a medium bowl and beat lightly with a fork. Add the biscuit crumbs and mix well. Press into the bottom and up the sides of the prepared pie plate. Mist the shell with non-stick spray.

4 Spoon the apple mixture into the shell. Bake for 45 minutes, or until the filling bubbles and the apples are tender when tested with the tip of a sharp knife.

Makes **6** servings.

Photograph on page 326

Photograph on page 326

Lynn's Fat-Free Flavour

The type of apple that you use in any cooked apple dessert makes a huge difference. So select cooking apples that are tart and aromatic, such as the Australian Braeburn, Winesap, McIntosh, Pippin and Granny Smith.

---

nutrition at a glance

per serving

0.4 g.	total fat
0.1 g.	saturated fat
347	calories
0 mg.	cholesterol
196 mg.	sodium
2.4 g.	protein
86.2 g.	carbohydrates
4.2 g.	dietary fibre

Chocolate-Banana Pie

Your family and friends will never guess that this creamy dream of a pie is free of fat. The shell and chocolate filling can be made well in advance. Top with the bananas and fat-free whipped topping just before serving.

Meringue Shell

3	egg whites, at room temperature
¼	teaspoon cream of tartar
100	g sugar
1	tablespoon cornflour

Chocolate Filling

4	ml cold water
1	envelope (7 g) powdered gelatine
1	can (440 g) fat-free sweetened condensed milk
4	tablespoons cocoa powder
1	teaspoon vanilla
500	ml fat-free soured cream
125	ml fat-free vanilla yogurt

Banana Topping

2	medium bananas, sliced
500	ml fat-free aerosol whipped topping or thawed frozen fat-free whipped topping

1   *To make the meringue shell*: Preheat the oven to 135°C, Gas 1. Coat a 25 cm pie plate with non-stick spray. Dust generously with flour, shaking out the excess.

2   Place the egg whites and cream of tartar in a large bowl. Beat with an electric mixer until foamy.

3   In a small bowl, combine the sugar and cornflour. Add to the egg whites, 1 tablespoon at a time, beating until stiff peaks form and the sugar dissolves. Spread the meringue carefully into the bottom and up the sides of the pie plate.

4   Bake for 1 hour. Turn the oven off and leave the meringue in the oven for at least 2 hours, or until completely cooled.

5 *To make the chocolate filling*: Place the water in a cup. Sprinkle with the gelatine and set aside for 5 minutes to soften.

6 In a medium saucepan, combine the condensed milk and cocoa. Whisk over low heat for 2 to 3 minutes, or until the cocoa is completely blended into the milk. Add the vanilla. Remove from the heat and stir in the gelatine mixture until dissolved.

7 Cool to room temperature. Add the soured cream and yogurt; mix until blended. Pour into the meringue shell. Chill for several hours, or until firm.

8 *To make the banana topping*: Just before serving, arrange the bananas in a single layer over the chocolate filling. Cover with the whipped topping.

Makes **8** servings.

Photograph on page 333

nutrition at a glance	
per serving	
0.5 g.	total fat
0.3 g.	saturated fat
357	calories
5 mg.	cholesterol
149 mg.	sodium
11 g.	protein
73.6 g.	carbohydrates
1.5 g.	dietary fibre

Fresh Berry Angel Tart

When early summer berries are in their prime, you won't find a more heavenly dessert.

Angel Tart

3	egg whites, at room temperature
½	teaspoon cream of tartar
	Pinch of salt
½	teaspoon vanilla
185	g sugar
100	g plain flour

Fresh Berry Topping

375	g sliced strawberries or raspberries
4	tablespoons red currant jelly
250	ml fat-free aerosol whipped topping or thawed frozen fat-free whipped topping

1 *To make the angel tart*: Preheat the oven to 190°C, Gas 5. Coat a 25 cm pie plate with non-stick spray. Dust generously with flour, shaking out the excess.

2 Place the egg whites, cream of tartar and salt in a large bowl. Beat with an electric mixer until soft peaks form. Beat in the vanilla. Gradually beat in 60 g of the sugar until the whites are stiff but not dry.

3 In a medium bowl, sift together the flour and the remaining sugar. Sift over the egg whites. Gently fold in with a large rubber spatula.

4 Spread the batter in the pie plate. Bake for 20 to 25 minutes, or until a wooden cocktail stick inserted in the centre comes out clean. Cool on a wire rack.

5 With a sharp knife, gently loosen the edges of the tart and place on a serving plate.

6 *To make the fresh berry topping*: Arrange the strawberries or raspberries over the top of the tart.

7 Place the jelly in a small microwaveable dish. Microwave on high power for 30 to 60 seconds, or until liquid. Spoon over the berries.

8 Top with the whipped topping just before serving.

Makes **8** servings.

Plum and Blueberry Tart

Top this luscious fruit tart with fat-free whipped topping, vanilla ice cream or frozen yogurt.

125	g sugar
3	tablespoons freshly squeezed lemon juice
1	tablespoon quick-cooking tapioca
½	teaspoon ground cinnamon
280	g fat-free lemon biscuit crumbs
4	medium purple plums, cut into quarters
250	g blueberries

Lynn's Lore

The classic saying should really be "as American as blueberry pie" since blueberries are native plants of North America, and apples are not.

1 Preheat the oven to 180°C, Gas 4.

2 In a small bowl, combine the sugar, lemon juice, tapioca and cinnamon. Cover and let stand, stirring occasionally, for 5 minutes.

3 Coat an 23 cm springform tin with non-stick spray. Press the biscuit crumbs over the bottom and 2 cm up the sides of the tin. Mist with non-stick spray. Bake for 7 minutes.

4 Remove the tin from the oven. Arrange the plums in concentric circles over the bottom of the tin. Spoon the tapioca mixture evenly over the plums. Sprinkle with the blueberries.

5 Bake for 45 to 50 minutes, or until the filling bubbles and the plums are soft. Cool on a wire rack. Remove the outer ring from the springform tin.

Makes **8** servings.

Summer Fruits in Phyllo

These flaky pastry bundles are best served warm and crisp from the oven. You can assemble them and hold them at room temperature for up to 2 hours before baking.

3	large peaches or nectarines, peeled and diced
155	g raspberries
1	package (100 g) fat-free instant vanilla pudding and pie filling mix
6	sheets frozen phyllo dough, thawed
	icing sugar
185	ml fat-free aerosol whipped topping or thawed frozen fat-free whipped topping

1 Preheat the oven to 190°C, Gas 5. Coat a baking tray with non-stick spray.

2 In a large bowl, combine the peaches or nectarines, raspberries and pudding mix. Fold with a rubber spatula until all the fruit is evenly coated with the dry pudding.

3 Unwrap the phyllo dough and cover it with a damp kitchen towel.

4 Remove 1 sheet from the stack and lay it on the work surface. Mist it with non-stick spray. Scoop out about a sixth of the fruit mixture and place it on one end of the phyllo sheet. Fold the lengthwise sides of the phyllo over the filling, then roll up, enclosing the filling. Place the bundle, seam side down, on the prepared baking tray.

5 Repeat with the remaining phyllo dough and filling to make a total of 6 individual pastry packets.

6 Bake for 25 to 35 minutes, or until the pastry is lightly browned. Dust with the icing sugar. Serve hot, topped with the whipped topping.

Makes **6** servings.

nutrition at a glance

per serving

0.7 g.	total fat
0.1 g.	saturated fat
92	calories
0 mg.	cholesterol
170 mg.	sodium
1 g.	protein
20.2 g.	carbohydrates
1.3 g.	dietary fibre

Raisin and Spice Oatmeal Biscuits

Stored in a tin in a cool spot, these wholesome biscuits keep beautifully. They're wonderful for packed lunches and snacks – try dunking them in a glass of cold skimmed milk.

155	g plain flour
1	teaspoon baking powder
½	teaspoon bicarbonate of soda
½	teaspoon salt
½	teaspoon ground cinnamon
250	g soft brown sugar
4	tablespoons unsweetened applesauce
1	egg white
2	tablespoons water
2	tablespoons rapeseed oil
1	teaspoon vanilla
125	g rolled oats
185	g raisins

1 Preheat the oven to 190°C, Gas 5. Coat 2 or 3 large baking trays with non-stick spray.

2 In a small bowl, combine the flour, baking powder, bicarbonate of soda, salt and cinnamon. Mix well.

3 In a large bowl, combine the brown sugar, applesauce, egg white, water, oil and vanilla. Mix well.

4 Stir in the flour mixture. Add the oats and raisins; mix well. (The mixture will look thinner than most biscuit doughs.)

5 Drop by rounded teaspoonfuls, 5 cm apart, on the prepared baking trays. Bake one tray at a time for 10 to 12 minutes, or until lightly browned.

6 Place the baking tray on a wire rack and let stand for 5 minutes. Remove the biscuits from the baking tray and let cool on the rack.

Makes **42** biscuits.

nutrition at a glance

per biscuit

0.9 g.	total fat
0.1 g.	saturated fat
58	calories
0 mg.	cholesterol
56 mg.	sodium
0.9 g.	protein
12 g.	carbohydrates
0.5 g.	dietary fibre

Chocolate-Cherry Biscuits

Glazed chocolate-and-fruit drops make a terrific snack or dessert. Be sure not to overbake to keep them tender. Kids love these. You can add 60 g chopped walnuts or pecans. The fat will rise – to slightly less than 2 grammes per biscuit – but so will the nutrients and fibre.

Chocolate-Cherry Biscuits

90	g dried cherries
4	tablespoons water
4	tablespoons skimmed milk
1½	teaspoons vanilla
190	g plain flour
250	g soft brown sugar
45	g cocoa powder
2	teaspoons baking powder
½	teaspoon salt
250	g sugar
4	egg whites, at room temperature
½	teaspoon cream of tartar

Chocolate Glaze

155	g icing sugar
1	teaspoon cocoa powder
1	teaspoon vanilla
2–3	teaspoons skimmed milk

1 *To make the chocolate-cherry biscuits*: Preheat the oven to 180°C, Gas 4. Coat a large baking tray with non-stick spray.

2 In a small non-stick saucepan, combine the cherries and water. Bring to a boil over medium-high heat. Reduce the heat and simmer for 15 minutes, or until all the water is absorbed. Cover and set aside for 30 minutes.

3 Pour the cherries into a blender or food processor. Process until puréed. (The cherries can also be puréed in the saucepan with a hand blender.) Add the milk and vanilla; blend to combine. Set aside.

4 In a medium bowl, sift together the flour, brown sugar, cocoa, baking powder, salt and 125 g of the sugar.

5 Place the egg whites and cream of tartar in a large bowl. Beat with an electric mixer until soft peaks form. Gradually beat in the remaining 125 g sugar until the egg whites are stiff but not dry.

6 Fold a third of the flour mixture and a third of the cherry mixture into the egg-white mixture. Repeat twice to use all the flour and cherries. The mixture will be thick.

7 Drop by level tablespoonfuls, 2.5 cm apart, on the prepared baking tray. Bake for 10 to 12 minutes, or until the edges are set (the centres will look moist).

8 Place the baking tray on a wire rack and let stand for 5 minutes. Remove the biscuits from the baking tray and let cool on the rack.

9 *To make the chocolate glaze*: In a small bowl, combine the icing sugar and cocoa. Add the vanilla and 2 teaspoons of the milk. Whisk until smooth. Add more milk if a thinner consistency is desired. Drizzle the glaze over the cooled biscuits.

Makes **24** biscuits.

nutrition at a glance

per biscuit

0.3 g.	total fat
0.1 g.	saturated fat
147	calories
0 mg.	cholesterol
100 mg.	sodium
2.9 g.	protein
34.6 g.	carbohydrates
0.9 g.	dietary fibre

Peppermint Rock Meringues

A properly baked meringue is crisp on the outside with an interior that literally melts on your tongue. The key ingredient is patience. Bake meringues slowly at a very low temperature. Bake on trays without sides to allow air to circulate around the biscuits. If you have only baking trays with sides, turn them upside down and bake the biscuits on the bottom. For best results, make meringues on a dry day. After baking, store in an airtight tin.

Today, mint is the most widely used of any aromatic herb. Some wild and delicate mints smell like oranges, lemons, apples and pineapples, but most mint grown commercially today is the brasher peppermint and spearmint. I grow a new hybrid called chocolate mint in my kitchen window box.

250	g sugar
1	tablespoon cornflour
3	egg whites, at room temperature
$\frac{1}{8}$	teaspoon salt
1	teaspoon vanilla
185	g crushed peppermint sweets or rock

1 Preheat the oven to 120°C, Gas ½. Coat 2 large baking trays with non-stick spray. Dust with flour, shaking off the excess.

2 In a small bowl, combine the sugar and cornflour. Set aside.

3 Place the egg whites and salt in a large bowl. Beat with an electric mixer until soft peaks form. Beat in the vanilla. Beat in the sugar mixture, 1 tablespoon at a time, until the whites are stiff but not dry. Fold in the peppermint.

4 Drop by rounded teaspoonfuls on the prepared baking trays. Place in the oven on two shelves.

5 Bake for 2½ hours, or until the meringues are dry. Turn the oven off and leave the meringues in the oven for several hours or overnight. Store in an airtight container.

Makes **72** meringues.

nutrition at a glance
per meringue
0 g.   total fat
0 g.   saturated fat
24   calories
0 mg.   cholesterol
7 mg.   sodium
0.1 g.   protein
6 g.   carbohydrates
0 g.   dietary fibre

Lemon Bars

Lemon yogurt adds a creamy texture and a pleasing tartness to these bars. For an even tangier filling, add an extra teaspoon of grated lemon zest. For best results, partially freeze these delicate bars before cutting.

Biscuit Shell

24	low-fat vanilla wafer biscuits
60	g icing sugar
1	teaspoon grated lemon zest
3	tablespoons applesauce

Lemon Filling

185	g sugar
2	egg whites
1	egg
185	ml fat-free lemon yogurt
3	tablespoons plain flour
2	tablespoons freshly squeezed lemon juice
1	teaspoon grated lemon zest
½	teaspoon baking powder
	icing sugar

1 *To make the biscuit shell:* Preheat the oven to 180°C, Gas 4. Coat an 20 x 20 cm baking dish with non-stick spray.

2 Break the wafers into pieces; place in a food processor or blender. Process to make crumbs. Add the icing sugar, lemon zest and applesauce; process to make a moist dough. Flour your fingers, then press the dough evenly into the prepared dish. Bake for 15 to 20 minutes, or until the shell feels firm and is lightly browned. Set aside. Do not turn off the oven.

3 *To make the lemon filling:* Place the sugar, egg whites and egg in a medium bowl. Beat with an electric mixer until thick and smooth. Add the yogurt, flour, lemon juice, lemon zest and baking powder. Mix until smooth. Spread over the baked shell.

(continued)

4   Bake for 25 to 30 minutes, or until set and lightly browned. Cool completely on a wire rack.

5   Place in the freezer for 1 hour before cutting into 16 bars. Refrigerate if not serving right away.

6   Sprinkle with the icing sugar just before serving.

Makes **16** bars.

Photograph on page 328

Pumpkin Pudding

Made for my 7-year-old friend Haley, this luscious dessert has all the comfort of pumpkin pie without the fatty shell. A dollop of fat-free topping makes it extra special.

500	g canned pumpkin
375	g fat-free liquid creamer
160	g fat-free egg substitute
125	g soft brown sugar
1½	teaspoons ground cinnamon
½	teaspoon ground ginger
¼	teaspoon ground nutmeg
⅛	teaspoon ground allspice
⅛	teaspoon ground cloves

1   Preheat the oven to 180°C, Gas 4.

2   In a large bowl, combine the pumpkin, creamer, egg substitute, brown sugar, cinnamon, ginger, nutmeg, allspice and cloves.

3   Pour the mixture into six 250-ml baking dishes or custard cups. Bake for 35 to 40 minutes, or until a knife inserted in the centre of a pudding comes out clean. Cool on a wire rack. Chill before serving.

Makes **6** servings.

Lynn's Nutrition Note
Canned pumpkin is a convenience product with class. It contains only cooked puréed pumpkin (not even sodium is added) and is an outstanding source of vitamin A.

Rice Pudding with Nectarines

Sliced ripe peaches or mangoes are also delicious with this pudding.

500	ml water
140	g long-grain white rice
1	can (440 g) fat-free sweetened condensed milk
2	egg whites
½	teaspoon ground cinnamon
3	nectarines, sliced

1   In a medium non-stick saucepan over medium-high heat, bring 440 ml of the water to a boil. Add the rice. Return to a boil. Reduce the heat to medium-low, cover and simmer for 15 to 20 minutes, or until the rice is tender and the water is absorbed.

2   Meanwhile, in a large non-stick saucepan, combine the condensed milk, egg whites, cinnamon and the remaining water. Cook over medium heat, stirring constantly, for 10 to 12 minutes, or until the mixture thickens slightly. Remove from the heat; stir in the rice. Refrigerate to chill completely.

3   Spoon the pudding into 8 dessert dishes. Top with the nectarines.

Makes **8** servings.

Lynn's Fat-Free Flavour

Fruits that aren't quite ripe can ruin the flavour of an otherwise fine dessert. To ripen nectarines or peaches after purchase, store in a brown paper bag for one to three days, or until the fruit yields to gentle pressure when squeezed. Placing bananas in the bag will accelerate the ripening process. After the fruit is ripened, store in the refrigerator until you're ready to use it.

nutrition at a glance

per serving

0.4 g.	total fat
0.1 g.	saturated fat
239	calories
5 mg.	cholesterol
67 mg.	sodium
6.6 g.	protein
51.8 g.	carbohydrates
1.2 g.	dietary fibre

Almond Tapioca and Lime-Blackberry Parfaits

Childhood favourite tapioca pudding grows up in these lovely parfaits. You can hold the parfaits for several hours in the refrigerator after assembling them.

500	ml fat-free liquid creamer
3	tablespoons quick-cooking tapioca
6	tablespoons + 60 g sugar
125	ml fat-free egg substitute
½	teaspoon almond essence
375	g blackberries
2	tablespoons freshly squeezed lime juice
½	teaspoon grated lime zest
	Pinch of ground cinnamon
1	tablespoon cornflour
1	tablespoon water

1 In a medium non-stick saucepan, combine the creamer, tapioca and 6 tablespoons of the sugar. Let stand for 5 minutes. Bring to the boiling point over medium heat. Cook, stirring constantly, for 5 minutes. Remove from the heat.

2 Place the egg substitute in a large bowl. Add a large spoonful of the hot tapioca; mix well. Continue adding tapioca by large spoonfuls until the mixture measures about 250 ml. Pour the egg mixture slowly into the saucepan and mix well. Cook over medium-low heat, stirring, for 2 minutes, or until thickened.

3 Cool to lukewarm. Stir in the almond essence. Cover and chill for several hours, or until thickened.

4 Meanwhile, in another medium non-stick saucepan, combine the blackberries, lime juice, lime zest, cinnamon and the remaining sugar. Cook over medium-low heat, stirring often, for 7 to 8 minutes, or until a sauce forms but the berries hold their shape.

5 Place the cornflour in a cup. Add the water and stir to dissolve the cornflour. Add to the blackberry mixture and cook over medium heat, stirring, for 1 minute, or until thickened.

6 Cool to lukewarm. Cover and chill for several hours.

7 To serve, spoon the tapioca and blackberry mixture alternately into 6 parfait dishes.

Makes **6** servings.

Photograph on page 331

nutrition at a glance
per serving
0.2 g. total fat
0.1 g. saturated fat
192 calories
0 mg. cholesterol
34 mg. sodium
2.4 g. protein
43.6 g. carbohydrates
2.1 g. dietary fibre

Lemon-Ginger Figs with Ice Cream

quick and easy

Poaching figs with ginger and lemon provides a counterpoint to the intense sweetness of the fruit. This sauce can be served warm or chilled. For a variation, serve the figs topped with fat-free whipped topping or custard sauce.

500 g dried figs (stems removed), cut into quarters
375 ml water
4 tablespoons sugar
Juice of 1 lemon
2 teaspoons thin lemon zest strips
1 tablespoon thinly sliced crystallised ginger
1 litre fat-free vanilla ice cream or fat-free vanilla frozen yogurt

1 In a large saucepan, combine the figs, water, sugar, lemon juice, lemon zest and ginger. Cover and simmer over low heat for 10 minutes. Remove the cover and simmer for 5 minutes, or until the figs are tender. Serve over the ice cream or frozen yogurt.

Makes **6** servings.

Lynn's Lore

In ancient times the figs grown in southern Europe, Asia and Africa were thought to be sacred and seen as a symbol of peace and prosperity

nutrition at a glance
per serving
0.9 g. total fat
0.2 g. saturated fat
361 calories
5 mg. cholesterol
75 mg. sodium
6.4 g. protein
86.5 g. carbohydrates
7.1 g. dietary fibre

Orange and Cinnamon Rhubarb

I like rhubarb plain and simple, not in a fatty shell or diluted with strawberries. I enjoy this easy dessert all by itself, but it's also terrific spooned over fat-free vanilla pudding, tapioca, vanilla ice cream or frozen yogurt.

500	g fresh rhubarb stalks, cut into 2.5 cm lengths, or 500 g frozen rhubarb pieces
4	tablespoons freshly squeezed orange juice
2	tablespoons freshly squeezed lemon juice (optional)
1	teaspoon grated orange zest
¼	teaspoon ground cinnamon
	Pinch of ground cloves (optional)
185 - 315	g sugar

1   In a large non-stick saucepan, combine the rhubarb, orange juice, lemon juice (if using), orange zest, cinnamon, cloves (if using) and 185 g of the sugar. Stir to combine. Bring to a boil over medium-high heat.

2   Reduce the heat to low, cover and simmer, stirring occasionally, for 25 to 30 minutes, or until the rhubarb is tender. Taste for sweetness. Add up to 125 g more sugar, if needed. Cook over low heat, stirring, for 2 to 3 minutes, or until the sugar dissolves. Serve warm or cold.

Makes **4** servings.

Lynn's Lore

Rhubarb is commonly referred to as a fruit, but it is a vegetable. The tart pink-and-green stalks are almost always cooked with some sweetener to make them palatable. The broad leaves attached to the stalks – which contain toxic oxalic acid – should always be discarded.

nutrition at a glance

per serving

0.3 g.	total fat
0.1 g.	saturated fat
178	calories
0 mg.	cholesterol
5 mg.	sodium
1.2 g.	protein
45 g.	carbohydrates
2.2 g.	dietary fibre

Holidays and Celebrations

To the Seasons

A Taste for Travel

Daily Dining

Menus for All Occasions

My fabulous fat-free dishes are made for feasting,

because they're a celebration of good health.

Although my recipes are intended as fat-free accompaniments to the foods that you normally serve – to help reduce your overall fat intake – they can also be paired to create whole meals that are hearty yet super-lean. So whether you're planning for a celebration dinner, a seasonal meal with friends, an exotic ethnic affair or daily suppers, you'll find a meal here to suit the occasion deliciously.

Unless otherwise noted, the portion size for recipes featured in these menus is one serving.

Easter Brunch

Springtime
Asparagus Soup
(page 65)

Salmon-Stuffed
Mushrooms
(page 312)

Spinach Quiche
in Potato Crust
(page 316)

Daffodil Cake
with Lemon
Sauce (page
354)

For each serving, plan on 2
Salmon-Stuffed Mushrooms.

nutrition at a glance

per serving

2 g.	total fat
0.6 g.	saturated fat
607	calories
4 mg.	cholesterol
958 mg.	sodium
31 g.	protein
116 g.	carbohydrates
6 g.	dietary fibre

Christmas Dinner

Mushroom and
Wild Rice Soup
(page 77)

Roast turkey
breast

Chicken Gravy
(page 293)

Potato-Carrot
Mash (page 222)

Creamed Pearl
Onions (page
215)

Brussels Sprouts
with Apples
(page 234)

Cran-Blackberry
Gelatine Salad
(page 110)

Pumpkin Pudding
(page 370)

For each serving, plan on 250 ml
Mushroom and Wild Rice Soup,
90 g roast turkey breast, and
60 ml Chicken Gravy.

nutrition at a glance

per serving

4.3 g.	total fat
0.9 g.	saturated fat
978	calories
77 mg.	cholesterol
650 mg.	sodium
49 g.	protein
191 g.	carbohydrates
23 g.	dietary fibre

Mid-summer's BBQ

Barbecued
halibut steaks

All-American
Barbecue Sauce
(page 292)

Potato Salad
with Caramelised
Onions (page
108)

Fresh Berry
Angel Tart (page
362)

For each serving, plan on 125 g
barbecued halibut and
60 ml All-American Barbecue
Sauce.

nutrition at a glance

per serving

4.4 g.	total fat
0.6 g.	saturated fat
636	calories
47 mg.	cholesterol
526 mg.	sodium
40 g.	protein
109 g.	carbohydrates
8 g.	dietary fibre

New Year's Day Lunch

Turkey and Black
Bean Stew (page
168)

Oriental Coleslaw
(page 107)

Citrus-Glazed
Carrot Cake
(page 352)

nutrition at a glance

per serving

2.1 g.	total fat
0.4 g.	saturated fat
518	calories
19 mg.	cholesterol
401 mg.	sodium
20 g.	protein
108 g.	carbohydrates
11 g.	dietary fibre

Mardi Gras Mirth

Assorted raw vegetables

Rémoulade Sauce (page 300)

Cajun Red Beans and Rice (page 278)

Pineapple-Caramel Cake (page 348)

For each serving, plan on 60 g mixed raw vegetable chunks or strips – such as carrots, broccoli, celery or sweet red peppers – to dip in the Rémoulade Sauce, as well as 2 servings Cajun Red Beans and Rice.

nutrition at a glance

per serving

2.6 g.	total fat
0.2 g.	saturated fat
680	calories
6 mg.	cholesterol
1,066 mg.	sodium
22 g.	protein
144 g.	carbohydrates
13 g.	dietary fibre

Salute to Spring

Parsleyed Queen Scallops (page 32)

Soufflé Primavera (page 174)

Dill Sauce (page 294)

Artichoke Salad (page 103)

For each serving, plan on 60 ml Dill Sauce.

nutrition at a glance

per serving

2.5 g.	total fat
0.6 g.	saturated fat
451	calories
14 mg.	cholesterol
843 mg.	sodium
42 g.	protein
65 g.	carbohydrates
14 g.	dietary fibre

Summer Luncheon

Gazpacho with Prawns and Avocado (page 66)

Turkey Salad with Orange Dressing (page 100)

Lemon Bars (page 369)

For each serving, plan on 250 ml Gazpacho with Prawns and Avocado and 2 Lemon Bars.

nutrition at a glance

per serving

3.6 g.	total fat
0.8 g.	saturated fat
363	calories
57 mg.	cholesterol
448 mg.	sodium
21 g.	protein
66 g.	carbohydrates
5 g.	dietary fibre

Harvest Garden Fest

Fresh Tomato Soup (page 67)

Garden and Grain Loaf (page 182)

Roasted Pepper Sauce (page 291)

Oven-Glazed Swedes (page 235)

Stacked-High Apple Pie (page 359)

For each serving, plan on 250 ml Fresh Tomato Soup and 125 ml Roasted Pepper Sauce.

nutrition at a glance

per serving

2.4 g.	total fat
0.4 g.	saturated fat
624	calories
0 mg.	cholesterol
481 mg.	sodium
150 g.	protein
145 g.	carbohydrates
15 g.	dietary fibre

Fireside Supper

Vegetable Stew with Beef (page 172)

Spinach-Orange Salad (page 109)

French bread

Baked Winter Fruits (page 310)

For each serving, plan on 2 slices (2.5 cm wide) French baguette.

nutrition at a glance

per serving

3.6 g.	total fat
1 g.	saturated fat
494	calories
13 mg.	cholesterol
706 mg.	sodium
17 g.	protein
104 g.	carbohydrates
11 g.	dietary fibre

Southwestern Sampler

Pinto Bean Dip (page 43)

Baked tortilla chips

Beef and Mushroom Fajitas (page 171)

Fruit Salad with Cantaloupe Dressing (page 112)

For each serving, plan on 125 ml Pinto Bean Dip, 14 tortilla chips (30 g), and 2 Beef and Mushroom Fajitas.

nutrition at a glance

per serving

4.2 g.	total fat
0.7 g.	saturated fat
640	calories
36 mg.	cholesterol
817 mg.	sodium
33 g.	protein
124 g.	carbohydrates
18 g.	dietary fibre

Florida Feast

Spicy Prawns (page 131)

Lemon-Dill Rice (page 277)

Baked Citrus Carrots (page 212)

Key Lime Cheesecake (page 347)

nutrition at a glance

per serving

2.2 g.	total fat
0.3 g.	saturated fat
552	calories
129 mg.	cholesterol
696 mg.	sodium
31 g.	protein
100 g.	carbohydrates
5 g.	dietary fibre

French Bistro Supper

Better-Than-French Onion Soup (page 72)

Turkey Cutlets Tarragon (page 165)

Scalloped Potatoes and Fennel (page 220)

Chocolate-Raspberry Cake (page 350)

For each serving, plan on 250 ml Better-Than-French Onion Soup.

nutrition at a glance

per serving

2.1 g.	total fat
0.8 g.	saturated fat
443	calories
58 mg.	cholesterol
564 mg.	sodium
30 g.	protein
78 g.	carbohydrates
6 g.	dietary fibre

Alfresco Italian

Mediterranean Prawns (page 37)

Orange-Rosemary Turkey (page 162)

Orzo with Asparagus (page 271)

Tomato, Basil and Mozzarella Salad (page 106)

nutrition at a glance

per serving

3.3 g.	total fat
0.5 g.	saturated fat
461	calories
142 mg.	cholesterol
445 mg.	sodium
49 g.	protein
62 g.	carbohydrates
7 g.	dietary fibre

Moroccan Magic

Couscous-Stuffed Peppers (page 188)

Mediterranean Vegetables (page 230)

Summer Fruits in Phyllo (page 364)

nutrition at a glance

per serving

2.4 g.	total fat
0.3 g.	saturated fat
439	calories
0 mg.	cholesterol
527 mg.	sodium
13 g.	protein
95 g.	carbohydrates
12 g.	dietary fibre

Greek Get-Away

Wild Mushroom Moussaka (page 194)

Greek Salad (page 104)

Lemon-Ginger Figs with Ice Cream (page 373)

nutrition at a glance

per serving

2.6 g.	total fat
0.8 g.	saturated fat
562	calories
7 mg.	cholesterol
546 mg.	sodium
20 g.	protein
122 g.	carbohydrates
13 g.	dietary fibre

Escape to the Islands

Hawaiian Mahimahi-Prawn Kebabs (page 130)

White rice

Sweet-and-Spicy Carrots (page 208)

Glazed Tropical Fruit Cake (page 356)

For each serving, plan on 2 Hawaiian Mahimahi-Prawn Kebabs and 90 g cooked white rice.

nutrition at a glance

per serving

3.3 g.	total fat
0.8 g.	saturated fat
600	calories
163 mg.	cholesterol
362 mg.	sodium
38 g.	protein
107 g.	carbohydrates
7 g.	dietary fibre

China Time

Lemongrass Egg-Drop Soup (page 73)

Peking Turkey and Vegetables (page 166)

White rice

Orange and Cinnamon Rhubarb (page 374)

For each serving, plan on 250 ml Lemongrass Egg-Drop Soup and 90 g cooked white rice.

nutrition at a glance

per serving
2.4 g.	total fat
0.5 g.	saturated fat
516	calories
34 mg.	cholesterol
437 mg.	sodium
23 g.	protein
104 g.	carbohydrates
8 g.	dietary fibre

Soup for Supper

Winter Potato and Fish Chowder (page 90)

Multigrain bread

Creamy Banana Bowl (page 316)

For each serving, plan on 500 ml Winter Potato and Fish Chowder and 1 slice multigrain bread.

nutrition at a glance

per serving
3 g.	total fat
0.9 g.	saturated fat
483	calories
19 mg.	cholesterol
324 mg.	sodium
24 g.	protein
88 g.	carbohydrates
6 g.	dietary fibre

Dinner for a Busy Weeknight

Garden Pita Pizza (page 177)

Tossed Antipasto Salad (page 97)

For each serving, plan on 2 servings Tossed Antipasto Salad.

nutrition at a glance

per serving
2.5 g.	total fat
0.3 g.	saturated fat
325	calories
1 mg.	cholesterol
528 mg.	sodium
21 g.	protein
62 g.	carbohydrates
11 g.	dietary fibre

Kids' Choice

Crispy Fish with Tartare Sauce (page 129)

Baby carrots

Western Fries (page 223)

Rice Pudding with Nectarines (page 371)

For each serving, plan on 3 baby carrots.

nutrition at a glance

per serving
1.9 g.	total fat
0.4 g.	saturated fat
602	calories
28 mg.	cholesterol
989 mg.	sodium
24 g.	protein
121 g.	carbohydrates
8 g.	dietary fibre

Index

M

Macaroni. *See also* Pasta
  Macaroni Cheese, 270
Mace, origins of, 310
Mackerel, fat content of, 123
Mahimahi, 130
  fat content of, *125*
  Hawaiian Mahimahi-Prawn
    Kebabs, 130–31
  Mahimahi with Prawns and
    Tropical Salsa,
    122–23
Malaysian-style dishes. *See*
    also Oriental-style
    dishes
  Malaysian Curried Rice,
    340–41
  Malaysian Prawn Fried Rice,
    135–36
Mangetout
  Oriental Vegetable Stir-Fry,
    219
Mangoes, dicing, 122
Marinara Sauce, 288
Mayonnaise, fat-free, 14
  salad dressings made with,
    108
Measuring jugs, 268
Meat(s). *See also specific*
    types
  removing fat from, 17,
    20–21
  selecting fat-free, 14–15
Meatloaf, meatless
  Garden and Grain Loaf,
    182–83
Mediterranean-style dishes.
    See also Greek-style
    dishes; Italian-style
    dishes; Moroccan-
    style dishes
  Mediterranean Beans, **250**,
    262
  Mediterranean Stuffed
    Tomatoes, 336
  Mediterranean Vegetables,
    230
Menus
  Alfresco Italian, 379
  China Time, 380

Christmas Dinner, 376
Dinner for a Busy
    Weeknight, 380
Easter Brunch, 376
Escape to the Islands,
    379
Fireside Supper, 378
Florida Feast, 378
French Bistro Sampler,
    378
Greek Getaway, 379
Harvest Garden Fest, 377
Kids' Choice, 380
Mardi Gras Mirth, 377
Midsummer's BBQ, 376
Moroccan Magic, 379
New Year's Day Lunch,
    376
Salute to Spring, 377
Soup for Supper, 380
Southwestern Sampler, 378
Summer Luncheon, 377
Meringue, 346
  Citrus-Glazed Carrot Cake,
    352–53
  Chocolate-Banana Pie, **333**,
    360–61
  Chocolate-Raspberry Cake,
    332, 350–51
  Coffee Angel Food Cake,
    351–52, 351
  Daffodil Cake with Lemon
    Sauce, **330**,
    354–55
  Fresh Berry Angel Tart,
    362–63
  Meringue Shell, 360
  Peppermint Rock
    Meringues, 368
  Pineapple Caramel Cake,
    327, 348–49
Mexican-style dishes. *See*
    Southwestern-style
    dishes
Microwave cooking, 20
Middle Eastern-style dishes
  Baba Ghannouj, 42
  Tabbouleh with Cucumbers,
    28
Milk
  buttermilk, 14, 350
  evaporated skimmed, 9
  skimmed, 14

Millet
  cooking guide, *281*
  leftover, 193
  nutritional qualities of,
    280
  Oriental Millet with Carrots,
    280
Mint, 11–12
  Autumn Couscous with Mint,
    267
  Peppermint Rock
    Meringues, 368
  Sugar Snap Peas with Mint,
    204
  varieties of, 368
Mole, 296
Moroccan-style dishes. *See*
    also Mediterranean-
    style dishes
  Moroccan Magic (menu),
    379
  Moroccan Vegetable Medley,
    153, 190
Moussaka
  Wild Mushroom Moussaka,
    158, 194–95
Muffins, fat substitutes in,
    353
Mushrooms
  closed cap
    canned, 271
    Dilled Squash with Mush-
      rooms, 216
    French Beans and Mush-
      rooms, 214
    Garden and Grain Loaf,
      182–83
    Hearty Vegetable Sauté,
      338
    Herbed Stuffed
      Mushrooms, 40
    history of, 40
    Hungarian Broccoli and
      Mushrooms, 228
    Mushroom and Bacon
      Sauce, 290
    Mushroom and Wild Rice
      Soup, 77
    Mushroom Omelette,
      315
    Mushroom Sauce, 294
    Scallop Risotto Primavera,
      134–35, **148**